osborne books

Computer Accounting
PLAIN GUIDE

Michael Fardon, Debbie Board

D1330355

© Michael Fardon, Debbie Board. First edition 2013.

Published by Osborne Books Limited
Unit 1B Everoak Estate
Bromyard Road
Worcester WR2 5HP
Tel 01905 748071
Email books@osbornebooks.co.uk
Website www.osbornebooks.co.uk

Graphic design by Jon Moore

Printed by CPI Group (UK) Limited, Croydon, CR0 4YY

British Library Cataloguing in Publication Data
A catalogue record for this book is available from the British Library

ISBN 978 1905777 914

CONTENTS

ACKNOWLEDGEMENTS

The authors wish to thank the following for their help with the reading, production and design of the text: Jon Moore and Cathy Turner. The authors also wish to thank Hania Lee for her technical editing of the text and test running of the Sage tasks.

Thanks are also due to Microsoft UK and to Sage (UK) Limited for their kind permission to use screen images within the text. It should be noted that Osborne Books Limited is a company which operates completely independently of Sage (UK) Limited.

AUTHORS

Debbie Board spent twenty-six years in the commercial sector before becoming a teacher and assessor of accounting in further education. While working in the commercial sector she was responsible as director and office manager for the introduction of computerised accounting in a multi-million pound business. She currently works in South Devon as a part-time AAT tutor and as the accounts manager of a small independent tool hire company.

Michael Fardon has had extensive teaching experience on a wide range of banking, business and accountancy courses at Worcester College of Technology where he also set up and ran computer accounting courses, using Sage software. He now specialises in writing business and financial texts and is currently General Editor at Osborne Books.

CONSULTANT

Hania Lee has worked within the accountancy profession for sixteen years. After gaining her ACCA qualification 10 years ago, she set up her own accountancy practice where she uses Sage on a daily basis. In addition to working as an accountant, she currently teaches all levels of the AAT qualification at South Devon College.

INTRODUCTION

Computer Accounting Plain Guide has been written to provide a Sage-based practical study resource for

- students taking first and second level courses offered by awarding bodies such as OCR, City & Guilds (Pitman) and IAB
- individuals wanting to learn how to use Sage 50 for business accounting

The major feature of this text is the use of Sage 50 Accounts Professional 2012 Version 18, which at the time of writing is widely used by businesses and by training providers.

The **text** of Computer Accounting Plain Guide contains clear and practical explanations of how to set up and run a Sage system. A Case Study – Pronto Supplies Limited – runs through the chapters.

Many of the teachers consulted in the writing process mentioned the need for an understanding by students of the theoretical background to computer accounting – in particular the use of financial documents and double-entry bookkeeping. The documents are explained as they are encountered in the text and a chapter on double-entry bookkeeping is included at the back of the book to help students who may not be studying it as part of their course.

The **processing activities** at the end of the chapters in this book have all been tried and tested a number of times. Trial balances and audit trails have been included periodically and also at the back of the book so that account balances and transactions can be checked. The end-of-chapter activities progressively build up the various processes needed to set up and run a Sage system.

The **Interlingo Extended Activity** at the end of the book is designed for extended study purposes and is standalone.

Chapter 8 is only relevant if the user wants to use the following modules in Sage 50:

- Products
- Sales Order Processing
- Invoicing
- Purchase Order Processing

The data is the same as in chapters 6 and 7 (where batch entry is used) but is processed using the above modules

Throughout this book the **standard VAT rate of 20%** has been used. This rate was applied at the time of writing and inputting the Sage transactions, but users of this book should note that it does vary from time-to time.

Michael Fardon, Debbie Board

Spring 2013

1 INTRODUCTION TO COMPUTER ACCOUNTING

Chapter introduction

- Computer accounting programs such as Sage 50 have many advantages over traditional manual bookkeeping and accounting systems, but their structure is based on the same principles and methods.

- Computers require input of data – which can either be carried out manually from sources such as financial documents or can be imported from other computer systems.

- Computers also output data in the form of 'hard copy' printouts and electronic data which can be emailed or exported to other computer programs.

INTRODUCTION TO COMPUTER ACCOUNTING PACKAGES

a growth area

Although some organisations, particularly small businesses, still use paper-based accounting systems, most are now operating computer accounting systems.

Small and medium-sized businesses can buy 'off-the-shelf' accounting programs from suppliers such as Sage while larger businesses may opt to have custom-designed programs.

links with traditional bookkeeping

If you study bookkeeping or accounting, your study is likely to concentrate initially on paper-based systems. The reason for this is that when you use a paper-based system you have to do all the work manually and so you can understand the theory that underlies the system: you prepare the documents, make entries in the accounts, balance the cash book, and so on. You know where all the figures are entered, and why they are entered. If you know how a paper-based system works, you will be in a much better position to be able to understand the operation of a computer-based system.

FEATURES OF COMPUTER ACCOUNTING

facilities

A typical computer accounting program will offer a number of facilities:

- on-screen input and printout of sales invoices and credit notes
- automatic updating of customer accounts with sales transaction values
- recording of suppliers' invoices
- automatic updating of supplier accounts with details of purchase values
- recording of money paid into bank or cash accounts
- recording of payments to suppliers and for expenses
- recording of product/stock movements
- sales and purchase order processing

Computerised accounting programs, including Sage, offer a generic structure that can be adapted and modified to suit any type of business.

Payroll can also be computerised – using a separate program.

management reports

A computer accounting program can provide instant reports for management, for example:

- an aged debtors summary – showing who owes you what and for what periods of time
- activity reports on customer and supplier accounts
- activity reports on expenses accounts
- VAT Return

advantages of a computer accounting program

Computer accounting programs are popular because they offer a number of distinct advantages over paper-based systems:

- they save time
- they save money
- they tend to be more accurate because they rely on single-entry input (one amount per transaction) rather than double-entry bookkeeping
- they can provide the managers of the organisation with a clear and up-to-date picture of what is happening

computer accounting and ledgers

The 'ledgers' of a business are basically the books of the business. 'The ledgers' is a term used to describe the way the accounts of the business are grouped into different sections.

There are four main ledgers in a traditional accounting system:

- **sales ledger** contains the accounts of debtors (customers)
- **purchases ledger** contains the accounts of creditors (suppliers)
- **cash book** contains the main cash book and the petty cash book
- **nominal ledger** (also called general or main ledger) contains the remaining accounts, eg expenses (including purchases), income (including sales), assets, loans, stock, VAT

A diagram illustrating these ledgers is shown on the next page. The structure of a computer accounting system is based on these ledgers. It may also include stock control and be linked to a payroll processing program.

A ledger-based computer system is designed to be user-friendly in Windows software. In Sage regular tasks can be performed by clicking on the Task options on the vertical panel on the left of the screen. These options change according to the module button selected at the bottom of the panel. The full range of modules within Sage (shown below) is accessed through the Modules drop-down menu on the menu bar. The notes to the side explain what the various modules are. Note that computer accounting packages vary in levels of sophistication; you may be working with one that does not include product records or invoice production.

Please note that the screens shown in these chapters may not necessarily be exactly the same as those on your computer because programs are regularly updated. This should not be a problem, however, because the basic principles of using the software are likely to remain exactly the same.

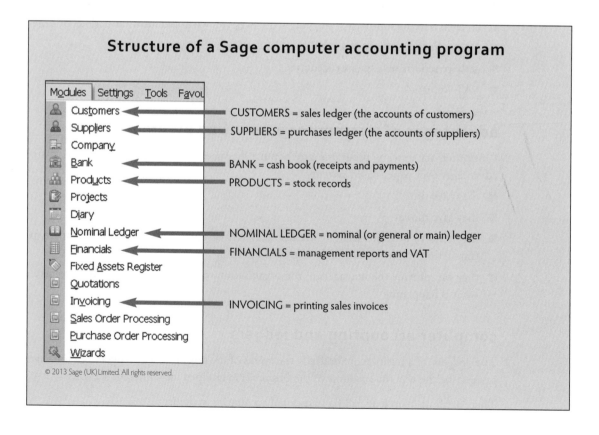

Structure of a Sage computer accounting program

| Modules | Settings | Tools | Favou |

- Customers → CUSTOMERS = sales ledger (the accounts of customers)
- Suppliers → SUPPLIERS = purchases ledger (the accounts of suppliers)
- Company
- Bank → BANK = cash book (receipts and payments)
- Products → PRODUCTS = stock records
- Projects
- Diary
- Nominal Ledger → NOMINAL LEDGER = nominal (or general or main) ledger
- Financials → FINANCIALS = management reports and VAT
- Fixed Assets Register
- Quotations
- Invoicing → INVOICING = printing sales invoices
- Sales Order Processing
- Purchase Order Processing
- Wizards

computerised ledgers – an integrated system

Before we look at the various functions on the toolbar, it is important to appreciate that a computerised ledger system is **fully integrated**. This means that when a business transaction is input on the computer it is normally recorded in two accounts at the same time, although only one amount is entered. Take the three transactions shown below:

■ a business buys from a supplier on credit (ie the business gets the goods but will pay later)

■ a business sells to a customer on credit (ie the business sells the goods but will receive payment later)

■ a business pays an advertising bill

At the centre of an integrated program is the nominal ledger which deals with all the accounts except customers' accounts and suppliers' accounts. It is affected one way or another by most transactions.

The diagram below shows how the three 'ledgers' link with the nominal ledger. Note in each case how an account in the nominal ledger is affected by each of the three transactions. This is the double-entry bookkeeping system at work. The advantage of the computer system is that in each case only one entry has to be made. Life is made a great deal simpler this way!

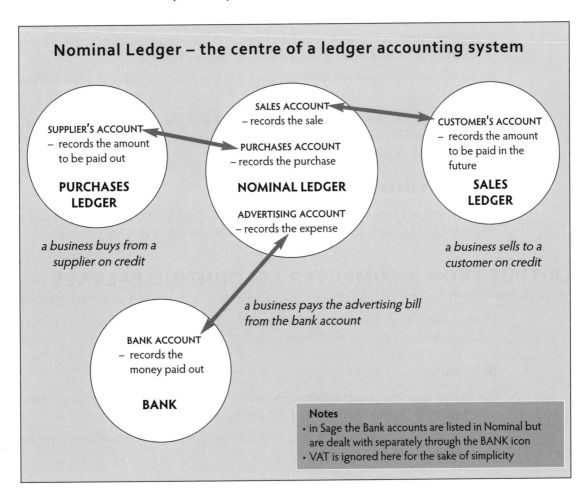

Nominal Ledger – the centre of a ledger accounting system

SUPPLIER'S ACCOUNT
– records the amount to be paid out

PURCHASES LEDGER

SALES ACCOUNT
– records the sale

PURCHASES ACCOUNT
– records the purchase

NOMINAL LEDGER

ADVERTISING ACCOUNT
– records the expense

CUSTOMER'S ACCOUNT
– records the amount to be paid in the future

SALES LEDGER

BANK ACCOUNT
– records the money paid out

BANK

a business buys from a supplier on credit

a business sells to a customer on credit

a business pays the advertising bill from the bank account

Notes
• in Sage the Bank accounts are listed in Nominal but are dealt with separately through the BANK icon
• VAT is ignored here for the sake of simplicity

INPUT INTO A COMPUTER ACCOUNTING PACKAGE

manual input

Input into a computer accounting package is normally made direct on screen from source documents or other data. If you are not familiar with financial documents, please read pages 69 to 73 before proceeding any further.

Typical transactions which form the 'bread and butter' of computer accounting input include:

- processing **sales invoices**, often in runs of several transactions known as 'batches' – the invoices are either produced before input or they can be input and printed out by the computer

- inputting **credit notes** from authorised documentation which says why the credit note has to be issued and a refund made – again the credit notes may be produced separately and used as a basis for input, or they may be printed out by the computer

- inputting **bank receipts** (money paid into the bank) – for example cheques or BACS payments received from customers in settlement of accounts due; the source document in this case is the remittance advice which comes with the cheque or advises the BACS payment, or the bank statement

- inputting details of **new customer accounts** – this is the input of text onto what is effectively a database screen in the computer accounting package

- setting up **product records** – inputting goods purchased and received, and goods sold and issued

There are, of course, many other types of transactions which you will input on the computer, but these are common examples. We will cover the input procedures in much greater detail in the individual chapters of this book.

importing data

Text files such as Customer, Supplier and Product details can be imported into a computer accounting package from other programs such as Microsoft Office or other software.

OUTPUT FROM A COMPUTER ACCOUNTING PACKAGE

Output of data from a computer accounting package can take a number of different formats and can be used in a number of different ways.

printouts

The familiar form of data output from a computer is the paper printout. This is often referred to as 'hard copy'. There are a number of different forms of printout:

- day-to-day lists of items processed, eg a list of invoices produced on a particular day, a list of cheques issued to pay suppliers

- financial documents such as invoices and credit notes
- reports for management, eg activity reports on accounts, aged debtors analysis (a list of who owes what – highlighting overdue accounts)

A printout of sales invoices produced is shown below.

Pronto Supplies Limited

Day Books: Customer Invoices (Detailed)

Transaction From:	1							N/C From:		
Transaction To:	99,999,999							N/C To:	99999999	

Dept From:	0
Dept To:	999

Tran No.	Type	Date	A/C Ref	N/C	Inv Ref	Dept.	Details	Net Amount	Tax Amount	T/C	Gross Amount	V	B
48	SI	05/02/2013	JB001	4000	10023	0	4 x Monitor 17 inch	400.00	80.00	T1	480.00	N	-
49	SI	06/02/2013	CH001	4000	10024	0	1 x Power lead 3 mtr	16.00	3.20	T1	19.20	N	-
50	SI	06/02/2013	CR001	4001	10025	0	1 x Macroworx software	450.00	90.00	T1	540.00	N	-
51	SI	08/02/2013	KD001	4002	10026	0	2 hours consultancy	120.00	24.00	T1	144.00	N	-
							Totals:	986.00	197.20		1,183.20		

faxed data

Data or documents can be faxed, for example, when a customer requests a copy of a sales invoice.

emailed data

Most current computer accounting packages have the facility for data to be exported to an email management program so that it can be emailed direct to the person who needs the information. Sage allows you to send invoices and statements direct to customers. Printouts and reports previewed on-screen can be emailed directly to external email addresses.

exporting data direct to other programs

Sage also allows you to export data to spreadsheet and word processing programs:

- export data to a Microsoft Excel spreadsheet, eg a list of the nominal accounts and their balances – this data will be placed directly into a spreadsheet grid from the Sage screen and can then be manipulated as required
- email reports in various formats from reports previewed on-screen
- export data in the form of a mailmerge to a Microsoft Word word processing file – for example, if a business wants to send a letter advertising a new product to all its customers, it can export the names and addresses from the customer details in the computer accounting program to a letter file in Word which will then print out personalised letters to all the customers
- export data files to your accountant

CHAPTER SUMMARY

■   A computer accounting program can record financial transactions, generate financial documents, provide management with financial reports and generally make running and managing the finances of any organisation a more efficient process.

■   Computer accounting programs are based on the ledger system of bookkeeping and link together accounts for customers (sales ledger), suppliers (purchases ledger), bank (cash book) and other payments, receipts and items owned or owed by the organisation (nominal ledger).

■   Additional facilities (optional modules) include sales order processing, purchase order processing and product control.

■   Input into a computer accounting program is normally carried out manually on the keyboard. Many programs will now accept data imported from other programs.

■   Output from a computer accounting program is in the form of reports. These can be printed on paper (hard copy), sent by email from within the program or sent to other computer programs such as a spreadsheet.

KEY TERMS

ledgers	the books of the accounting system which contain individual accounts – the sales ledger, for example, contains the individual accounts of customers who buy on credit (ie they pay later)
integrated system	a computer accounting system which links together all the ledgers and accounts so that a transaction on one account will always be mirrored in another account
double-entry bookkeeping	the method of manual bookkeeping from which the integrated system has been developed – it involves the making of two entries in the accounts for every financial transaction
hard copy	a paper document containing data – often a printout from a computer
data export	the transfer of data from one computer program to another

2 LOOKING AFTER THE COMPUTER AND DATA

Chapter introduction

- Before looking in detail at the setting up of a computer accounting system it is important to establish the principles of good housekeeping for computer data.

- The issues we will look at in this chapter include:

  - the use of passwords and access rights to the computer accounting system

  - logging onto the computer and dealing with dates

  - saving and backing up data

  - restoring data in Sage

  - getting help when things go wrong

  - closing down

  - password protection

  - dealing with security risks

  - legal regulations relating to computer operation

COMPUTER CARE

An organisation that uses computers will have invested thousands of pounds in buying equipment and in training staff to operate it. A business that fails to look after the equipment and the data that it holds is potentially throwing this money down the drain.

USING PASSWORDS

Before getting going on the computer, you are likely to have to use passwords to enable you to gain access to:

- the computer itself, for example if you are using a work station on a network – this is a system password
- particular computer programs, some of which may enable you to access sensitive or confidential information – eg the accounting software – this is a software password

We will deal with the security aspect of passwords later in this chapter. We will concentrate here on the practical aspects of passwords as part of the starting up procedure.

system passwords – logging on

If you are working on a network you have to 'log on' as a user before you can use a computer work station. You may have to give a user name and also a unique password. The user name will normally show on the screen as you input it, but the password will show as a series of dots or asterisks. The example on the right shows someone logging onto a computer in the production department. Logging on is a simple process, and you may well be familiar with it because it is normally used when you log onto the internet.

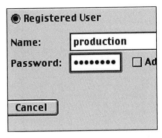

logging onto the system

software passwords – accessing a program

One solution to the problem of unauthorised employees gaining access to sensitive financial and personal data is the use of **passwords** to gain access to the computer program. Many larger businesses will employ a number of people who need to operate the computer accounting system; they will be issued with an appropriate password. Businesses can also set up **access rights** which restrict certain employees to certain activities and prevent them from accessing more sensitive areas such as the making of payments from the bank account.

When an employee comes to operate, for example, a Sage computer accounting package, he or she will be asked to 'log on'. In the example from Sage 50 shown below a person called Tom enters his logon name and a password (COBBLY).

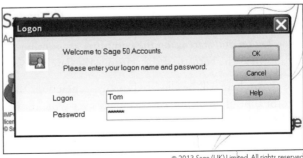

The screen from Sage 50 (see below) shows that Ben, another employee, has partial access to the Sage accounts. He is allowed to deal with Customers, Suppliers, the Nominal (Main) Ledger, Products and Invoicing. He cannot, however, access the Bank records.

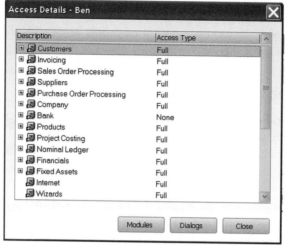

LOGGING ON AND DEALING WITH DATES

the different dates

One potential problem area for the operator of a computer accounting system is the use of dates when inputting. There are a number of dates that need to be borne in mind:

- the **actual date** – most people can manage this concept
- the **system date** – this is the date that the computer thinks is the actual date – the computer is normally right
- the **program date** – the date which you can instruct the accounting software to use as the actual date
- the **financial year start date** – the month in which the financial year of the business starts

logging on and using dates

When you log on and start using the computer accounting software, you should check that the date shown at the bottom of the screen is the date you want to use for your input.

The date shown here will be allocated to any transactions that you input into the computer unless, at the time of inputting, you manually over-write the date. Normally this is the **system date** (the date the computer thinks it is).

You should then ask yourself if you want your transactions to be allocated any other date. This might be the case if...

- you are inputting a batch of transactions which went through last week – for example a number of cheques received from customers – and you want the transactions to show on the records as going through last week

■ you are in a training situation and you have been given a specific date for input

If you are using Sage software in these cases you should change the program date through the SETTINGS menu. The program date lets you set any date to be 'today's date'.

You will be prompted to close any open modules before changing the program date. When inputting the program date you can either use the calendar – by clicking on the icon to the right of the date box and clicking on the date you want – or simply overtype the date shown. In the case of the example below a date of 1 February 2013 has been entered by keying 010213.

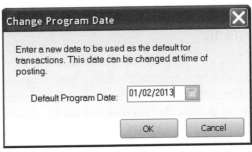

financial year

A business will use a financial year for accounting purposes. The financial year, like the calendar year, may run from January through to December. But the financial year can start anytime during the year; some businesses end their financial year on 31 March or 30 June, for example. When setting up the data in a computer accounting program you have to state when the financial year starts. In Sage this is normally entered during the company set up (see Chapter 3) but can be accessed from the SETTINGS menu as shown below.

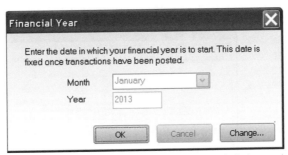

The financial year is important for the management of the business. The end-of-year routines run on the computer provide the data from which the end-of-year financial statements and management reports can be produced.

SAVING AND BACK-UP

The computer accounting program you are using will prompt you to save your work. This is normally done after inputting a group of transactions and before passing on to the next task.

backing up files

You will also need to **back-up** the data generated by the computer. There is no set rule about when you should do this, but it should be at least at the end of every day and preferably when you have completed a long run of inputting.

back-up media

If you are working on a network, you can normally save to your files, to your work station's hard disk and also to the server. If you have a standalone computer system, the back-up files should be saved to some form of storage device. This may take the form of a disk drive in the work station itself or it may be an external drive.

Data can be backed up onto a variety of media:

- writable or rewritable CDs (cheap and disposable)
- tape drive
- portable hard disk drive
- writable or rewritable DVDs
- USB memory stick

Another back-up option is to send files by email and keep them secure at a remote location, although this option would be limited by file size.

back-up in Sage

Back-up in Sage is carried out from the FILE menu, or on the prompt when you close down. The screen gives you a choice of file name (by default the date) and asks to which drive you want the data saved. In the Sage screen shown below it is an external USB drive.

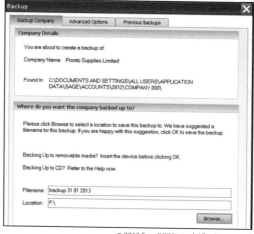

You are recommended to run the ERROR CHECKING routine from MAINTENANCE (from the FILE menu) before backing up. This will check the data files and ensure that you do not back-up any corrupted data. The screen after a check looks like this:

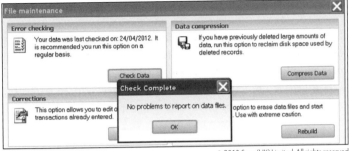

back-up policy

It is important that an organisation works out a systematic policy for back-up of its data. This should involve:

- more than one back-up held at any one time
- back-up media held off the premises
- periodic back-up (eg back-ups at the end of each month) stored securely

One solution is for the business to keep a set of back-up media (eg tapes) for each working day, labelled with the name of the day.

At the end of each working day the data is backed up on the appropriate back-up media, which are kept securely on site, preferably under lock and key.

As a further security measure, a second set of back-ups could be kept as an off-site security back-up. These would be backed up at the end of each day and taken off-site by an employee.

With this system in place the business has double security for its valuable data.

It should also be mentioned that the back-up media should be replaced periodically (every three months, for example) as they wear out in time and the data can become corrupted.

restoring data from a back-up

In the unfortunate event that the accounting data on your computer has been corrupted, you can restore the data from an earlier date from the appropriate back-up media. This is carried out in Sage from RESTORE in the FILE menu. Note that all the data is restored in this process;

it is not possible to restore selected files. You should then run ERROR CHECKING routine from FILE MAINTENANCE to make sure the restored data is not corrupted.

Note that Sage provides a history of previous back-up files to choose from in the RESTORE screen.

GETTING HELP

software failure

Software problems can occur. If it is a case of not knowing how to carry out a particular operation, refer the matter to someone who does. Help is always at hand through HELP menus, online support or telephone technical support to which the business is likely to have subscribed. If a program crashes, it may be necessary to restart the computer. If the program refuses to work after repeated attempts, it may have become corrupted, in which case it may need to be reinstalled by a technician.

corrupted, deleted or overwritten data files

Problems can also be caused if a data file you are using

- becomes **corrupt**, ie it becomes unusable and will not open or print, or both

- gets **deleted** by accident when you are tidying up your computer desktop and sending what you think are redundant files into the recycle bin

- is accidentally **overwritten** by an older version of a file, and in the process wipes out the work you may have done on the file

In these cases you have to rely on your back-up files.

CLOSING DOWN THE PROGRAM

Closing down Sage correctly is important because a variety of problems can arise if the correct procedures are not followed.

When you wish to close Sage you should exit using the **Exit** command in the FILE menu or by clicking "X" in the top right of the screen – this will warn you if you have any unsaved files still open and will enable you to save your work; it will also make sure that the program starts up properly next time the computer is used.

If you are using a work station on a network and need to keep the computer turned on – perhaps for someone else to use – you should log off, making sure that all your files are closed, saved and backed up.

DATA SECURITY

dangers to the data

The data held on the computer is irreplaceable once lost and so must be kept securely both on the computer system and also in the form of back-ups.

Back-up systems have already been discussed in this chapter. An essential element of data security is the maintenance of a foolproof back-up system and the secure location of back-up media, both on-site and off-site.

The data must be kept securely and protected from unauthorised users outside and inside the business:

- people such as competitors or criminals outside the business may try to gain access to the data either directly (through 'hacking' if the computer is linked to the internet) or through an employee who can be persuaded to obtain the information

- employees of the business may try to access the data in order to work a fraud – through the payroll, for example, or by making bogus payments to external bank accounts which they control

In this section we look at the various precautions that can be taken to minimise these risks.

PASSWORD PROTECTION

We have seen earlier in this chapter that passwords are needed to access:

- the computer system itself (system passwords)
- the software run on the computer system (software passwords)

The organisation can also increase security by ensuring that passwords are changed regularly and also that they are 'unbreakable'.

basic rules of choosing an individual password

1 Do not use an obvious word like 'password'.

2 Combine letters and numbers if possible.

3 Do not use your own name or date of birth.

4 Make it so that you can remember the password easily and avoid forgettable combinations such as z9ad2w8y7d – try the name and birthday of your first girlfriend/boyfriend, Lisa0511, for example, but avoid using similar details relating to your present partner (because people will guess them).

5 Never write the password down where people can see it, and never put it on a post-it note stuck on the computer monitor (it does happen!)

When you have chosen a password, make sure that nobody stands watching you when you are logging on; the password appears as dots on the screen, but people can work out what you are typing on the keyboard.

An organisation should ensure that if there is any suspicion that a password has been 'leaked', there should be a wholesale change of passwords.

IDENTIFYING SECURITY RISKS

Data on computer files needs to be protected against:

- **corruption** – ie when the file goes 'wrong' and does not work properly – either because of a virus or because of poor storage facilities

- **loss** – when the file is deleted, accidentally or intentionally – by an employee or by a virus introduced from outside

- **illegal copying** – by an employee copying a program or by someone 'hacking in' from outside through the internet connection

Clearly the threats to data therefore come both internally, from employees, and externally, from hackers or viruses.

protecting data from internal risks

Much of the data held on computer file is sensitive and confidential in nature, for example:

- payroll details of employees
- financial details relating to customers

It is an unfortunate possibility that employees may be persuaded or paid by outsiders to obtain this information. As a result all employees should take reasonable precautions to prevent data that they are working from being used in this way. For example:

- if you leave your computer, do not leave sensitive data on-screen, or the program running
- use a screensaver
- use passwords wherever possible
- if you print out a document with confidential information on it, do not leave it on the printer (or the photocopier!)

Another internal risk is **illegal copying** of computer data – often program files – by employees who 'borrow' disks to take home or 'lend' to friends. The answer here is to keep these types of files under strict control. A business using software will in any event have been granted a licence to use it, and any unauthorised copying will be a breach of that licence.

Careful and safe **storage** of computer data on various forms of media is also important. Heat and radiation can damage files held on disk, and the surface of CDs and DVDs can easily be scratched, causing corruption and data loss.

protecting data from external risks

External risks to data include:

- thieves who steal data by stealing the computers on which it is held
- external hackers who access files within an organisation by 'hacking in' from the internet and accessing files held – often on a network
- viruses sent into the computer system, either on a disk or through the internet

Protection against thieves can be achieved by rigorous security at the premises. CCTV is now commonly used to guard against crime. Laptops away from the premises should be kept under lock and key wherever possible, and preferably not left in cars. Hackers can be kept at bay by a 'firewall' on the internet portal of a computer network. A 'firewall' is software which keeps out all external interference and unwanted emails.

Computer viruses are dealt with in the next section.

VIRUS AND MALWARE PROTECTION

Computers are vulnerable to viruses and malware, such as spyware. These are destructive programs which can be introduced into the computer either from a disk, USB memory stick, an internet download, email attachment or from another computer.

Some viruses are relatively harmless and may merely display messages on the screen, others can be very damaging and destroy operating systems and data, putting the computer system completely out of action. Most computers are now sold already installed with virus protection software which will:

- establish a **firewall** to repel viruses
- check for existing viruses
- destroy known viruses
- check for damage to files on the hard disk
- repair damage to files on the hard disk where possible

This software should be run and updated regularly so that it can deal with the latest viruses.

precautions against viruses

There are a number of precautions which you can take against viruses:

- be wary of opening any unidentified email attachments which arrive
- use protective software to inspect any disk or memory stick received from an outside source before opening up any file saved onto it
- make sure that your protective software is up-to-date – very often it will update automatically over the internet

If your protective software announces that you have a virus, you should report it at once in your workplace and stop using your computer.

LEGAL REGULATIONS

Any organisation using computer systems of any type must comply with a number of legal requirements.

Businesses inevitably keep records of their customers and suppliers on file – either manually – a card index system, for example – or, more likely, on computer file. This is 'personal data'.

The **Data Protection Act (1998)** establishes rules for the processing of personal data. The Act follows the guidelines of an EC Directive and brings the UK in line with European legal principles. The Act applies to a filing system of records held on **computer**, eg a computer database of customer names, addresses, telephone numbers, sales details, or a **manual** set of accessible records.

People have the legal right to know what personal details about them are held by an organisation. They can apply in writing for a copy of the personal data held on file by the organisation; they may have to pay a fee.

The Act states that an organisation should not without permission reveal:

- information about one customer to another customer
- information about its employees

This applies directly to data held on a computer accounting system: for example, sensitive customer information such as credit limits and account balances.

Other regulations include the **Health and Safety at Work Act 1974** and **Display Screen Equipment Regulations 1992** which require that employers maintain computer equipment in good and safe condition, making sure that the risk of eyestrain and backstrain to employees is minimised.

CHAPTER SUMMARY

- A business which has invested in a computer accounting system needs to ensure that both the equipment and the data held on it are well maintained.

- Passwords and access rights can be set up on the computer system to restrict access to the data to authorised employees.

- A number of different dates are involved when logging onto the system: system dates, program dates and financial year dates.

- Data should be backed up regularly and a back-up routine established. In the case of data corruption, data can be restored from the back-up media.

- When operating a computer system it is important to know where help can be obtained when things go wrong, eg hardware failure, software failure and corruption of data.

- It is important to follow the correct close down procedure for a computer system in order to avoid creating problems for the software and hardware.

- Accounting data kept on a computer is valuable and vulnerable. Outsiders can use it to fraudulently obtain money and information about customers. Employees can log into the system to set up fraudulent money transfers.

- Accounting data can be protected with virus protection software.

KEY TERMS

system password	a code word used to allow an employee to 'log on' to access the computer accounting system
software password	a code word used to allow an employee to 'log on' to access a particular computer accounting program, such as Sage 50
access rights	the right of an employee to access specified areas of the computer accounting program
system date	the date allocated by the operating system of the computer – normally the actual date
program date	the date which you can tell the computer accounting software to use as 'today's' date
financial year	the twelve month period used by the business to record its financial transactions
back-up	to copy the computer data onto a separate storage medium in order to ensure that the data is not lost
restore	to copy the back-up data back onto the computer when the original data has been lost or corrupted
corrupt data	data which has become unusable because it will not open, or print, or both
malware	malicious software, for example: computer viruses, worms, trojan horses, spyware and adware
virus	a computer program introduced into the computer system which then disrupts or destroys the operation of the system
Data Protection Act	the law which establishes the regulations for the protection of personal data held by organisations on computer (and paper-based) files

3 SETTING UP THE BUSINESS IN SAGE

Chapter introduction

■ Setting up a computer accounting program for a business or other organisation will take some time, but as long as the correct data is entered in the correct format there should be no problem.

■ We will assume here that the organisation setting up the computer accounting program is a business. Sage software always calls a business a 'company' – so we will adopt that term.

■ The chapter introduces a Case Study business – Pronto Supplies Limited – which will be used through this book to show how computer accounting works.

■ There is plenty of help around when you are setting up accounts on the computer. In Sage, for example, there is the user guide, the 'Help' function, Tutorial simulations, and on-screen step-by-step instruction procedures known as 'Wizards'.

■ The data that will have to be input includes:

- the 'company' details such as name and address, financial year and VAT status

- the customer details and any sales transactions already carried out

- the supplier details and any purchases transactions already carried out

- details of accounts for income and expenses, assets (items owned), liabilities (loans) and capital (money put in by the owner) – this is all contained in the nominal ledger

■ This chapter concentrates on setting up the company details. The other data – customer and supplier details and balances and the nominal ledger – will be covered in the next two chapters.

WHERE ARE YOU STARTING FROM?

If you are reading this book you are likely to be in one of two situations:

1   You are in a real business and looking for guidance in setting up a computer accounting system.

2   You are a student in a training situation and will have the program already set up for you on a training centre network. You will be given exercises to practise the various functions of a computer accounting program.

In the first case – the real business – you may be starting from scratch and will have to go through the whole installation and set-up procedure. This is not at all difficult. The software itself will take you through the various steps.

In the second case – the training centre situation – the computer may already have accounting records on it, possibly another student's work. What you may be required to do, by agreement with your tutor, is to remove the data (making sure it is backed up first!) and then start again. This is done using a 'rebuild' procedure. There is more about this on pages 203-204.

The Case Study which follows on the next page – Pronto Supplies Limited – assumes that you are in business setting up computer accounts for the first time using Sage software. It is important for your studies that you know how this is done, even if you may not carry out in the training centre all the procedures explained in the Case Study.

WHY SAGE AND WHICH SAGE?

Osborne Books (the publisher of this book) has chosen Sage software for this book for two very good reasons:

1   Sage software is widely used in business and is recognised as a user-friendly and reliable product.

2   Osborne Books has used Sage itself for over fifteen years and is well used to the way it works.

The Sage software used as a basis for this book is Sage 50 Accounts Professional 2012 (Version 18). The screens displayed in this book are taken from this version by kind permission of Sage (UK) Limited.

screen illustrations

It should be appreciated that some training centres and businesses may be using older and slightly different versions and so some of the screens may look slightly different. This does not matter however: using Sage is like driving different models of car – the controls may be located in slightly different places and the dashboard may not look exactly the same, but the controls are still there and they still do the same thing. So if the screens shown here look unfamiliar, examine them carefully and you will see that they will contain the same (or very similar) Sage icons and functions as the version you are using.

PRONTO SUPPLIES LIMITED:
SETTING UP THE COMPANY IN SAGE

the business

Pronto Supplies is a limited company run by Tom Cox who has worked as a computer consultant for over ten years. Pronto Supplies provides local businesses and other organisations with computer hardware, software and consumables needed in offices. It also provides consultancy for computer set-ups through its proprietor, Tom Cox. Pronto Supplies has eight employees in total. The business is situated on an industrial estate, at Unit 17 Severnvale Estate, Broadwater Road, Mereford, Wyvern, MR1 6TF.

the accounting system

Pronto Supplies Limited started business on 1 January 2013. The business is registered for VAT (ie it charges VAT on its sales) and after a month of using a manual accounting system Tom has decided to transfer the accounts to Sage 50 software and sign up for a year's telephone technical support. Tom has also decided to put his payroll onto the computer, but this will be run on a separate Sage program.

Tom has chosen Sage 50 because it will enable him to:

- record the invoices issued to his customers to whom he sells on credit
- pay his suppliers on the due date
- keep a record of his bank receipts and payments
- record his income and expenses, business assets and loans in a nominal ledger

In short he will have an integrated computer accounting package which will enable him to:

- record all his financial transactions
- print out reports
- manage his business finances
- save time (and money) in running his accounting system

getting started

Tom has decided to use just one machine in the office to run Sage and so he has bought a 'single user' package together with telephone technical support for a year.

He installs the program from his CD and uses the ActiveSetup Wizard to take him through the procedure.

Note

A Wizard is a series of dialogue boxes on the screen which take you step-by-step through a particular procedure. The ActiveSetup Wizard is one of a number of Wizards in Sage. Wizards generally appear automatically on screen when you need to carry out a complicated procedure.

The ActiveSetup Wizard takes Tom through a series of screens by which he can personalise Sage to his business. In the first he chooses to set up a new company as shown below.

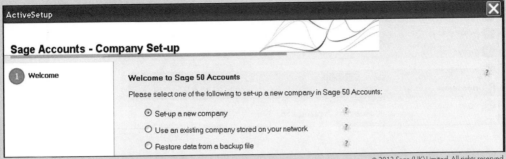

Next he must enter his company details

ActiveSetup

Sage Accounts - Company Set-up

1 Welcome	**Enter Company Details**
2 Network Sharing	Company Name : Pronto Supplies Limited
3 **Company Details**	Street 1 : Unit 17 Severnvale Estate
4 Business Type	Street 2 : Broadwater Road
5 Financial Year	Town : Mereford
6 VAT	County : Wyvern
7 Currency	Post Code : MR1 6TF
8 Confirm Details	Country : United Kingdom GB
	Telephone Number : 01908 748071
	Fax Number : 01908 748951
	Email Address : mail@prontosupplies.co.uk
	Website Address : www.prontosupplies.co.uk

As Pronto Supplies is a limited company, in the next screen Tom chooses the "Limited Company" option. The list of accounts will cover all his business needs such as sales, purchases, bank accounts and expenses.

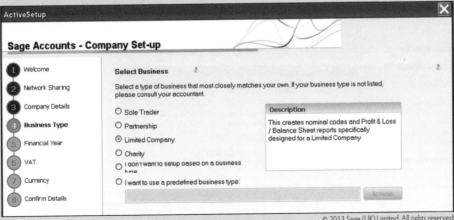

Next he sets up his financial year start date: January 2013

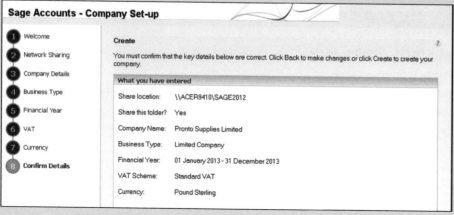

Sage Accounts - Company Set-up

1 Welcome	**Select Financial Year** ?
2 Network Sharing	Choose when your company financial year begins. If you are not sure when your financial year begins, please contact your accountant for guidance before you proceed any further.
3 Company Details	Month January
4 Business Type	Year 2013
5 **Financial Year**	
6 VAT	**Financial year range**
	01 January 2013 - 31 December 2013

The next two screens require Tom to enter the business VAT details and the currency he trades in.

Sage Accounts - Company Set-up

1 Welcome	**Select VAT Details** ?
2 Network Sharing	Is your company VAT registered? ⊙ Yes ○ No
3 Company Details	Enter your VAT registration number 404 7106 52
4 Business Type	VAT Scheme Standard VAT
5 Financial Year	Enter your standard VAT rate % 20.00
6 **VAT**	

Sage Accounts - Company Set-up

1 Welcome	**Select Currency**
2 Network Sharing	Select the currency your accounts will be prepared in.
3 Company Details	If the currency is not shown in the list select Unlisted Currency.
4 Business Type	Base Currency Pound Sterling

Tom must now confirm the details he has entered.

Sage Accounts - Company Set-up

1 Welcome	**Create** ?
2 Network Sharing	You must confirm that the key details below are correct. Click Back to make changes or click Create to create your company.
3 Company Details	**What you have entered**
4 Business Type	Share location: \\ACER9410\SAGE2012
5 Financial Year	Share this folder? Yes
6 VAT	Company Name: Pronto Supplies Limited
7 Currency	Business Type: Limited Company
8 **Confirm Details**	Financial Year: 01 January 2013 - 31 December 2013
	VAT Scheme: Standard VAT
	Currency: Pound Sterling

Finally, Tom must enter a logon name and also a password if he wants to restrict the use of the program.

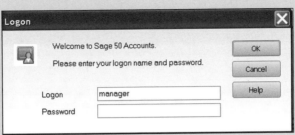

The welcome screen now opens showing that Sage is ready for use.

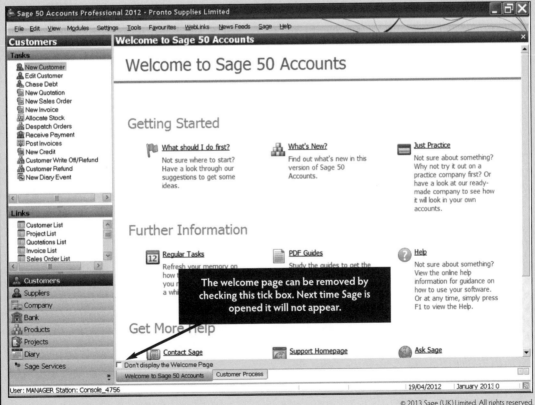

Tom should now check his VAT codes. This is done by selecting CONFIGURATION from the SETTINGS menu. This shows the various tax codes used, eg T1 for standard rated transactions, T0 for zero-rated transactions (eg sales of books). The screen appears as follows ...

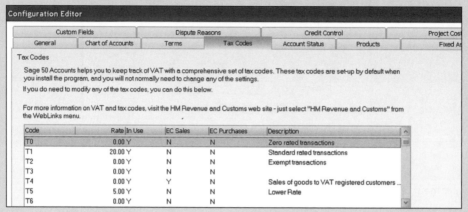

Tom can at any time check and amend if necessary his company details. This is done in COMPANY PREFERENCES which can also be found in the SETTINGS menu. This screen is illustrated below.

There are a number of tabs, including 'Details'. The address entered here will automatically be printed by the program, as required, on business documents such as invoices and credit notes. Tom has the option to enter a different delivery address, but this is unlikely in his case, as all the deliveries from his suppliers will be made to his warehouse at Unit 17 Severnvale Estate. He decides not to bother with this option.

Tom will work with the default Sage settings in the other tabs.

Tom's Company Preferences screen appears as follows ...

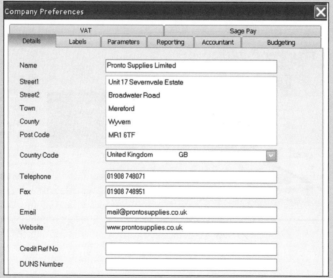

Tom also needs to set up the passwords for members of his staff so that access to the Sage accounts can be restricted to authorised people. Adjustments to access rights and passwords are carried out through ACCESS RIGHTS and CHANGE PASSWORD in SETTINGS.

The screen below shows how Tom creates a new log-on name and password for Ben James, his assistant.

Tom subsequently restricts Ben's access to the Bank accounts in ACCESS RIGHTS. He does this by clicking on the Details button, then on Modules, highlighting Bank and clicking NO ACCESS.

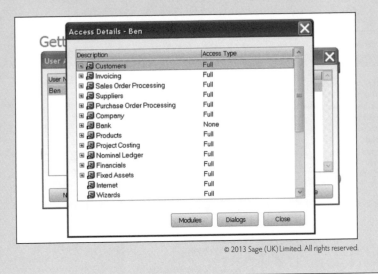

HELP!

Tom now has his business details set up on the computer but he still has to install his account balances and get to know how the system works. Sage provides a number of facilities which help the user when he or she needs information: Wizards, a user guide, and an on-screen Help function.

wizards

Wizards, as seen in the Case Study, help the user step-by-step through difficult procedures. We will encounter Wizards in later chapters.

user guide

The Sage User Guide is a useful reference source. It can be accessed from within the program and printed if required. Less experienced users may find on-screen guidance more helpful.

on-screen help

On-screen help can be accessed through either the help menu or by pressing the F1 function key. It works with three tabs, all of which will enable the user to access information. Look at the diagram below.

tutorials

Visual simulations of inputting and processing tasks accessed through the Help menu.

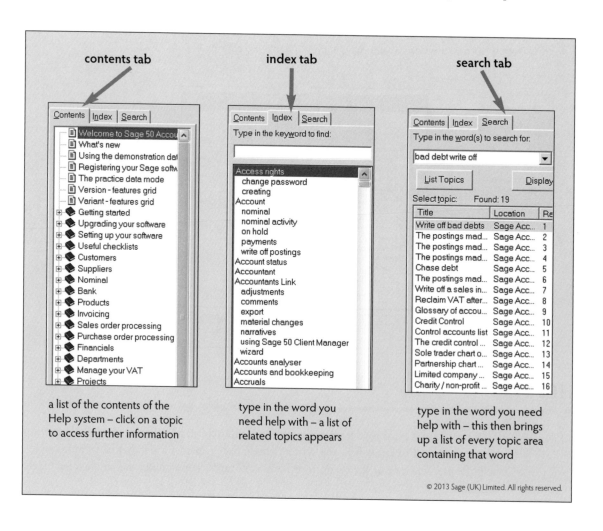

contents tab

index tab

search tab

a list of the contents of the Help system – click on a topic to access further information

type in the word you need help with – a list of related topics appears

type in the word you need help with – this then brings up a list of every topic area containing that word

TRANSFERRING DATA INTO SAGE

When a business first sets up a computer accounting system a substantial amount of data will need to be transferred onto the computer, even if the business is in its first week of trading. A summary of this data is shown in the diagram below.

The names of Sage modules shown on the right of the diagram represent the different operating areas within Sage. As you can see they relate to the ledger structure of a manual bookkeeping system.

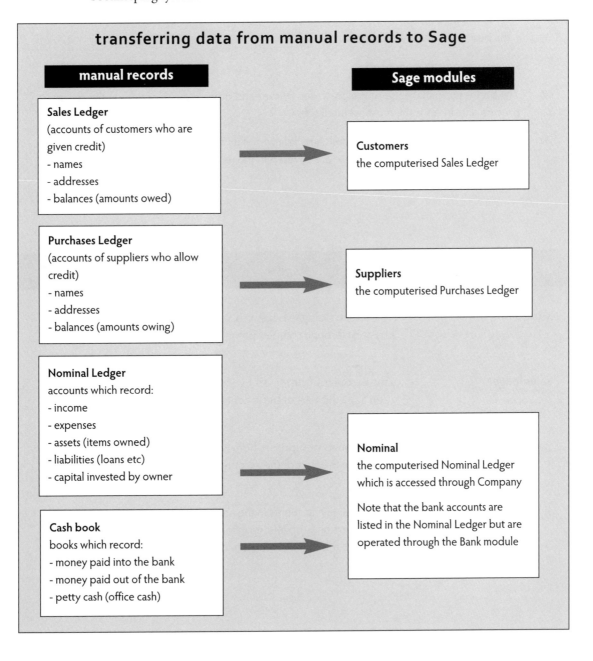

transferring data from manual records to Sage

manual records

Sage modules

Sales Ledger
(accounts of customers who are given credit)
- names
- addresses
- balances (amounts owed)

Customers
the computerised Sales Ledger

Purchases Ledger
(accounts of suppliers who allow credit)
- names
- addresses
- balances (amounts owing)

Suppliers
the computerised Purchases Ledger

Nominal Ledger
accounts which record:
- income
- expenses
- assets (items owned)
- liabilities (loans etc)
- capital invested by owner

Cash book
books which record:
- money paid into the bank
- money paid out of the bank
- petty cash (office cash)

Nominal
the computerised Nominal Ledger which is accessed through Company

Note that the bank accounts are listed in the Nominal Ledger but are operated through the Bank module

CHAPTER SUMMARY

- A business setting up a Sage computer accounting program for the first time will have to enter the details of the company on-screen, for example

  - the program serial number and Activation Key code

  - the start date of the financial year of the business

  - the business VAT registration number and VAT Status (where applicable)

  - the business name and address

  - any passwords that are needed

- The business can make use of the on-screen Wizard and other 'Help' functions in the set-up process. The index is the most useful of these.

- The business will need to enter details and balances of its customers, suppliers and its nominal accounts (the other accounts). These are covered in the next two chapters.

KEY TERMS

wizard	on-screen dialogue boxes in a Sage program which take you step-by-step through complex procedures
sales ledger	the accounts of customers to whom a business sells on credit – in Sage this part of the accounting system is known as 'Customers'
purchases ledger	the accounts of suppliers from whom a business buys on credit – in Sage this part of the accounting system is known as 'Suppliers'
nominal ledger	the remaining accounts in the accounting system which are not Customers or Suppliers, eg income, expenses, assets, liabilities – in Sage this is known as 'Nominal'

EXERCISES

Warning note!

This activity involves you setting up a new company in Sage and inputting live data into the computer.

Remember to save your data and keep any printouts as you progress through the tasks.

Task 1

Set the program date as 31 January 2013. Set up the company details of Pronto Supplies Limited in Sage.

The details are:

Address/contact	Unit 17 Severnvale Estate, Broadwater Road, Mereford, Wyvern, MR1 6TF.
Telephone	01908 748071
Fax	01908 748951
Email	mail@prontosupplies.co.uk
	www.prontosupplies.co.uk
Financial year start	January 2013 (if not already input)
VAT Registration number	404 7106 52
VAT rate	20%
Business Type	Limited Company

NB If you are using a multi-user version of Sage (for instance in a college environment), you may see an additional screen during set up called Network Sharing (at point 2 after the Welcome Screen). Accept the defaults if this is the case.

Task 2

Check the business details in the first tab of COMPANY PREFERENCES in SETTINGS.

Reminder! Have you made a back-up?

4 SETTING UP RECORDS FOR CUSTOMERS AND SUPPLIERS

Chapter introduction

- The term 'Customers' is a word which in Sage means people to whom a business sells on credit. In other words, the goods or services are supplied straightaway and the customer is allowed to pay at a specified later date – often a month or more later.

- A business keeps running accounts for the amounts owed by individual customers – much as a bank keeps accounts for its customers. The accounts are maintained by the business in the 'Sales Ledger'.

- The term 'Suppliers' is a word which in Sage means people from whom a business buys on credit. In other words, the goods or services are supplied straightaway and the business is allowed to pay at a specified later date.

- A business keeps running accounts for the amounts owed to individual suppliers. The accounts are maintained by the business in the 'Purchases Ledger'.

- This chapter continues the Pronto Supplies Limited Case Study and shows how the business sets up its Customer and Supplier records on the computer.

- When the accounts have been set up on the computer the business will need to input the amounts owed by Customers and owing to Suppliers.

- The next step – dealt with in the next chapter – is to input the Nominal ledger accounts. When this has been done, the set up is complete and the system will be ready for the input of transactions such as sales and purchases.

CASH AND CREDIT SALES

cash and credit – the difference

When businesses such as manufacturers, shops and travel agents sell their products, they will either get their money straightaway, or they will receive the money after an agreed time period. The first type of sale is a **cash sale**, the second is a **credit sale**. These can be defined further as:

cash sale   A sale of a product where the money is received straightaway – this can include payment in cash, or by cheque or by credit card and debit card. The word 'cash' means 'immediate' – it does not mean only notes and coins.

credit sale   A sale of a product where the sale is agreed and the goods or services are supplied but the buyer pays at a later date agreed at the time of the sale.

buying and selling for cash and on credit

Businesses are likely to get involved in cash and credit sales not only when they are selling their products but also when they are buying. Some goods and services will be bought for cash and some on credit. Buying and selling are just two sides of the same operation.

You will see from this that it is the nature of the business that will decide what type of sales and purchases it makes. A supermarket, for example, will sell almost entirely for cash – the cash and cheques and credit/debit card payments come in at the checkouts – and it will buy from its suppliers on credit and pay them later. It should therefore always have money in hand – which is a good situation to be in for a business.

SETTING UP CUSTOMER AND SUPPLIER ACCOUNTS

accounting records for customers

You will first need to learn some accounting terminology.

Customers who buy from a business on credit are known as **debtors** because they owe money to the business.

The amounts owed by customers (debtors) are recorded in individual customer accounts in the **Sales Ledger**. In double-entry terms these customer account balances are **debit balances** (remember debtors = debits).

The total of all the customer (debtor) accounts in the Sales Ledger is recorded in an account known as **Debtors Control Account**. This is the total amount owing by the customers of a business.

accounting records for suppliers

When a business purchases goods and services from its suppliers on credit the suppliers are known as **creditors** because the business owes them money.

The amounts owed to suppliers (creditors) are recorded in individual supplier accounts in the **Purchases Ledger**. In double-entry terms these supplier account balances are **credit balances** (remember creditors = credits).

The total of all the supplier (creditor) accounts in the Purchases Ledger is known as **Creditors Control Account**. This is the total amount owing to the suppliers of a business.

All this is summarised in the table set out below.

Customers	**Suppliers**
• buy from the business	• sell to the business
• have individual accounts in the Sales Ledger	• have individual accounts in the Purchases Ledger
• are also known as 'debtors'	• are also known as 'creditors'
• normally have debit balances on their accounts	• normally have credit balances on their accounts

credit references

A business is only likely to sell to customers on credit (ie receive the money at a later date) if it is reasonably sure that the money will come in. When an account is opened the seller should obtain credit references to make sure the customer can pay. These references can include:

bank reference   can the customer meet his or her financial obligations?

trade references   references from other suppliers to this customer – does the customer have a good history of paying up on time?

credit bureau   a reference from a business (a credit bureau) which specialises in assessing the credit risk of customers

credit limits

When a business is opening a new account it will need to establish a **credit limit**. A credit limit is the maximum amount of credit a seller is willing to grant to a customer. For example if a credit limit of £5,000 is set up by the seller, the customer can owe up to £5,000 at any one time – for example two invoices of £2,500. A well-managed business will keep an eye on situations where a credit limit might be exceeded.

credit terms

The seller will need to establish its **terms** of trading with its customers and the customer will have to agree. The terms are normally set out on the invoice (the invoice is the document issued when the goods or services are sold and supplied). They include:

- **trade discount** given to the customer based on the selling price, for example a customer with a 30% trade discount will pay £70 for goods costing £100, ie £100 minus £30 (30% discount)

- the **payment terms** – the length of credit allowed to the customer, ie the number of days the customer is allowed to wait before paying up – this is commonly 30 days after the invoice date

- **settlement discount** (also known as **cash discount**) sometimes given to a customer who settles up early within a specified number of days, for example a 2.5% reduction for settlement within 7 days

day-to-day customer/supplier information

A business will need information on file relating to its day-to-day dealings with customers and suppliers. For example:

- the name and address of the customer
- telephone, fax and email details and website address (if there is one)
- contact names
- credit limit, trade discount, payment terms and any settlement discount agreed

setting up the accounts in Sage

As you will see from the last three pages, there is a great deal of information that has to be input when setting up accounts for customers and suppliers on a computer accounting program such as Sage.

In the Case Study which follows on page 38 we will follow the steps taken by Pronto Supplies Limited in setting up its Customers and Suppliers records.

SETTING UP THE COMPUTER FILES

There are two methods in Sage for setting up new records for customers or suppliers. If, for example, you wanted to set up a new Customer's account you could click on CUSTOMERS in the vertical toolbar and then either…

1   Click New Customer in the Tasks pane. A Wizard will take you through the process, or

2   Change the View in the top right-hand corner of the screen to CUSTOMERS, then click on RECORD for direct entry of details

The Wizard screen is shown below and the second method is illustrated in the Case Study, as the process is very simple.

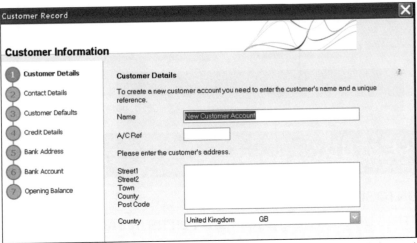

Whether you are using the Wizard or just setting up a new record through RECORD, you will need to have to hand all the customer details you have on file. These are the type of details covered earlier in this chapter.

customer and supplier reference codes

You will see from the Wizard screen shown above that you need to decide on a unique reference code for each customer and supplier account. This code can be letters, numbers, or a mixture of both. If letters are used they are often an abbreviation of the account name. This process, using both letters and numbers, will be illustrated in the Case Study.

customer and supplier record defaults

If you are setting up a number of customer and supplier accounts it is possible that the terms agreed – discounts and payment periods – will be the same for each customer or supplier account. To save you entering these in each and every account (which can take a lot of time!) you can establish a default set of terms which will apply to all accounts. These can be set up from the 'terms' tab of the CONFIGURATION EDITOR in SETTINGS.

It is also important to establish the standard VAT rate to be used in transactions (currently 20%) and also the default account number used for sales to customers (usually account number 4000). This is carried out from the 'Record' tab in CUSTOMER DEFAULTS in SETTINGS. In the illustration below note the default VAT code (T1, 20%) and the 'Def N/C' default Sales Account number 4000 ('N/C' stands for 'Nominal Code').

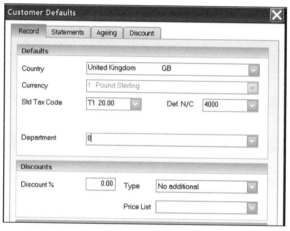

CASE STUDY

PRONTO SUPPLIES LIMITED:

SETTING UP CUSTOMERS AND SUPPLIERS IN SAGE

Tom Cox at Pronto Supplies has decided to input his customer and supplier records into the computer first, and will then afterwards input the Nominal balances.

During the month of January Tom had set up accounts for customers and suppliers which at the end of the month (31 January) have balances as follows:

Customers   6 accounts in the Sales Ledger   Total now outstanding £29,534

Suppliers   3 accounts in the Purchases Ledger   Total now outstanding £18,750

Tom has kept the relevant financial documents – sales and purchase invoices and purchase order forms – in two separate files marked 'Credit Sales' and 'Credit Purchases'. The accounts are as follows:

customers

account reference	account name	amount outstanding (£)
JB001	John Butler & Associates	5,500.00
CH001	Charisma Design	2,400.00
CR001	Crowmatic Ltd	3,234.00
DB001	David Boossey	3,400.00
KD001	Kay Denz	6,500.00
LG001	L Garr & Co	8,500.00
Total	(Debtors Control Account)	29,534.00

suppliers

account reference	account name	amount outstanding (£)
DE001	Delco PLC	5,750.00
EL001	Electron Supplies	8,500.00
MA001	MacCity	4,500.00
Total	(Creditors Control Account)	18,750.00

entering the customer defaults

Tom sets his program date to 31 January 2013. He decides that he will save time by setting up his standard terms in the CONFIGURATION EDITOR in SETTINGS:

Payment due days	30 days
Terms of payment	Payment 30 days of invoice

He then clicks Apply and Close.

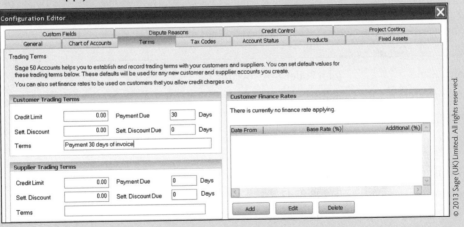

He also checks his default VAT code (T1) and rate (20%) and Sales Account number (4000) in CUSTOMER DEFAULTS (reached through SETTINGS):

VAT rate	Standard rate of 20% (this is Tax Code T1)
Default nominal code	4000

Tom decides not to set a default credit limit as this will vary from customer to customer and will be input with the individual customer details.

Note also that as Tom has not long been in business he does not allow discounts on his sales nor receive discounts on his purchases. These will be negotiated as time goes on.

Tom prefers the View that shows a list of customers (and suppliers) on the screen rather than the Process or Dashboard options. He goes to Tools/Options on the menu bar and clicks on View to change the default views.

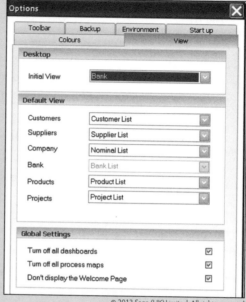

entering customer details and opening balances

Tom will now enter the details and the opening balance for each customer. He does this by clicking on RECORD in CUSTOMERS. The first customer to input is John Butler & Associates. The information he wants to input (including the invoice issued in January) is as follows:

Account name	John Butler & Associates
Account reference	JB001
Address	24 Shaw Street
	Mereford
	MR4 6KJ
Contact name	John Butler
Telephone	01908 824342
Fax	01908 824295
	www.jbutler.co.uk, Email mail@jbutler.co.uk
Credit limit	£10,000

Invoice reference 10013 for £5,500.00 issued on 05 01 13

Tom inputs the data on the 'Details' screen.

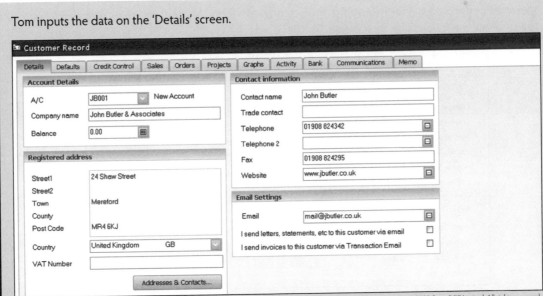

He now has to input the details of the invoice which he had issued on 5 January and which has not yet been paid. He does this by clicking the O/B button in the Balance box which brings up the screen shown below. When prompted to Save the new record, Tom clicks 'Yes'.

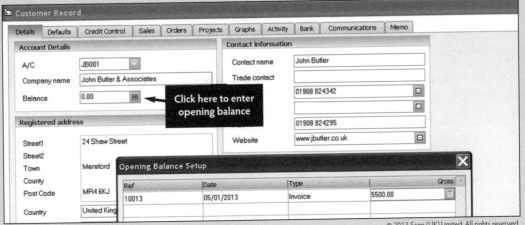

The data Tom inputs into the above screen is:

Ref: the invoice number

Date: the date the invoice was issued

Type: the transaction was the issue of an invoice

Gross: the total amount of the invoice

Having saved this data, Tom will go to the CREDIT CONTROL screen and input the credit limit, the payment period and the terms, and tick the box marked 'Terms Agreed' and then Save again. Some of these details may already be on screen if Tom has used the CONFIGURATION EDITOR (see page 38).

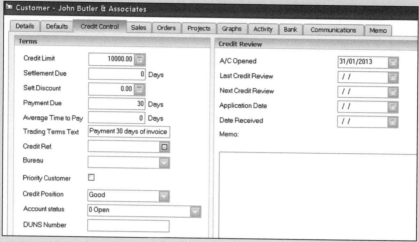

Tom will now repeat this process with the other five customer records, checking carefully as he goes and saving each record as it is created.

entering supplier details and opening balances

Tom can now carry out the same process for supplier details and opening balances. He will first ensure that the Supplier Defaults in SETTINGS include T1 as the default tax code and 5000 as the default Nominal Account number.

He sets up his Supplier accounts by clicking on RECORD in SUPPLIERS. The first supplier to input is Delco PLC. The information he wants to input (including the invoice issued by the supplier) is as follows:

Account name	Delco PLC
Account reference	DE001
Address	Delco House
	Otto Way
	New Milton
	SR1 6TF
Contact name	Nina Patel

Telephone 01722 295875, Fax 01722 295611, www.delco.co.uk
Email sales@delco.co.uk

Credit limit granted £10,000, payment terms 30 days of invoice date

Invoice reference 4563 for £5,750.00 issued by Delco PLC on 04 01 13

Tom will now input the supplier details and opening balances, starting with Delco PLC. The completed Delco PLC details screen is shown below.

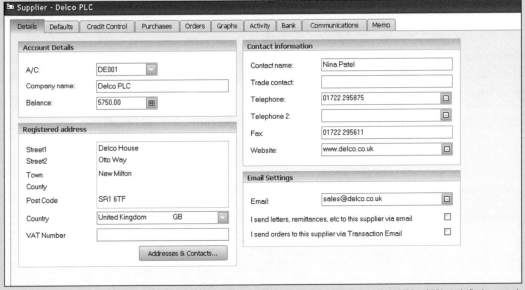

Tom will now input the credit limit and payment terms agreed on the CREDIT CONTROL screen of the Supplier record. These are not held as defaults because they may well vary from supplier to supplier. The 'terms agreed' box will also be ticked.

Tom will now repeat this process with the other supplier records, checking carefully as he goes and saving each record as it is created.

the final checks

Tom will need to ensure that his input is correct and that the customer and supplier accounts are accurate.

Tom will now check the individual account entries by comparing his original paper-based records with reports printed from CUSTOMERS and SUPPLIERS.

The input of customer invoices can be checked from the Day Books: Customer Invoices (Summary) Report, which can be printed from the list of reports accessed through the REPORTS icon on the CUSTOMERS menu bar.

Pronto Supplies Limited
Day Books: Customer Invoices (Summary)

Customer From:
Customer To: ZZZZZZZ

Transaction From: 1
Transaction To: 99,999,999

Tran No.	Items	Tp	Date	A/C Ref	Inv Ref	Details	Net Amount	Tax Amount	Gross Amount
1	1	SI	05/01/2013	JB001	10013	Opening Balance	5,500.00	0.00	5,500.00
2	1	SI	05/01/2013	CH001	10014	Opening Balance	2,400.00	0.00	2,400.00
3	1	SI	09/01/2013	CR001	10015	Opening Balance	3,234.00	0.00	3,234.00
4	1	SI	10/01/2013	DB001	10016	Opening Balance	3,400.00	0.00	3,400.00
5	1	SI	10/01/2013	KD001	10017	Opening Balance	6,500.00	0.00	6,500.00
6	1	SI	17/01/2013	LG001	10019	Opening Balance	8,500.00	0.00	8,500.00
						Totals:	29,534.00	0.00	29,534.00

The input of supplier invoices can be checked from the Day Books: Supplier Invoices (Summary) Report accessed through REPORTS on the SUPPLIERS menu bar.

Pronto Supplies Limited
Day Books: Supplier Invoices (Summary)

Supplier From:
Supplier To: ZZZZZZZ

Transaction From: 1
Transaction To: 99,999,999

Tran No.	Item	Type	Date	A/C Ref	Inv Ref	Details	Net Amount	Tax Amount	Gross Amount
7	1	PI	04/01/2013	DE001	4563	Opening Balance	5,750.00	0.00	5,750.00
8	1	PI	05/01/2013	EL001	8122	Opening Balance	8,500.00	0.00	8,500.00
9	1	PI	09/01/2013	MA001	9252	Opening Balance	4,500.00	0.00	4,500.00
						Totals	18,750.00	0.00	18,750.00

Lastly Tom will print out a **trial balance**. He does this by clicking on Company on the vertical toolbar, then Financials in the Links section above and finally the Trial icon on the horizontal toolbar. In the criteria window he chooses January 2013 in the drop-down menu. A trial balance is a list of the account balances of the company. It shows the control (total) accounts as follows.

Debtors Control Account £29,534 (the total of the customer invoices)

Creditors Control Account £18,750 (the total of the supplier invoices)

The Suspense Account has been created automatically and shows the arithmetic difference (£10,784) between the two control accounts. It is put in automatically by the system to make the two columns balance.

Pronto Supplies Limited
Period Trial Balance

To Period: Month 1, January 2013

N/C	Name	Debit	Credit
1100	Debtors Control Account	29,534.00	
2100	Creditors Control Account		18,750.00
9998	Suspense Account		10,784.00
	Totals:	29,534.00	29,534.00

conclusion

The Customer and Supplier records are now installed and their account balances summarised in the two Control 'total' Accounts.

The trial balance is far from complete, however, and Tom's next task will be to input the Nominal Ledger balances – eg income received, expenses paid, loans, items purchased. When these items have all been entered the Trial Balance should 'balance' – the two columns will have the same total and the Suspense Account will disappear. This will be dealt with in the next chapter.

AMENDING RECORDS

As well as setting up customer and supplier records, an organisation operating a computer accounting system will from time-to-time need to amend its records. For example amending records:

■ to take account of changes of address, contact names, terms of supply

■ by indicating that the account is no longer active

■ by deleting the account (if the system allows you to – see page 47)

amending records in Sage

The procedures in Sage are very straightforward:

■ select either CUSTOMERS or SUPPLIERS as appropriate

■ highlight the record that needs amending, click Record and go to the

   - DETAILS screen (for customer or supplier details) or

   - CREDIT CONTROL screen (for terms of supply, eg credit limit)

■ make the necessary change on-screen

■ SAVE and BACK UP

In the following example, the name of a customer contact at L Garr & Co has been changed from Ted Nigmer to Win Norberry.

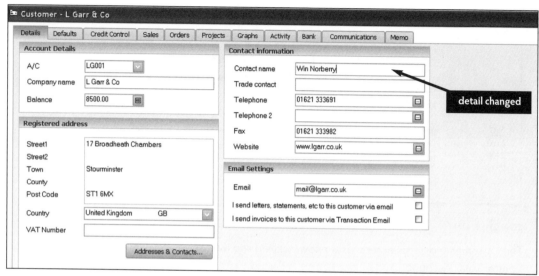

In the example below, the credit limit of £10,000 given to customer John Butler & Associates has been increased to £15,000.

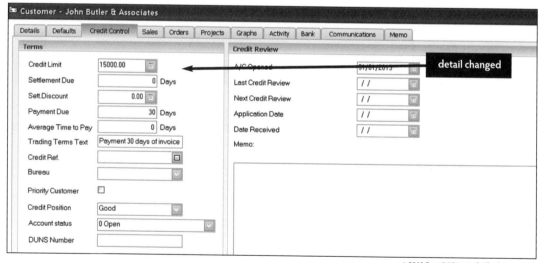

'closing' a customer or supplier account

The question may well arise "What should we do if a customer has ceased trading, or if we no longer use a particular supplier?" The logical answer is to close the account.

Sage does not allow you to **delete** an account when there are transactions recorded on it, even if the balance is nil. Instead you should **amend** the name of the account on the Customer or Supplier Record to something anonymous like 'Closed Account' so that it cannot be used again.

If, on the other hand, the account has no transactions on it (eg it may have been opened and not used), it may be closed by clicking on the Delete button at the bottom of the Details tab of the Record (see below).

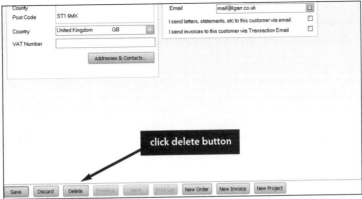

CHAPTER SUMMARY

- Businesses buy and sell products either on a cash basis (immediate payment) or on credit (payment made later).

- The accounting records for selling on credit comprise the accounts of customers (debtors) contained in the Sales Ledger.

- The accounting records for buying on credit comprise the accounts of suppliers (creditors) contained in the Purchases Ledger.

- A business will also have to agree the terms of trading with a customer – the credit limit, the level of discounts and the payment period it allows.

- In the Sage accounting system the Sales Ledger is known as 'Customers' and the Purchases Ledger as 'Suppliers'.

- Setting up Customer and Supplier records in Sage involves the input of details such as names, addresses and outstanding financial transactions.

- Records set up in this way should be carefully checked against printed out reports such as the Day Book report and the Trial Balance.

- Customer and Supplier records in Sage can also be amended or deleted (where allowable) as required.

KEY TERMS

cash sale	a sale where payment is immediate
credit sale	a sale where payment follows after an agreed period of time
debtors	customers who owe money to a business
creditors	suppliers who are owed money by a business
debtors control account	the total of the balances of debtors' accounts
creditors control account	the total of the balances of creditors' accounts
credit terms	discounts and extended payment periods allowed to customers who make purchases
defaults	sets of data on the computer which are automatically applied

EXERCISES

PRONTO SUPPLIES INPUTTING TASKS

> **Warning note!**
>
> This activity involves you setting up Customer and Supplier records in Sage and inputting live data into the computer.
>
> Ensure that you have changed your program date to 31 January 2013 in SETTINGS.
>
> Also check that the Customer and Supplier Defaults are set to Nominal accounts 4000 and 5000 respectively. The default tax code should be T1 (standard rate). The Customer Defaults can also be set up for payment due days as 30 days and terms of payment 30 days of invoice.

Task 1

Enter the customer details into the Customers screens as indicated in the Case Study.

The six customer records are as follows:

JB001   John Butler & Associates
         24 Shaw Street
         Mereford
         MR4 6KJ

Contact name: John Butler

Telephone 01908 824342, Fax 01908 824295, www.jbutler.co.uk

Email mail@jbutler.co.uk

Credit limit £10,000

Invoice 10013 issued, 05 01 13, £5,500.00

CH001   Charisma Design
         36 Dingle Road
         Mereford
         MR2 8GF

Contact name: Lindsay Foster

Telephone 01908 345287, Fax 01908 345983, www.charisma.co.uk

Email mail@charisma.co.uk

Credit limit £5,000

Invoice 10014 issued, 05 01 13, £2,400.00

CR001   **Crowmatic Ltd**
Unit 12 Severnside Estate
Mereford
MR3 6FD

Contact name: John Crow

Telephone 01908 674237, Fax 01908 674345, www.crowmatic.co.uk

Email mail@crowmatic.co.uk

Credit limit £5,000

Invoice 10015 issued, 09 01 13, £3,234.00

DB001   **David Boossey**
17 Harebell Road
Mereford Green
MR6 4NB

Contact name: David Boossey

Telephone 01908 333981, Fax 01908 333761, Email dboossey@swoopwing.com

Credit limit £5,000

Invoice 10016 issued, 10 01 13, £3,400.00

KD001   **Kay Denz**
The Stables
Martley Hillside
MR6 4FV

Contact name: Kay Denz

Telephone 01908 624945, Fax 01908 624945, Email kdenz@centra.com

Credit limit £10,000

Invoice 10017 issued,10 01 13 , £6,500.00

LG001   **L Garr & Co**
17 Broadheath Chambers
Stourminster
ST1 6MX

Contact name: Ted Nigmer

Telephone 01621 333691, Fax 01621 333982, www.lgarr.co.uk

Email mail@lgarr.co.uk

Credit limit £15,000

Invoice 10019 issued, 17 01 13, £8,500.00

Task 2

Enter the supplier details into the Suppliers screens as indicated in the Case Study.

The three supplier records are as follows:

DE001   Delco PLC
Delco House
Otto Way
New Milton
SR1 6TF

Contact name: Nina Patel

Telephone 01722 295875, Fax 01722 295611, Email sales@delco.co.uk

www.delco.co.uk

Credit limit £10,000, payment period 30 days.

Invoice 4563 issued, 04 01 13, £5,750.00

EL001   Electron Supplies
17 Maxim Way
Manchester
M1 5TF

Contact name: Jon Summers

Telephone 0161 628 2151, Fax 0161 628 2161, Email sales@electronsupplies.co.uk

www.electronsupplies.co.uk

Credit limit £15,000, payment period 30 days.

Invoice 8122 issued 05 01 13, £8,500.00

MA001   MacCity
Unit 15 Elmwood Trading Estate
RoughWay
RM2 9TG

Contact name: Josh Masters

Telephone 01899 949233, Fax 01899 949331, Email sales@maccity.co.uk

www.maccity.co.uk

Credit limit £10,000, payment period 30 days.

Invoice 9252 issued 09 01 13, £4,500.00

Task 3

Print out a Day Books: Customer Invoices (Summary) Report for the new Customer accounts and check and agree the amounts you have input. Check it against the printout on page 271.

Task 4

Print out a Day Books: Supplier Invoices (Summary) Report for the new Supplier accounts and check and agree the amounts you have input. Check it against the printout on page 271.

Task 5

Print out a Trial Balance for January 2013 and check that the Debtors and Creditors Control Account balances agree with the figures on page 271 and the totals shown on the Day Book reports produced in Tasks 3 and 4.

Task 6

At the end of January, Ted Nigmer, who is your named contact at L Garr & Co, retires. He has been replaced by Win Norberry. You are asked to amend the customer details as appropriate.

Task 7

At the end of January, Tom of Pronto Supplies has had discussions with a good customer, John Butler & Associates, and has agreed to amend their credit limit to £15,000. You are asked to amend the customer record as appropriate.

Task 8

Tom asks you how you would delete a customer or supplier record on the Sage system if you ceased to deal with the customer or supplier. What would be your reply?

Would your reply be any different if the account had not been used at all, and had no transactions recorded on it?

Reminder! Have you made a back-up?

5 SETTING UP THE NOMINAL LEDGER

Chapter introduction

- In the last two chapters we have set up the company in Sage and entered details of Customers and Suppliers. All that remains to be done is to set up the Nominal Ledger on the computer.

- The Nominal Ledger contains all the other accounts in the accounting system:

  - income accounts, including Sales

  - purchases accounts for goods that the company trades in

  - expenses and overheads accounts

  - asset accounts (for items the business owns)

  - liability accounts (for items the business owes)

  - capital accounts (the investment of the business owner)

- The Nominal Ledger lists the bank accounts of the business, but they are operated through a separate BANK module, just as in a manual accounting system the bank accounts are recorded in a Cash Book, kept separately from the Nominal Ledger accounts.

- The accounts in the Nominal Ledger are set up in Sage using the structure of a 'Chart of Accounts' provided by the program. This allocates suitable reference numbers to the various accounts which are grouped in categories (eg expenses, assets, liabilities) so that the computer program knows where to find them in the system and can then provide suitable reports to management.

- One of the reports produced by the computer is the Trial Balance, which lists the nominal account balances in two balancing columns. When the balances of all the nominal accounts have been entered on the computer, the two columns should balance and the Suspense Account (which records any difference) should disappear.

NOMINAL ACCOUNTS

nominal accounts

An account in an accounting system records financial transactions and provides a running balance of what is left in the account at the end of each day. The **nominal ledger** accounts in any accounting system are the accounts which are not Customer accounts (sales ledger) or Supplier accounts (purchases ledger). They may also be referred to as 'main ledger' or 'general ledger' accounts. The nominal accounts record:

- income – eg sales, rent received
- expenses – eg wages, advertising
- assets – items that a business owns or amounts that it is owed
- liabilities – money that a business owes, eg loans or creditors
- capital – money invested by the owner(s) and profits made

bank accounts

In a manual accounting system the bank accounts are kept in a separate Cash Book and are not strictly speaking part of the Nominal Ledger. In Sage the bank accounts of the business are *listed* in NOMINAL, but they are *operated* through a separate BANK module.

the default nominal accounts

When Tom in the Case Study set up his company he chose the set of nominal accounts automatically provided by the Sage program.

If you click on the Company button in the Sage opening screen the accounts are to be found in the Nominal opening screen (see below). You can scroll down this screen to see the whole list (summarised on the next page). Note that the full list of nominal accounts for a Limited Company supplied in Sage 2012 may not appear if data has been restored from previous versions of Sage.

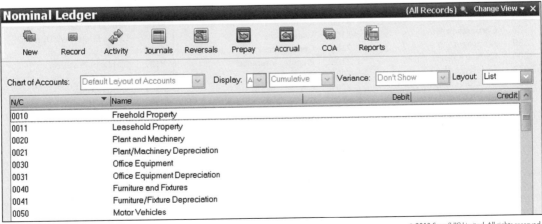

Nominal Account List

0010	Freehold Property	4099	Flat Rate – Benefit/Cost	7350	Scale Charges
0011	Leasehold Property	4100	Sales Type D	7400	Travelling
0020	Plant and Machinery	4101	Sales Type E	7401	Car Hire
0021	Plant/Machinery Depreciation	4200	Sales of Assets	7402	Hotels
0030	Office Equipment	4400	Credit Charges (Late P'ments)	7403	U.K. Entertainment
0031	Office Equipment Depreciation	4900	Miscellaneous Income	7404	Overseas Entertainment
0040	Furniture and Fixtures	4901	Royalties Received	7405	Overseas Travelling
0041	Furniture/Fixture Dpn	4902	Commissions Received	7406	Subsistence
0050	Motor Vehicles	4903	Insurance Claims	7500	Printing
0051	Motor Vehicles Depreciation	4904	Rent Income	7501	Postage and Carriage
1001	Stock	4905	Distribution and Carriage	7502	Office Stationery
1002	Work in Progress	5000	Materials Purchased	7503	Books etc
1003	Finished Goods	5001	Materials Imported	7550	Telephone and Fax
1004	Raw materials	5002	Miscellaneous Purchases	7551	Internet Charges
1100	Debtors Control Account	5003	Packaging	7552	Computers and Software
1101	Sundry Debtors	5009	Discounts Taken	7553	Mobile Charges
1102	Other Debtors	5100	Carriage	7600	Legal Fees
1103	Prepayments	5101	Import Duty	7601	Audit Fees
1104	Inter-company Debtors	5102	Transport Insurance	7602	Accountancy Fees
1105	Provision for Credit Notes	5200	Opening Stock	7603	Consultancy Fees
1106	Provision for Doubtful Debts	5201	Closing Stock	7604	Professional Fees
1200	Bank Current Account	6000	Productive Labour	7605	Mgt Charges Payable
1210	Bank Deposit Account	6001	Cost of Sales Labour	7606	Software Subscriptions
1220	Building Society Account	6002	Sub-Contractors	7700	Equipment Hire
1230	Petty Cash	6100	Sales Commissions	7701	Office Machine Maintenance
1235	Cash Register	6200	Sales Promotions	7702	Equipment Leasing
1240	Company Credit Card	6201	Advertising	7703	Leasing Costs
1250	Credit Card Receipts	6202	Gifts and Samples	7800	Repairs and Renewals
2100	Creditors Control Account	6203	P.R.(Literature & Brochures)	7801	Cleaning
2101	Sundry Creditors	6900	Miscellaneous Expenses	7802	Laundry
2102	Other Creditors	7000	Gross Wages	7803	Premises Expenses
2109	Accruals	7001	Directors Salaries	7900	Bank Interest Paid
2200	Sales Tax Control Account	7002	Directors Remuneration	7901	Bank Charges
2201	Purchase Tax Control Acc.	7003	Staff Salaries	7902	Currency Charges
2202	VAT Liability	7004	Wages-Regular	7903	Loan Interest Paid
2204	Manual Adjustments	7005	Wages-Casual	7904	H.P. Interest
2210	P.A.Y.E.	7006	Employers N.I.	7905	Credit Charges
2211	National Insurance	7007	Employers Pensions	7906	Exchange Rate Variance
2220	Net Wages	7008	Recruitment Expenses	7907	Other Interest Charges
2230	Pension Fund	7009	Adjustments	7908	Factoring Charges
2300	Loans	7010	SSP Reclaimed	8000	Depreciation
2310	Hire Purchase	7011	SMP Reclaimed	8001	Plant/Machinery Depreciation
2320	Corporation Tax	7012	Employers NI (Directors)	8002	Furniture/Fitting Depreciation
2330	Mortgages	7100	Rent	8003	Vehicle Depreciation
3000	Ordinary Shares	7102	Water Rates	8004	Office Equipment Dpn
3010	Preference Shares	7103	General Rates	8100	Bad Debt Write Off
3060	Directors Loan Acc (Dir 1)	7104	Premises Insurance	8102	Bad Debt Provision
3061	Directors Loan Acc (Dir 2)	7200	Electricity	8200	Donations
3100	Reserves	7201	Gas	8201	Subscriptions
3101	Undistributed Reserves	7202	Oil	8202	Clothing Costs
3200	Profit and Loss Account	7203	Other Heating Costs	8203	Training Costs
4000	Sales Type A	7300	Vehicle Fuel	8204	Insurance
4001	Sales Type B	7301	Vehicle Repairs & Servicing	8205	Refreshments
4002	Sales Type C	7302	Vehicle Licences	8206	Cash Register Discrepancies
4009	Discounts Allowed	7303	Vehicle Insurance	8250	Sundry Expenses
4010	Mgmt Charges Receivable	7304	Misc Motor Expenses	9001	Taxation
		7305	Congestion Charges	9998	Suspense Account
		7306	Mileage Claims	9999	Mispostings Account

CHART OF ACCOUNTS

If you look at the nominal account list you will see that a four digit code is given to each nominal account in the nominal ledger. These account number codes range from 0010 to 9999. Tom is very unlikely to use all these accounts and may even want to change some.

What is important, however, is that Tom – or any user of Sage – must appreciate that these accounts are organised into categories by account number. These categories are set out in the **Chart of Accounts**. They can be accessed in the Nominal Ledger by clicking on the COA (chart of accounts) icon and then EDIT . . .

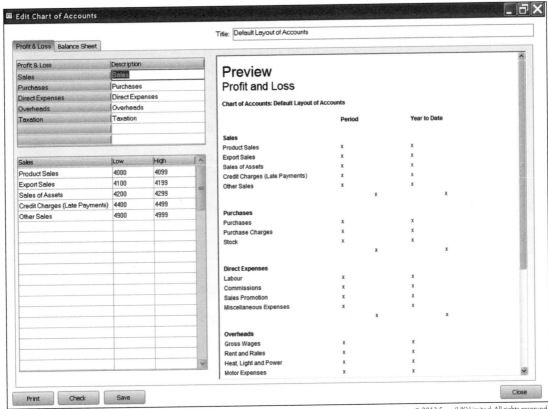

The left-hand panel shows the **categories** of account, eg Sales, Purchases. If you click on a category you will see the ranges of accounts and account numbers covered by that category displayed in the right-hand panel.

In this case the Sales category has been selected and the types of Sales listed on the right. This panel tells you that all Product Sales should have an account number between 4000 and 4099. When you set up the Customer records in the last chapter you chose 4000 as the default number (see page 38) for sales to customers.

If you wanted to categorise customer sales (by area or type of product, for example) you could choose to have three accounts running for Product Sales: 4000 Sales Type A, 4001 Sales Type B, 4002 Sales Type C.

reports from nominal

The Sage nominal accounts are used as the basis for a number of computer-generated management reports telling the owner about subjects such as the profit and the value of the business. If accounts get into the wrong category, the reports will also be wrong.

a summary of categories

It may be that a new business will adopt all the default nominal accounts (see list on page 56) because it does not need any others, but if a new account has to be set up it is critical that the new account is in the right category. The business owner will therefore need to understand what the categories mean and what they include.

The nominal categories and account number ranges are:

Sales	4000 - 4999	income from sales of goods or services
Purchases	5000 - 5299	items bought to produce goods to sell
Direct Expenses	6000 - 6999	expenses directly related to producing goods
Overheads	7000 - 8299	expenses the business has to pay anyway

*These are used to produce the **profit and loss statement** which shows what profit (or loss) the business has made.*

Fixed Assets	0010 - 0059	items bought to keep in the business long-term
Current Assets	1000 - 1250	items owned by the business in the short-term
Current Liabilities	2100 - 2299	items owed by the business in the short-term
Long Term Liabilities	2300 - 2399	items owed by the business in the long-term
Capital & Reserves	3000 - 3299	the financial investment of the owner(s)

*These are used to produce the **balance sheet** which gives an idea of the value of the business and shows the owner what is represented by the capital investment (the money put in by the owner).*

We will now put this theory into practice with a continuation of the Pronto Supplies Limited Case Study.

CASE STUDY

PRONTO SUPPLIES LIMITED:
SETTING UP THE NOMINAL ACCOUNTS

Pronto Supplies Limited was set up in January 2013 and during that month operated a **manual** book-keeping system using hand-written double-entry ledger accounts.

It was a busy month for Tom Cox . . .

financing	Tom paid £75,000 into the bank as ordinary share capital to start up the limited company business.
	Tom also raised a £35,000 business loan from the bank.

assets   The finance raised enabled Tom to buy:

office computers	£35,000
office equipment	£15,000
furniture for the office	£25,000

purchases   Tom's total purchases of goods for resale in January was £69,100.

sales   Tom divided his sales into three types:

Computer hardware sales

Computer software sales

Computer consultancy

overheads   Tom also had to pay fixed expenses including:

Wages	£16,230
Advertising	£12,400
Rent	£4,500
Rates	£450
Electricity	£150
Telephone	£275
Stationery	£175

Pronto Supplies Trial Balance

Tom at the end of January listed all the balances of his accounts in two columns, using a spreadsheet. This is his trial balance and will form the basis of the entries to the Sage system. The columns are headed up Debit (Dr) and Credit (Cr) and they have the same total. In double-entry bookkeeping each debit entry in the accounts is mirrored by a credit entry. (Refer to Chapter 14 if you are not sure about this). If the bookkeeping is correct, the total of debits should be the same as the total of the credits. The spreadsheet is shown below. Note that:

- **debits** = assets and expenses   **credits** = liabilities, capital and income

- the control (total) account for debtors shows the total amount owed by all Tom's customers; it is a debit balance because it is money owed to the business

- the control (total) account for creditors shows the total amount owed by Tom to his suppliers; it is a credit balance because it is money owed by the business

- Tom is registered with HM Revenue & Customs for Value Added Tax (VAT). This means that he has to quote his registration number on all his documents and also

  - charge VAT on his sales – this is due to HM Revenue & Customs and so is a credit balance – Sales tax control account

  - reclaim VAT on what he has bought – this is due from HM Revenue & Customs and so is a debit balance – Purchase tax control account

	A	B	C	D	E	F	G	H	I	J
1	TRIAL BALANCE		Dr	Cr						
2										
3	Plant and machinery		35000							
4	Office equipment		15000							
5	Furniture and fixtures		25000							
6	Debtors control account		29534							
7	Bank current account		14656							
8	Creditors control account			18750						
9	Sales tax control account			17920						
10	Purchase tax control account		26600							
11	Loans			35000						
12	Ordinary shares			75000						
13	Computer hardware sales			85000						
14	Computer software sales			15000						
15	Computer consultancy sales			2400						
16	Materials purchased		69100							
17	Advertising		12400							
18	Gross wages		16230							
19	Rent		4500							
20	General rates		450							
21	Electricity		150							
22	Office stationery		175							
23	Telephone		275							
24										
25	Total		249070	249070						
26										
27										
28										

inputting the accounts into Sage Nominal

The date is 31 January 2013.

Tom uses his trial balance as the source document for inputting his nominal account balances. The procedure he adopts is:

1   He clicks on the Company button on the vertical toolbar and examines the nominal accounts list which appears on the Nominal Ledger screen. He allocates the accounts in his existing books with computer account numbers as follows:

Plant and machinery	0020
Office equipment (photocopiers, phones etc)	0030
Furniture and fixtures	0040
Debtors control account	1100
Bank current account	1200
Creditors control account	2100
Sales tax control account	2200
Purchase tax control account	2201
Loans	2300
Ordinary Shares	3000
Sales Type A (hardware)	4000
Sales Type B (software)	4001
Sales Type C (consultancy)	4002
Materials purchased	5000
Advertising	6201
Gross wages	7000
Rent	7100
General rates	7103
Electricity	7200
Office stationery	7502
Telephone and fax	7550

Note: earlier versions of Sage used account number 7502 for Telephone and fax, and 7504 for Office Stationery. These numbers can be used instead of the ones shown here.

2   Tom scrolls down the screen and clicks on all the accounts that he is going to need – they then show as selected.

But – importantly – he does not click on the following two accounts:

Debtors Control Account – the total of the Customers' accounts

Creditors Control Account – the total of the Suppliers' accounts

This is because he has already input the debtors' (Customers') and creditors' (Suppliers') balances (see the last chapter). If he inputs these totals now they will be entered into the computer twice and cause havoc with the accounting records!

The NOMINAL screen is shown below.

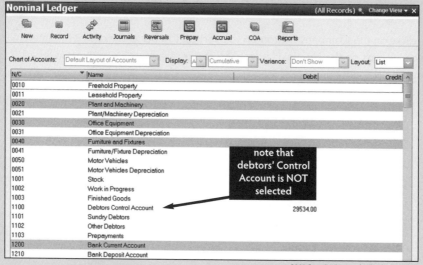

3   Tom is now ready to input the balances of these accounts. To do this he will

-    Select the RECORD icon which will bring up a RECORD window.

-    Click on O/B on the balance box which asks him to enter the date (31/01/2013) and the balance which must go in the correct box: debits on the left, credits on the right. He should ignore the 'ref' box. The first account entry will look like this:

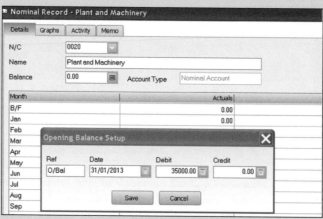

This record should then be saved.

Tom should repeat this for all the selected accounts (using the Next button to move to the next one), making sure that he is saving all the data as he goes along.

checking the input – the trial balance

Tom needs to check that what he has input is accurate. He needs to check his original list of balances – his trial balance (see page 60) – against the computer trial balance.

The trial balance is produced through clicking Financials in the Links pane and clicking on the Trial icon. The printout produced is shown below.

The date chosen is January 2013.

Pronto Supplies Limited
Period Trial Balance

Page: 1

To Period: Month 1, January 2013

N/C	Name	Debit	Credit
0020	Plant and Machinery	35,000.00	
0030	Office Equipment	15,000.00	
0040	Furniture and Fixtures	25,000.00	
1100	Debtors Control Account	29,534.00	
1200	Bank Current Account	14,656.00	
2100	Creditors Control Account		18,750.00
2200	Sales Tax Control Account		17,920.00
2201	Purchase Tax Control Account	26,600.00	
2300	Loans		35,000.00
3000	Ordinary Shares		75,000.00
4000	Sales Type A		85,000.00
4001	Sales Type B		15,000.00
4002	Sales Type C		2,400.00
5000	Materials Purchased	69,100.00	
6201	Advertising	12,400.00	
7000	Gross Wages	16,230.00	
7100	Rent	4,500.00	
7103	General Rates	450.00	
7200	Electricity	150.00	
7502	Office Stationery	175.00	
7550	Telephone and Fax	275.00	
	Totals:	249,070.00	249,070.00

Is the input accurate? Yes, because all the figures agree with the original trial balance figures and they are all in the correct column. The totals also agree.

You will see that the Suspense Account which the system created in the last chapter (see page 45) has now disappeared because the total of the debits now equals the total of the credits, as on Tom's spreadsheet shown on page 60.

Tom is now ready to input February's transactions – new sales invoices, new purchase invoices and payments in and out of the bank. These will be dealt with in the chapters that follow.

CHANGING NOMINAL ACCOUNT DETAILS

It is possible to change the names of accounts in the Nominal Ledger if they do not fit in with the nature of your business. If, for example, you run a travel agency your Nominal account names may be very different from the names used by an insurance broker.

The important point to remember is that if you change your account names they must fit in with the categories in the Chart of Accounts. Much of this should be common sense.

adding new nominal accounts

Accounts can be added to the Nominal Ledger. Again, care should be taken to ensure that any new account fits into the Chart of Accounts structure (see page 57).

entering budgets

Target figures or budgets for each month can be entered in the nominal records. These can then be compared to actual results to measure the progress of the business.

Budget figures can be entered on a month by month basis or by putting a total for the year in the Total box of the Budgets column in the nominal record. This is then divided by 12 and distributed automatically throughout the months of the year.

Details	Graphs	Activity	Memo		
N/C	4000				
Name	Computer hardware sales				
Balance	85000.00 Cr	Account Type	Control Account		

Month		Actuals	Budgets
B/F		0.00	0.00
Jan		85000.00 Cr	75000.00
Feb		0.00	75000.00
Mar		0.00	75000.00
Apr		0.00	75000.00
May		0.00	75000.00
Jun		0.00	75000.00
Jul		0.00	75000.00
Aug		0.00	75000.00
Sep		0.00	75000.00
Oct		0.00	75000.00
Nov		0.00	75000.00
Dec		0.00	75000.00
Future		0.00	0.00
Total		85000.00 Cr	900000.00

In the Case Study continuation on the next page, Tom changes the names of his sales accounts to reflect more accurately what is going on in his business. Tom also plans to offer a computer helpline to customers and so decides to add this to his sales accounts.

CASE STUDY

PRONTO SUPPLIES LIMITED:
CHANGING NOMINAL ACCOUNT NAMES

Tom looks at his Trial Balance (see page 63) and realises that his sales accounts are named 'Type A' and 'Type B' and 'Type C'. This does not really tell him much about what he is actually selling, so he decides that he will change the names as follows:

account number	old name	new name
4000	Sales Type A	Computer hardware sales
4001	Sales Type B	Computer software sales
4002	Sales Type C	Computer consultancy

He selects the three accounts in the NOMINAL list screen, goes to RECORD in NOMINAL and overwrites the old name in the name box for each account and Saves. The amended screen for Account 4000 (Computer hardware sales) is shown below.

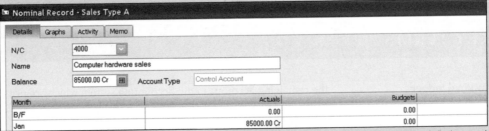

To add a new nominal account, Tom clicks RECORD and types 4003 into the N/C box. Sage recognises this as a New Account. Tom enters 'Computer helpline' in the account name box. There is no opening balance so Tom saves the new record. The new account now appears in the nominal list.

CHAPTER SUMMARY

- When a business sets up its accounts on a Sage computer accounting package it will normally set up its Customer and Supplier records first.

- The next stage will be for the business to set up its Nominal accounts, adopting the default list of accounts supplied by Sage in its 'Chart of Accounts' structure.

- If the business has already started trading it should input all its Nominal account balances (except for the Debtors and Creditors control accounts).

- The input balances should be checked carefully against the source figures. The Sage program can produce a trial balance which will show the balances that have been input.

- Account names can be changed and new accounts added to suit the nature of the business – but it is important that the type of account should be consistent with the appropriate category in the 'Chart of Accounts'.

- Target figures in the form of budgets can be entered into the nominal accounts for comparison with actual results in the future.

KEY TERMS

nominal ledger	the remaining accounts in the accounting system which are not Customers or Suppliers, eg income, expenses, assets, liabilities – in Sage this is known as 'Nominal'
chart of accounts	the structure of the nominal accounts, which groups accounts into categories such as Sales, Purchases, Overheads . . . and so on
categories	subdivisions of the Chart of Accounts (eg Sales, Purchases) each of which is allocated a range of account numbers by the computer
trial balance	a list of the accounts of a business divided into two columns: debits – mostly assets and expenses credits – mostly income and liabilities The two columns should have the same total, reflecting the workings of the double-entry bookkeeping system
budget	A forecast of the likely value that will be entered in the accounts in the future. Actual results can then be compared to the forecast to monitor how the business is performing against targets

EXERCISES

PRONTO SUPPLIES INPUTTING TASKS

> **Warning note!**
> This activity involves inputting live data into the computer.
> Remember to save your data and keep your printouts as you progress through the tasks.

Task 1

Make sure the program date is set to 31 January 2013.

Open up the nominal ledger and select accounts in the computer nominal ledger list screen for the accounts included on the spreadsheet trial balance (see page 60).

But do not select Debtors Control Account or Creditors Control Account as they already have balances on them.

Task 2

Enter the balances from the spreadsheet trial balance (see page 60) into the appropriate nominal accounts as opening balances – but do not input the Debtors Control Account and the Creditors Control Account.

Make sure that debits are entered as debits and credits as credits.

Task 3

Print out a trial balance for January 2013 from the computer and check it against the trial balance on page 63, or have it checked by your tutor. The suspense account should have disappeared.

Task 4

Change the names of the three sales accounts you have chosen as follows:

number	old name	new name
4000	Sales Type A	Computer hardware sales
4001	Sales Type B	Computer software sales
4002	Sales Type C	Computer consultancy

Task 5

Add new account number 4003 Computer helpline to the Nominal list.

> **Reminder! Have you made a back-up?**
> This back-up is very important as you may need to restore it at the beginning of Chapter 8 on page 96.

6 SELLING TO CUSTOMERS ON CREDIT

This chapter explains the use of the 'batch entry' method for entering customer invoices and credit notes. It presumes that the sales invoices are not produced within Sage and that the Products module is not used to record stock movements. If you want to use the Products, Sales Order Processing, Invoicing and Purchase Order Processing modules, skip this chapter and Chapter 7 and go straight to Chapter 8.

Chapter introduction

- A business that sells on credit will invoice the goods or services supplied and then receive payment at a later date.

- The invoice is an important document because it sets out the details of the goods or services supplied, the amount owing, and the date by which payment should be made.

- It is therefore essential that details of the invoice are entered in the computer accounting records so that the sale can be recorded and the amount owed by the customer logged into the accounting system.

- In this chapter we look at entering details of sales invoices produced outside the Sage program. This is known as 'batch entry'.

- A business that sells on credit may have to issue a refund for some or all of the goods or services supplied. They may be faulty or the sale may be cancelled. As payment has not yet been made, the 'refund' takes the form of a deduction from the amount owing. The document that the seller issues in this case is a credit note.

- A credit note is dealt with by a computer accounting program in much the same way as an invoice. This chapter deals with the 'batch entry' of sales credit notes.

- Processing invoices may involve the use of discounts. There are two main types of discount:

  - Trade discount, a percentage reduction in the price of goods or services

  - Cash discount (also know as settlement discount), a percentage reduction in the price of goods or services allowed for early settlement of an invoice

- This chapter continues the Pronto Supplies Case Study and shows how details of invoices and credit notes are entered into the computer accounting records.

- The next chapter looks at how the invoices and credit notes issued by suppliers are dealt with by a computer accounting program.

BACKGROUND TO FINANCIAL DOCUMENTS

When a business sells goods or services it will use a number of different financial documents. A single sales transaction involves both seller and buyer. In this chapter we look at the situation from the point of view of the seller of the goods or services. Documents which are often used in the selling process for goods include:

- **purchase order** which the seller receives from the buyer
- **delivery note** which goes with the goods from the seller to the buyer
- **invoice** which lists the goods and tells the buyer what is owed
- **credit note** which is sent to the buyer if any refund is due
- **statement** sent by the seller to remind the buyer what is owed
- **remittance advice** sent by the buyer with the payment

Study the diagram below which shows how the documents 'flow' between buyer and seller.

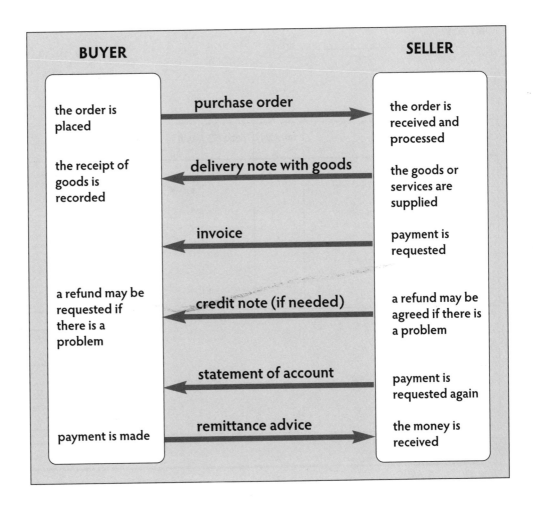

INVOICE

The main document we will deal with in this chapter is the **invoice** which is sent by the seller to the buyer to state what is owing and when it has to be paid. An invoice is illustrated below and explained on the next page.

INVOICE

DELCO PLC

Delco House, Otto Way, New Milton SR1 6TF
Tel 01722 295875 Fax 01722 295611 Email sales@delco.co.uk
VAT Reg GB 0745 4672 76

invoice to

Pronto Supplies Limited Unit 17 Severnvale Estate Broadwater Road Mereford MR1 6TF	invoice no	12309
	account	3993
	your reference	47609
	date	02 10 13

product code	description	quantity	price (£)	unit	total	discount %	net
Z324	Zap USB Flash Memory Drive	20	11.00	pack of 5	220.00	0.00	220.00

terms		
30 days	goods total	220.00
	VAT	44.00
	TOTAL	264.00

The invoice here has been issued by Delco PLC for some Zap USB Flash Drives ordered by Pronto Supplies on a purchase order.

The reference number quoted here is the order number on Pronto Supplies' original purchase order.

The date here is the date on which the goods have been sent. It is known as the 'invoice date'.

The date is important for calculating when the invoice is due to be paid. In this case the 'terms' (see the bottom left-hand corner of the invoice) are 30 days. This means the invoice is due to be paid within 30 days of the invoice date.

The arithmetic and details in this line must be checked very carefully by Pronto Supplies to make sure that they pay the correct amount:

- **product code** – this is the catalogue number for the Zap Drives which Pronto put on the original purchase order
- **description** – this describes the goods ordered – the Zap Drives
- **quantity** – this should be the same as the quantity on the purchase order
- **price** – this is the price of each unit shown in the next column
- **unit** is the way in which the unit is counted up and charged for, eg single items or packs (as here)
- **total** is the price multiplied by the number of units
- **discount** % is the percentage allowance (known as trade discount) given to customers who regularly deal with the supplier, ie they receive a certain percentage (eg 10%) deducted from their bill
- **net** is the amount due to the seller after deduction of trade discount, and before VAT is added on

The Goods Total is the total of the column above it. It is the final amount due to the seller before VAT is added on.

Value Added Tax (VAT) is calculated and added on – here it is 20% of the Goods Total, ie

$£220.00 \times \dfrac{20}{100} = £44.00$

The VAT is then added to the Goods Total to produce the actual amount owing:
$£220.00 + £44.00 = £264.00$

The 'terms' explain the conditions on which the goods are supplied. Here '30 days' mean that Pronto has to pay within 30 days of 2 October.

CREDIT NOTE

The other document we will deal with in this chapter is the **credit note**.

The **credit note** is issued when some form of refund has to be given to the buyer of goods or services. As payment has not yet been made the credit note allows the buyer to deduct an amount from the invoice when settlement is finally made.

Note that it is never acceptable practice to change the amounts on an invoice; a credit note is always required.

The credit note illustrated below has been issued by Delco PLC because one of the packs of Zap drives ordered by Pronto Supplies was damaged. Pronto Supplies has returned the box, asking for a reduction in the amount owing.

Study the document below and read the notes which follow.

CREDIT NOTE

DELCO PLC

Delco House, Otto Way, New Milton SR1 6TF
Tel 01722 295875 Fax 01722 295611 Email sales@delco.co.uk

to

Pronto Supplies Limited
Unit 17 Severnvale Estate
Broadwater Road
Mereford
MR1 6TF

credit note no	12157
account	3993
your reference	47609
our invoice	12309
date/tax point	10 10 13

product code	description	quantity	price	unit	total	discount %	net
Z324	Zap USB Flash Memory Drive	1	11.00	pack of 5	11.00	0.00	11.00

Reason for credit
1 pack received damaged and returned.

GOODS TOTAL	11.00
VAT	2.20
TOTAL	13.20

notes on the credit note

You will see from the credit note on the previous page that the credit note total is £13.20. This can be deducted from the invoice total (see page 70) of £264.00. In other words, Pronto Supplies now owes £264.00 minus £13.20 = £250.80.

Note in particular from the credit note opposite:

■ The format of the credit note is very much the same as the invoice.

■ The reference quoted is Pronto Supplies' purchase order number.

■ The columns (eg 'product code') are identical to those used on the invoice and work in exactly the same way.

■ VAT is also included – it has to be refunded because the goods have not now been supplied.

■ If there was any discount this should also be refunded – but there is no discount here.

■ The reason for the credit note (the 'reason for credit') is stated at the bottom of the document. Here it is a box of faulty Zap Drives that has been returned to Delco PLC by Pronto Supplies.

INVOICES, CREDIT NOTES AND SAGE

the bookkeeping background

The totals of invoices and credit notes have to be entered into the accounting records of a business. They record the sales and refunds made to customers who have bought on credit – the **debtors** of the business (known in Sage as Customers). The amounts from these documents combine to provide the total of the **Sales Ledger**, which is the section of the accounting records which contains all the debtor (Customer) balances. This is recorded in the **Debtors Control Account** which tells the business how much in total is owing from customers who have bought on credit.

methods of recording invoices and credit notes

When a business uses a computer accounting program such as Sage, it will have to make sure that the details of each invoice and credit note issued are entered into the computer accounting records. Businesses using Sage accounting programs have two alternatives: batch entry and computer printed invoices.

batch entry

The business produces the invoices independently of the computer program (for example, it may write them out) and then, using the actual invoices as the source documents, enters the invoice details into the computer accounting program on a **batch invoice** screen. A 'batch' is simply a group of items (eg a 'batch' of cakes in the oven). The term is used in this context to describe a group of invoices which are all input at one time. This may not be the day that each invoice is produced – it may be the end of the week, or even the month.

It is normal practice to add up the totals of all the actual invoices that are being input – the 'batch total' – and check this total against the invoice total calculated by the computer from the actual input. This will pick up any errors.

A batch invoice entry screen with four invoices input is shown below.

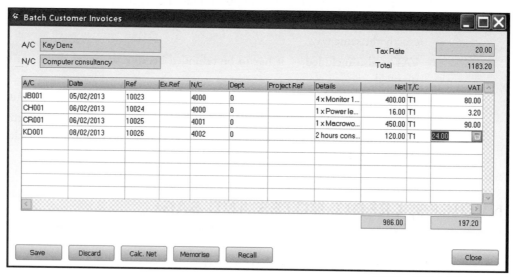

notes on the data entry columns:

■ 'A/C' column contains the customer account reference

■ 'Date' is the date on which each invoice was issued

■ 'Ref' column is the invoice number (note that they are consecutive)

■ 'Ex.Ref' is optional – it could be used for the purchase order number

■ 'N/C' column is the nominal account code which specifies which type of sale is involved

■ 'Dept' is 0 by default and is not used here

■ 'Project ref' is optional and is not used here

■ 'Details' describes the goods that have been sold

■ 'Net' is the amount of the invoice before VAT is added on

■ 'T/C' is the tax code which sets up the VAT rate that applies – here T1 refers to Standard Rate VAT, and is the default rate set up in Customer Preferences in SETTINGS

■ 'VAT' is calculated automatically

When the operator has completed the input and checked the batch totals with the computer totals, the batched invoices can be saved.

computer printed invoices

Most versions of Sage include an invoicing function which requires the business to input the details of each invoice on-screen. The computer system will then print out the invoices on the office printer – exactly as input. The invoices can either be for stock or for a service provided. If the invoice is for stock, 'product' records with product codes will normally have to be set up in Sage, and the product code used each time stock is invoiced.

Service invoices do not require a product code, because no stock is involved in the transaction. A service invoice input screen is shown below.

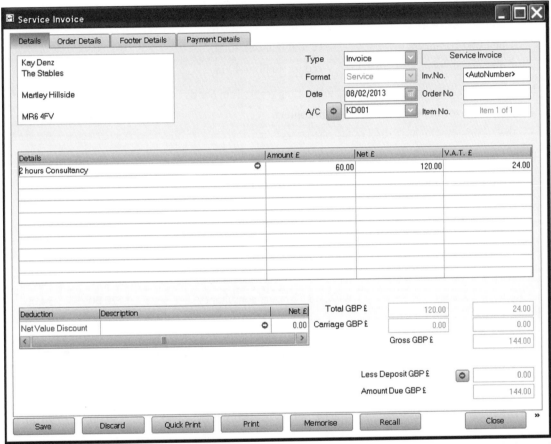

important note: treatment of invoicing in this book

In this chapter we concentrate on the batch entry method of recording invoices and credit notes. Chapter 8 deals with producing invoices within Sage.

CASE STUDY

PRONTO SUPPLIES LIMITED:

PROCESSING SALES INVOICES AND CREDIT NOTES

Tom Cox runs Pronto Supplies Limited which provides computer hardware, software and consultancy services. At the end of January he input his nominal accounts and his Customer and Supplier details and balances into his Sage accounting program. He has set up four Sales Accounts in his Nominal Ledger:

Computer hardware sales   Account number 4000

Computer software sales   Account number 4001

Computer consultancy   Account number 4002

Computer helpline   Account number 4003

It is now February 8, the end of the first full trading week. Tom needs to input

- the sales invoices he has issued to his customers
- the credit notes he has issued to his customers

He has the documents on file and has collected them in two batches . . .

sales invoices issued

invoice	name	date	details	net amount	VAT
10023	John Butler & Associates	5/02/13	4 x monitor 17"	400.00	80.00
10024	Charisma Design	6/02/13	1 x power lead 3 mtr	16.00	3.20
10025	Crowmatic Ltd	6/02/13	1 x Macroworx software V9	450.00	90.00
10026	Kay Denz	8/02/13	2 hours consultancy	120.00	24.00
Subtotals				986.00	197.20
Batch total					1183.20

credit notes issued

credit note	name	date	details	net amount	VAT
551	David Boosey	6/02/13	1 x Macroworx software V9	450.00	90.00
552	L Garr & Co	6/02/13	2 x Zap USB flash memory drv	40.00	8.00
Subtotals				490.00	98.00
Batch total					588.00

batch invoice entry

Tom will start by opening up the Customers screen in Sage and clicking on the INVOICE icon. This will show the screen shown on the next page. He will then

- identify the account references for each of the four customers
- enter each invoice on a new line

- take the data from the invoice: date, invoice no ('Ref'), product details and amounts

- enter the appropriate Sales account number ('N/C') for the type of sale

- enter the T1 tax code for standard rate VAT and check that the VAT amount calculated on-screen is the same as on the invoice

When the input is complete Tom should check his original batch totals (Net, VAT and Total) against the computer totals. Once he is happy that his input is correct he should SAVE.

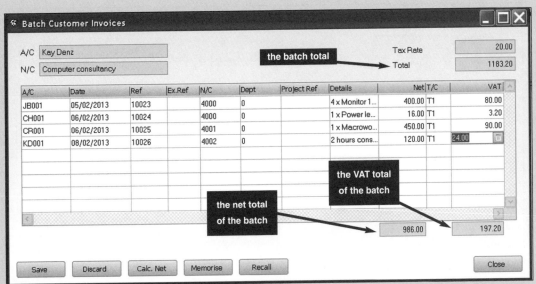

checking the invoices are on the system

As a further check Tom could print out a Day Book Report. This can be obtained through the REPORTS icon on the CUSTOMERS menu bar. The title of the report is 'Day Books: Customer Invoices (Detailed)'. The transaction date range is 05/02/2013 to 08/02/2013. The report appears as follows:

Pronto Supplies Limited
Day Books: Customer Invoices (Detailed)

Date From:		05/02/2013							Customer From:				
Date To:		08/02/2013							Customer To:		ZZZZZZZZZ		
Transaction From:		1							N/C From:				
Transaction To:		99,999,999							N/C To:		99999999		
Dept From:		0											
Dept To:		999											

Tran No.	Type	Date	A/C Ref	N/C	Inv Ref	Dept.	Details	Net Amount	Tax Amount	T/C	Gross Amount	V	B
48	SI	05/02/2013	JB001	4000	10023	0	4 x Monitor 17 inch	400.00	80.00	T1	480.00	N	-
49	SI	06/02/2013	CH001	4000	10024	0	1 x Power lead 3 mtr	16.00	3.20	T1	19.20	N	-
50	SI	06/02/2013	CR001	4001	10025	0	1 x Macroworx software	450.00	90.00	T1	540.00	N	-
51	SI	08/02/2013	KD001	4002	10026	0	2 hours consultancy	120.00	24.00	T1	144.00	N	-
							Totals:	986.00	197.20		1,183.20		

batch credit note entry

Tom will input the details from the two credit notes in much the same way as he processed the invoices. He will start by opening up the Customers screen in Sage and clicking on the CREDIT icon. This will show the screen shown below. He will then identify the account references for each of the two customers and the Sales account numbers and input the credit note details as shown on the screen. When the input is complete Tom should check his original batch totals (Net, VAT and Total) against the computer totals. Once he is happy that his input is correct he should SAVE.

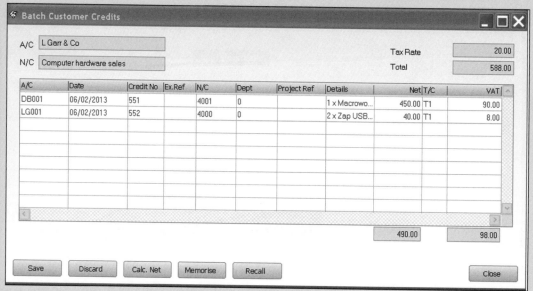

checking the credit notes are on the system

As a further check Tom could print out a Day Book Report for Credit notes. This can be obtained through the REPORTS icon on the CUSTOMERS menu bar. The title of the report is 'Day Books: Customer Credits (Detailed)'.

The report appears as follows:

Pronto Supplies Limited

Day Books: Customer Credits (Detailed)

Date From:	06/02/2013			Customer From:	
Date To:	06/02/2013			Customer To:	ZZZZZZZZZ
Transaction From:	1			N/C From:	
Transaction To:	99,999,999			N/C To:	99999999
Dept From:	0				
Dept To:	999				

Tran No.	Type	Date	A/C Ref	N/C	Inv Ref	Dept.	Details	Net Amount	Tax Amount	T/C	Gross Amount	V	B
52	SC	06/02/2013	DB001	4001	551	0	1 x Macroworx software Version 9	450.00	90.00	T1	540.00	N	-
53	SC	06/02/2013	LG001	4000	552	0	2 x Zap USB flash memoray drive	40.00	8.00	T1	48.00	N	-
							Totals:	490.00	98.00		588.00		

DISCOUNTS ON INVOICES

A **discount** is a reduction in the selling price of goods or services. The discount will always be shown on the invoice. There are two main types of discount given by sellers:

■ **Trade discount** is a percentage reduction in the price of goods and services, for example in return for large orders.

For example, a supplier may give customers an overall 20% discount. A sale of goods with a list price of £100 would therefore cost

£100 less £20 (20% trade discount) = £80

■ **Cash discount** (also known as **settlement discount**) is a percentage reduction in the price of goods and services allowed to customers who pay the invoice early, for example within seven days, rather than the usual thirty days. (Remember that 'cash' means immediate payment).

For example, a supplier may allow a 2.5% cash discount if a customer pays up within seven days rather than the usual agreed credit period of 30 days. If the original invoice was for £100, the customer could pay within seven days

£100 less £2.50 (2.5% cash discount) = £97.50

Remember, however, that VAT will normally have to be added on to these amounts.

VAT and discount

The normal practice on an invoice is for VAT to be calculated on the sales amount **after** the discount has been deducted.

In the examples given the total amount charged will be (assuming 20% standard rate VAT):

■ **Trade discount**

£80 (ie £100 minus £20) + VAT of £16 = total of £96

■ **Cash discount**

£97.50 (ie £100 minus £2.50) + VAT of £19.50 = total of £119.50

The important thing to remember here is that **the VAT is always calculated on the amount after the discount has been deducted, even if the cash discount is not taken.** It may seem odd and illogical but the printed invoice will always show the **pre-discount total** (in this case £100) as the net total (ie the higher amount) but will then add on the VAT calculated on the amount **after the discount has been deducted**

discounts and computer accounting

One of the advantages of using a computer accounting package such as Sage is that the program calculates discount automatically and accurately. There are a number of ways in which to input the discount details: using Customer Defaults, amending the Customer Record and editing the invoice itself.

customer defaults

It is possible to set up discount rates on the computer which will apply to all customer accounts unless the user specifies otherwise.

Trade discounts can be set up in CUSTOMER DEFAULTS under SETTINGS. This would be useful if the business sold goods in a trade where there was a common trade discount rate.

Cash (settlement) discounts can be set up on the Terms tab in the CONFIGURATION EDITOR. In the example shown below a cash (settlement) discount of 2.5% is given if payment is received within 14 days rather than the normal 30 days.

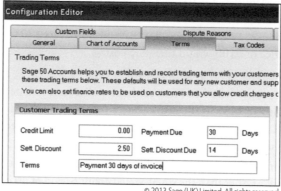

customer record – special terms agreed

The default rates could, if required, be over-ridden by amending the RECORD in CUSTOMERS.

The Defaults tab in the Customer Record will enable the user to set up a special trade discount for an individual customer. The screen below shows the application of a 10% trade discount.

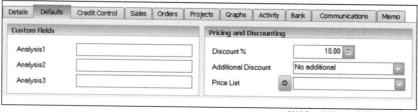

The Credit Control tab in the Customer Record will enable the user to set up a revised cash (settlement) discount; in the case shown below the discount is 5% for payment within 14 days of invoice.

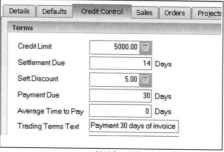

customer invoice

Further changes can be made at the invoicing stage, if required. The cash discount can be amended on the invoice footer tab and the trade discount can be amended on the Edit Item screen. A one-off percentage or value discount on the whole invoice value can be given using the net value discount box on the invoice screen.

CASE STUDY

PRONTO SUPPLIES LIMITED:
APPLYING DISCOUNTS

It is 11 February 2013. Tom Cox has negotiated 10% **trade discount** for two of his customers:

JB001   John Butler & Associates

LG001   L Garr & Co

Tom amends the customer records as shown below:

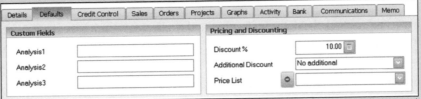

Tom has also offered a 3% **cash discount** to customer Kay Denz for settlement within 7 days of invoice. He enters this in the customer record as shown below:

CHAPTER SUMMARY

- When a business sells on credit it will issue an invoice to the buyer. This sets out the amount owing and the date by which it has to be paid.

- When a business has to make a refund to a customer to whom it sells on credit it will issue a credit note to the customer. This sets out the amount by which the amount owing is reduced.

- Sales invoices and credit notes are part of the 'flow of documents' which occurs when a sale is made on credit. The full list is purchase order, delivery note, invoice, credit note, statement, and remittance advice with payment. Not all of these will be used all of the time.

- The details of invoices and credit notes must be entered into the accounting records of a business. If a computer program is used the details will be input on-screen.

- Computer accounting programs will either print out the invoices after input, or will need to have the details of existing invoices input, commonly in batches.

- It is essential to check the details of invoices and credit notes which have been input. This can be done by printing out a daybook report.

- Processing invoices may also involve the use of discounts. There are two main types of discount: trade discount and cash discount.

KEY TERMS

credit sale	a sale made where payment is due at a later date
debtors	customers who owe money to a business
sales ledger	the part of the accounting system where the debtors' accounts are kept – it records the amounts that are owed to the business
purchase order	the financial document which requests the supply of goods or services and specifies exactly what is required
invoice	the financial document which sets out the details of the goods sold or services provided, the amount owing and the date by which the amount is due
credit note	the financial document – normally issued when goods are returned – which reduces the amount owing by the customer
batch	a group of documents, eg invoices or credit notes
batch entry	the input of a number of documents in a group
trade discount	a percentage reduction in the price of goods and services, eg in return for large orders
cash discount	a percentage reduction in the price of goods and services allowed to customers who pay an invoice early (also known as settlement discount)

EXERCISES

Task 1

Making sure that you have set the program date to 8 February 2013, enter the following invoice details into the computer. Check your totals before saving and print out a Day Books: Customer Invoices (Detailed) Report to confirm the data that you have saved. The transaction date range should be 05/02/2013 to 08/02/2013. Check this report against the report on page 77.

SALES INVOICES issued

invoice	name	date	details	net amount	VAT
10023	John Butler & Associates	5/02/13	4 x monitor 17"	400.00	80.00
10024	Charisma Design	6/02/13	1 x power lead 3 mtr	16.00	3.20
10025	Crowmatic Ltd	6/02/13	1 x Macroworx software V9	450.00	90.00
10026	Kay Denz	8/02/13	2 hours consultancy	120.00	24.00
Subtotals				986.00	197.20
Batch total					1183.20

Task 2

Enter the following credit note details into the computer. Check your totals before saving and print out a Day Books: Customer Credits (Detailed) Report. Check this report against the report on page 78.

CREDIT NOTES issued

credit note	name	date	details	net amount	VAT
551	David Boosey	6/02/13	1 x Macroworx software V9	450.00	90.00
552	L Garr & Co	6/02/13	2 x Zap USB flash memory drv	40.00	8.00
Subtotals				490.00	98.00
Batch total					588.00

Task 3

Amend customer discounts as shown in the Case Study on page 81.

Task 4

It is now a week later and the date is 15 February 2013. Change your program date setting. You have a further batch of invoices to process. Enter the details into the computer. Check your totals before saving and print out a Day Books (Detailed) Report (11 to 15 Feb) and check it against the report on page 272.

account	invoice date	number	details	net	VAT
David Boossey	11 02 13	10027	1 x Printer EF102 Multi	600.00	120.00
L Garr	12 02 13	10028	2 x Zap external drive	162.00	32.40
Kay Denz	13 02 13	10029	1 x Macroworx software V9	450.00	* 87.30
Charisma Design	15 02 13	10030	2 x Monitor 17 inch	200.00	40.00
John Butler & Associates	15 02 13	10031	2 hours consultancy	108.00	21.60
				1520.00	301.30
					18214.30

*The reduced VAT is due to the settlement discount now offered. You will need to overwrite the figure calculated by Sage.

Task 5

You also on the same date have two credit notes to process. Enter the details shown below into the computer. Check your totals before saving and print out a Day Books (Detailed) Report (12 to 13 Feb) to confirm the data that you have saved. Check your printout against the report on page 272.

Finally, print out a Trial Balance for February and check it against the Trial Balance on page 273.

account	date	reference	details	net	VAT
Charisma Design	12 02 13	553	1 x Power lead 3 mtr	16.00	3.20
Crowmatic Ltd	13 02 13	554	1 x Zap USB flash mem drv	20.00	4.00
				36.00	7.20
					43.20

Reminder! Have you made a back-up?

BUYING FROM SUPPLIERS ON CREDIT

This chapter explains the use of the 'batch entry' method for entering supplier invoices and credit notes. It presumes that the Purchase Order Processing module is not used to generate purchase invoices. If you want to use the Products and Purchase Order Processing modules, skip this chapter and go to Chapter 8.

Chapter introduction

■ This chapter should be read in conjunction with the last chapter 'Selling to customers on credit' as it represents 'the other side of the coin' – the invoice and the credit note as they are dealt with by the purchaser.

■ A business purchaser that buys on credit will receive an invoice for the goods or services supplied and will then have to pay at a later date.

■ Details of invoices and any credit notes received are entered by the purchaser into the account of the supplier in the computer accounting records. In this way the credit purchase and any credit due are recorded and the total amount owing by the purchaser logged into the accounting system.

■ This chapter continues the Pronto Supplies Case Study and shows how details of invoices and credit notes received are entered into supplier accounts in the computer accounting records.

INVOICES AND CREDIT NOTES

Make sure that you are familiar with the two types of financial document we will be dealing with – the invoice and the credit note. Read the descriptions below and remind yourself of the 'flow of documents' by studying the diagram on the opposite page.

invoice

The main document we will deal with in this chapter is the **invoice** which is sent by the seller to the buyer to state the amount that is owing and the date by which it has to be paid. See page 70 for an illustration.

credit note

The **credit note** is issued by the seller when some form of refund has to be given to the buyer of goods or services. As payment has not yet been made the credit note allows the buyer to deduct an amount from the invoice when settlement is finally made. See page 72 for an illustration.

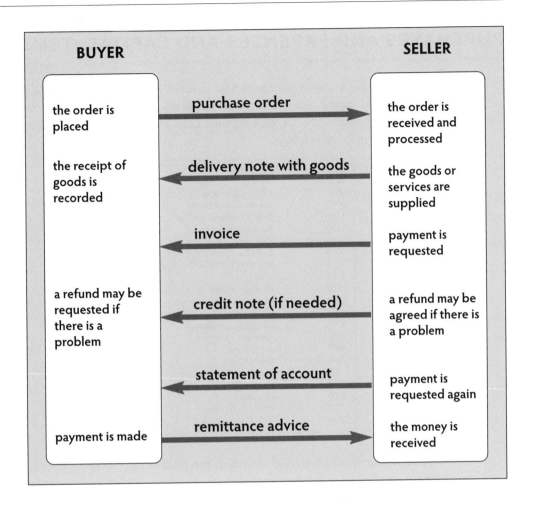

THE BOOKKEEPING BACKGROUND

Details of invoices and credit notes have to be entered into the accounting records of a business that buys on credit. They record the sales and refunds made by suppliers who have sold on credit – the **creditors** of the business, known in Sage as 'Suppliers'.

The amounts from these documents combine to provide the total of the **Purchases Ledger**, which is the section of the accounting records which contains all the supplier accounts and their balances. The total of the **Purchases Ledger** (recorded in the **Creditors Control Account**) tells the business how much in total it owes to suppliers.

The documents received from the suppliers – invoices and credit notes – are recorded in the computer accounting system on the **batch** basis illustrated in the Case Study in the last chapter. The important point about receiving documents from a seller is that they have to be checked very carefully before input – is the buyer being overcharged, for example?

PURCHASES AND EXPENSES AND CAPITAL ITEMS

One point that is very important to bear in mind is the difference between **purchases** and **expenses** and **capital items**, as it affects the nominal account codes used when inputting invoices and credit notes on the computer. Look at the Pronto Supplies account list (with account numbers) shown below.

N/C	Name
0020	Plant and Machinery
0030	Office Equipment
0040	Furniture and Fixtures
1100	Debtors Control Account
1200	Bank Current Account
2100	Creditors Control Account
2200	Sales Tax Control Account
2201	Purchase Tax Control Account
2300	Loans
3000	Ordinary Shares
4000	Computer hardware sales
4001	Computer software sales
4002	Computer consultancy
5000	Materials Purchased
6201	Advertising
7000	Gross Wages
7100	Rent
7103	General Rates
7200	Electricity
7502	Office Stationery
7550	Telephone and Fax

Purchases are items a business buys which it expects to turn into a product or sell as part of its day-to-day business. For example:

- a business that makes cheese will buy milk to make the cheese
- a supermarket will buy food and consumer goods to sell to the public

All these items are bought because they will be sold or turned into a product that will be sold. In Sage these purchases will be recorded in a **purchases account**, normally 5000, or a number in that category. In the list shown above Pronto Supplies uses account 5000 for 'Materials Purchased'.

Expenses, on the other hand, are items which the business pays for which form part of the business running expenses (overheads), eg rent and electricity. They all have separate nominal account numbers.

Capital items are 'one off' items that the business buys and intends to keep for a number of years, for example office equipment and furniture. These categories of asset all also have separate nominal account numbers.

conclusion

The important point here is that all of these items may be bought on credit and will have to be entered into the computer accounting records, **but with the correct nominal account number.**

CASE STUDY

PRONTO SUPPLIES LIMITED:
PROCESSING PURCHASES INVOICES AND CREDIT NOTES

It is 25 February 2013. Tom has a number of supplier invoices and supplier credit notes to enter into the computer accounting system.

He has the documents on file and has collected them in two batches.

PURCHASES INVOICES RECEIVED

invoice	name	date	details	net amount	VAT
11365	Delco PLC	20/02/13	10 x Desktop Computer 3000i	3,600.00	720.00
8576	Electron Supplies	25/02/13	4 x Processor G240	2,000.00	400.00
2947	MacCity	25/02/13	16 x Macroworx Software Version 9	3,680.00	736.00
Subtotals				9,280.00	1,856.00
Batch totals					11,136.00

CREDIT NOTES RECEIVED

credit note	name	date	details	net amount	VAT
7223	Delco PLC	6/02/13	1 x Pro 704 Computer	480.00	96.00
552	MacCity	8/02/13	1 x 10 Optical Mouse	38.00	7.60
Subtotals				518.00	103.60
Batch total					621.60

batch invoice entry

Tom will start by opening up the SUPPLIERS screen in Sage and clicking on the INVOICE icon. This will show the screen shown on the next page. He will then

- identify the account references for each of the three suppliers

- enter each invoice on a new line

- take the data from the invoice: date, invoice no ('Ref'), product details and amounts

- ignore the Dept (0 by default), Project Ref and Cost Code columns

- enter the Materials Purchased account number 5000 under 'N/C'

- enter the T1 tax code for standard rate VAT and check that the VAT amount calculated on-screen is the same as on the invoice – if there is a difference it should be queried (there could, for example, be a calculation mistake on the original invoice or a 'rounding' difference might occur)*

When the input is complete Tom should check his batch totals (Net, VAT and Total) against the computer totals. Once he is happy that his input is correct he should SAVE.

*   Sometimes the VAT on the document will vary by a penny from the VAT on the screen. This is because Sage 'rounds' VAT
        up or down to the nearest penny, whereas the VAT authorities require that VAT is rounded **down** to the nearest penny. These
        one penny differences can be altered on the input screen to tally with the document VAT amount.

The batch suppliers' invoice screen will appear like this:

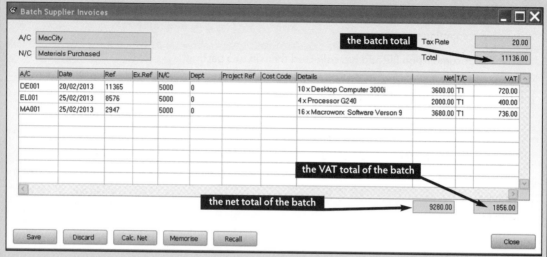

checking the invoices are on the system

As a further check Tom could print out a Day Book Report. This can be obtained through the REPORTS
icon on the SUPPLIER menu bar. The title of the report is 'Day Books: Supplier Invoices (Detailed)'. The
transaction date range is 20/02/2013 to 25/02/2013. The report appears as follows:

Pronto Supplies Limited   Page: 1

Day Books: Supplier Invoices (Detailed)

Date From:	20/02/2013						Supplier From:	
Date To:	25/02/2013						Supplier To:	ZZZZZZZZ
Transaction From:	1						N/C From:	
Transaction To:	99,999,999						N/C To:	99999999
Dept From:	0							
Dept To:	999							

Tran No.	Type	Date	A/C Ref	N/C	Inv Ref	Dept	Details	Net Amount	Tax Amount	T/C	Gross Amount	V	B
61	PI	20/02/2013	DE001	5000	11365	0	10 x Desktop Computer 3000i	3,600.00	720.00	T1	4,320.00	N	-
62	PI	25/02/2013	EL001	5000	8576	0	4 x Processor G240	2,000.00	400.00	T1	2,400.00	N	-
63	PI	25/02/2013	MA001	5000	2947	0	16 x Macroworx Software	3,680.00	736.00	T1	4,416.00	N	-
							Totals	9,280.00	1,856.00		11,136.00		

batch credit note entry

Tom will input the details from the two credit notes in much the same way as he processed the invoices. He will open up the SUPPLIERS screen in Sage and click on the CREDIT icon. This will show the screen shown on the next page. He will then identify the account references for each of the two customers and input the credit note details as shown on the screen. He will use the Materials Purchased account number 5000. When the input is complete he should again check his original totals (Net, VAT and Batch total) against the computer totals. Once he is happy that his input is correct he should SAVE.

The batch suppliers' credit note screen will appear like this:

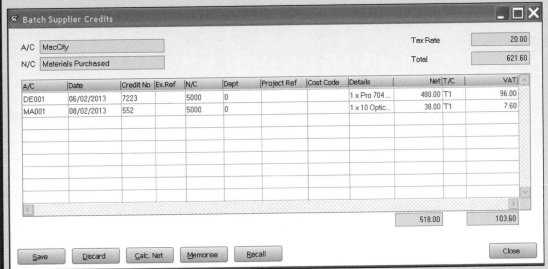

checking the credit notes are on the system

As a further check Tom could print out a Day Book Report for Supplier Credit notes. This can be obtained through the REPORTS icon on the SUPPLIERS menu bar. The title of the report is 'Day Books: Supplier Credits (Detailed)'. The transaction date range is 06/02/2013 to 08/02/2013. The report appears as follows:

Pronto Supplies Limited

Day Books: Supplier Credits (Detailed)

Date From:	06/02/2013					Supplier From:		
Date To:	08/02/2013					Supplier To:	ZZZZZZZZ	
Transaction From:	1					N/C From:		
Transaction To:	99,999,999					N/C To:	99999999	
Dept From:	0							
Dept To:	999							

Tran No.	Type	Date	A/C Ref	N/C	Inv Ref	Dept	Details	Net Amount	Tax Amount	T/C	Gross Amount	V	B
64	PC	06/02/2013	DE001	5000	7223	0	1 x Pro 704 Computer	480.00	96.00	T1	576.00	N	-
65	PC	08/02/2013	MA001	5000	552	0	1 x 10 Optical Mouse	38.00	7.60	T1	45.60	N	-
							Totals	518.00	103.60		621.60		

Tom needs to buy a new laptop and printer for use in his office. He has spoken to Delco PLC and agreed a cash (settlement) discount of 2.5% for settlement within 14 days of invoice for purchases on or after 25 February. Tom amends the supplier record as shown below:

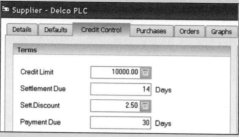

He then enters the following invoice, received from Delco PLC.

INVOICE

DELCO PLC

Delco House, Otto Way, New Milton SR1 6TF
Tel 01722 295875 Fax 01722 295611 Email sales@delco.co.uk
VAT Reg GB 0745 4672 76

invoice to

Pronto Supplies Limited
Unit 17 Severnvale Estate
Broadwater Road
Mereford
MR1 6TF

invoice no	11377
account	3993
date	25 02 13

product code	description	quantity	price (£)	unit	net	VAT
X70	Laptop X70	1	400.00	each	400.00	78.00
P28	Laser multi-printer P28	1	360.00	each	360.00	70.20

goods total	760.00
VAT	148.20
TOTAL	908.20

terms

2.5% settlement discount for payment
within 14 days of invoice date

As there are two items on the invoice, Tom enters each line on the batch supplier invoices screen but copies the same details in the account, date and reference columns. He is careful to code the invoice with the nominal code for office equipment (rather than purchases for resale), ie 0030. Tom notes that the VAT is reduced because of the settlement discount so he overwrites the amount that the Sage program generates in the VAT column.

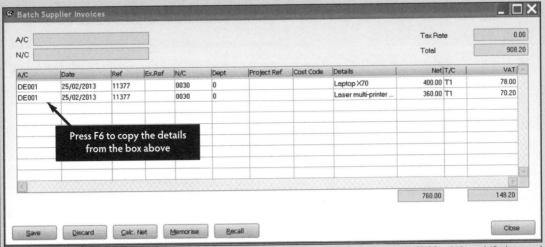

what next?

Tom has now entered into his computer:

- his company details and nominal accounts and balances

- customer and supplier details

- customer and supplier invoices

- customer and supplier credit notes

The next chapter shows how he enters details of payments made to suppliers and payments received from customers. The 'flow of documents' will be complete.

CHAPTER SUMMARY

- When a business buys on credit it will receive invoices and possibly credit notes from its suppliers as part of the 'flow of documents'.

- The details of invoices and credit notes must be entered into the accounting records of a business. If a computer program is used the details are normally input on-screen on the batch basis.

- In the case of supplier invoices and credit notes it is important that the correct Nominal account number is used to describe whether the transaction relates to purchases, expenses or capital items.

- It is essential to check the details of invoices and credit notes before input and the details of input by printing out, for example, a day book report.

KEY TERMS

credit sale	a sale made where payment is due at a later date
creditors	suppliers to whom the business owes money
purchases ledger	the part of the accounting system where the suppliers' accounts are kept
purchases	items bought which will be turned into a product or be sold as part of day-to-day trading
expenses	payments made which relate to the running of the business – also known as overheads
capital items	items bought which the business intends to keep
batch	a group of documents, eg invoices or credit notes

EXERCISES

PRONTO SUPPLIES INPUTTING TASKS

Task 1

Set the program date to 25 February 2013. Enter the following invoice details into the computer. Check your totals before saving and print out a Day Books: Supplier Invoice (Detailed) Report. Choose the appropriate date range. Check this against the report on page 90.

PURCHASES INVOICES RECEIVED					
invoice	name	date	details	net amount	VAT
11365	Delco PLC	20/02/13	10 x Desktop Computer 3000i	3,600.00	720.00
8576	Electron Supplies	25/02/13	4 x Processor G240	2,000.00	400.00
2947	MacCity	25/02/13	16 x Macroworx Software Version 9	3,680.00	736.00
Subtotals				9,280.00	1,856.00
Batch totals					11,136.00

Task 2

Enter the following credit note details into the computer. Check your totals before saving and print out a Day Books: Supplier Credits (Detailed) Report. Choose the appropriate date range. Check this against the report on page 91.

CREDIT NOTES RECEIVED					
credit note	name	date	details	net amount	VAT
7223	Delco PLC	6/02/13	1 x Pro 704 Computer	480.00	96.00
552	MacCity	8/02/13	1 x 10 Optical Mouse	38.00	7.60
Subtotals				518.00	103.60
Batch total					621.60

Task 3

On the same day Tom receives a supplier invoice from Delco for the purchase of office equipment. Enter the details as shown in the case study on page 89 including the amendment to Delco's supplier record for settlement discount. Take care to use the correct nominal code when entering the purchase invoice.

When the input is complete, the details should be checked and a Day Books Supplier Invoice (Detailed) Report printed. Limit the supplier and date range so that only invoice 11377 from Delco PLC appears, ie by entering a Supplier Ref range from Delco to Delco and a date range of 25 02 13 to 25 02 13. Check your report against the one on page 273.

Now print a Trial Balance. Check it against the one on page 274.

Reminder! Have you made a back-up?

8 PRODUCTS, ORDER PROCESSING AND INVOICING

This chapter is relevant if the user wants to use the following modules in Sage:

- Products
- Sales Order Processing
- Invoicing
- Purchase Order Processing

The data is the same as in chapters 6 and 7 but is processed using the above modules rather than by 'batch entry'. If you have already worked through chapters 6 and 7 you will need to restore the backup taken at the end of chapter 5 on page 67 (see page 15 for how to restore).

Chapter introduction

- In Chapter 6 – 'Selling to customers on credit' – we looked at the way in which customers are invoiced for goods and services sold using the 'batch' method where invoices are produced independently of the computer program. In this chapter we illustrate the way in which sales invoices for stock and non-stock items can be produced by the computer program and customer account details updated automatically.

- Items sold by a business – whether products or services – can be set up in Sage using product codes. Sales Order Processing and Sales Invoicing can be linked to the products.

- Purchase Order Processing can be used to order new stock from suppliers. Details of the purchase order can be used to create a batch supplier invoice for updating accounting records.

- We will again look at the business in the Case Study – Pronto Supplies Limited – and see how Tom deals with managing stock, processing sales and purchase orders and sales and purchase invoices.

PRODUCTS

The products module is reached by clicking on Products in the vertical toolbar. This allows details of products to be entered into a database where stock levels, stock sales and stock purchases can be controlled. The Products module can also be used for non-stock items where it is useful to be able to use a pre-loaded description of a service sold.

coding and categories of products

It is important to give some thought to a system of coding for products. Each product must have its own unique code. Codes are usually a combination of letters and numbers. Products can be grouped for reporting purposes by setting up categories in the Configuration Editor/Products.

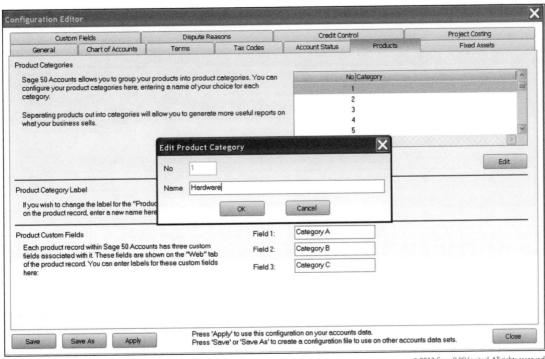

entering new product details

The New Product Wizard may be used for entering new products but the examples shown here use the Record option to make entries in all the relevant fields.

Below is the record for a Power Lead, product code AP300. The following details have been directly entered:

Product code:	AP300
Item type:	Stock item
Description:	Power lead 3 mtr
Category:	3
Sales nominal code:	4000
Tax code:	T1 20%
Purchase nominal code:	5000
Sales price and unit:	£16.00 each
In stock:	6 (this is entered as an opening balance with a cost price of £9.50 using the OB button)

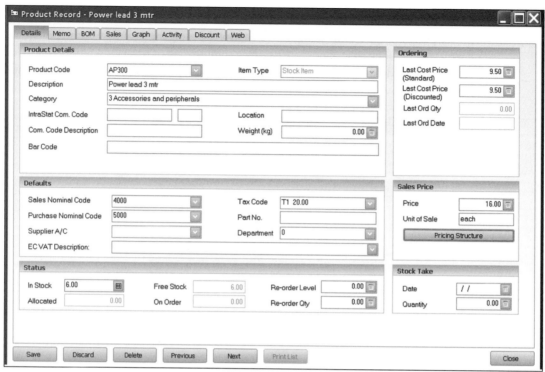

Once all these details have been entered the record is saved.

CASE STUDY

PRONTO SUPPLIES LIMITED:

SETTING UP PRODUCTS

It is 1 February 2013. Tom is going to set up his product records. He has decided to use a coding system that prefixes numerical codes with letters that designate the product categories that he stocks. So first of all he sets up these categories in Configuration Editor in the Settings menu. On the Products tab he enters the following categories:

1. Hardware

2. Software

3. Accessories and peripherals

(See illustration on page 97)

Now he enters each of his products by clicking the Record icon in the Products module and entering the product details. The list of product details is as follows:

Product code	Description	Category	Nominal code	Opening balance	Cost price	Sales Price
AP300	Power lead 3 mtr	3	4000	6	9.50	16.00 each
AP301	Zap external drive	3	4000	5	52.00	90.00 each
AP302	Zap USB flash memory drive	3	4000	9	11.00	20.00 pack 5
H200	Desktop computer 3000i	1	4000	2	360.00	600.00 each
H201	Monitor 17 inch	1	4000	7	65.00	100.00 each
H202	Processor G240	1	4000	2	500.00	799.00 each
H203	Printer EF102 Multi	1	4000	3	420.00	600.00 each
S100	Macroworx software Version 9	2	4001	5	230.00	450.00 each

(See illustration opposite)

Once he has entered all his products and their opening balances, the Products module screen looks like this:

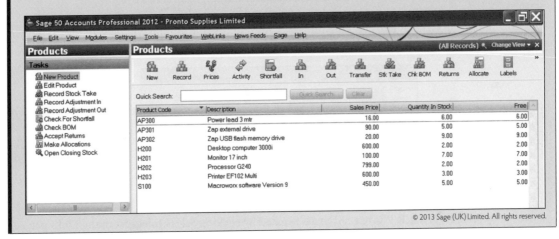

SALES ORDER PROCESSING

numbering

Sage will automatically allocate a number to each order. If a system of numbering is already in place, a starting number can be set on the Options tab of Invoice & Order Defaults under Settings on the menu bar. The screen below shows invoice-numbering starting at 10023, credit notes at 551, sales orders at 1000 and purchase orders at 2000.

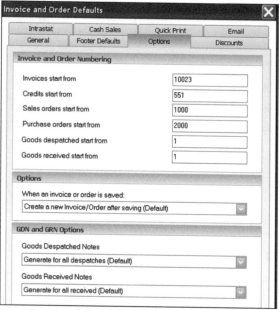

On the General tab, checking the 'Lock Autonumbering' option will prevent over-typing of document numbers when details are entered.

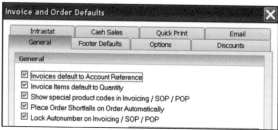

SALES ORDER PROCESSING is reached by clicking Sales Order List in the Links pane of CUSTOMERS, or through Modules on the Menu bar. A new sales order can be processed by clicking New Sales Order in the Tasks pane or New/Edit on the SALES ORDER PROCESSING toolbar.

entering a sales order

The procedure for entering a new sales order is:

1. On the Product sales order form enter details as follows:

Date:	Enter the date of the order
A/C:	Enter the customer account reference. The customer name & address appears top left
Product code:	Enter the product code (or click the drop-down arrow or press F4 for choices). This will automatically complete a description of the product in the next field. Clicking on the little arrow in the

description field will open a window giving details of the product. Here price or trade discount can be amended.

Quantity:
Enter the number required. The pricing and value columns will be automatically completed.

Additional lines can be entered for more product sales to the same customer.

The example below shows the sales order for four 17" monitors, product code H201, to customer John Butler & Associates.

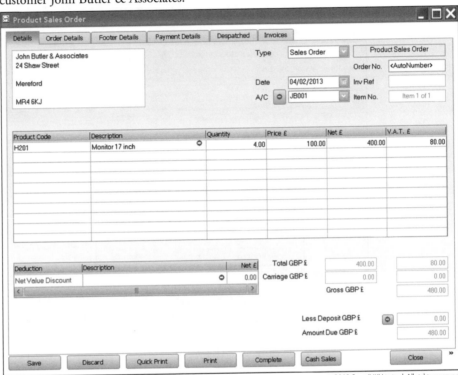

Other tabs in the order window allow additional information to be added. On the Order Details tab a different delivery address can be entered and a customer order number inserted. On the Footer Details tab any carriage charge and settlement discount can be added. Other tabs include details of payment (in the case of immediate payment) and document reference numbers generated by the system once the order has been despatched, eg delivery note and sales invoice numbers.

Click Save when the order is complete. The order can be printed if required at this point. It now appears on the SALES ORDER PROCESSING module screen.

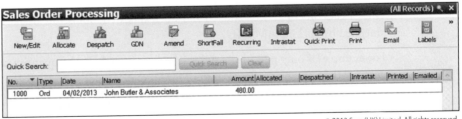

2. The next step is to allocate the stock to the order by highlighting the order in the SALES ORDER PROCESSING screen and clicking Allocate (on the module toolbar) and Yes. The SOP screen will now show "FULL" in the Allocated column.

   Until the goods are despatched (see number 3 below) the sales order details can be amended, for example, for quantity or price.

3. At present goods have been reserved against the order. The next stage is to despatch them by highlighting the order again and clicking DESPATCH. At this point a delivery note can be printed and a sales invoice is automatically created.

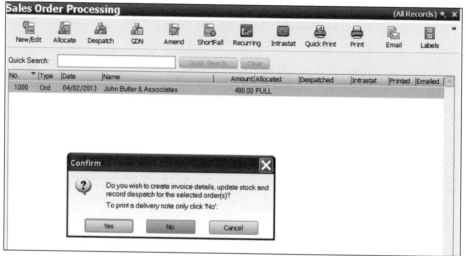

4. The Sales Order will now show as COMPLETE in the Despatched column of the SALES ORDER PROCESSING screen (unless only part of the order has been despatched in which case it will show as PART).

amending a sales order

Once a sales order has been entered and stock allocated, but before despatch, its status can be amended by clicking AMEND.

For example, if only part of the order is to be despatched, the quantity can be amended by entering the appropriate figure in the This Despatch field.

The AMEND option can also be used to cancel or hold an order and to unallocate stock.

SALES INVOICING

The invoices created from sales orders will already appear in the INVOICING module (reached through Modules/Invoicing or by clicking Invoice List in the Links pane of the CUSTOMERS window). The date of the invoice can be changed before printing if required.

processing the product invoice

Invoices are normally better printed in batches rather than one by one. To print invoices, select the ones to print and click Print. Choose the format required and click Preview to check the appearance of the invoice. Invoices in Sage normally require preprinted invoice forms with headings and boxes in place so the printer just puts in the figures and details. It is possible to design an invoice, or adapt the built-in designs, in the Report Designer module (within the Sage program) but that is a whole new topic that is not dealt with here.

When you are satisfied that the invoices are correct, they should be selected and updated (or 'posted') to the Sales Ledger by clicking Update on the INVOICING module toolbar. An Update Ledgers report is automatically generated and can be printed. Alternatively Day Books reports can be printed to record the transactions in the ledgers.

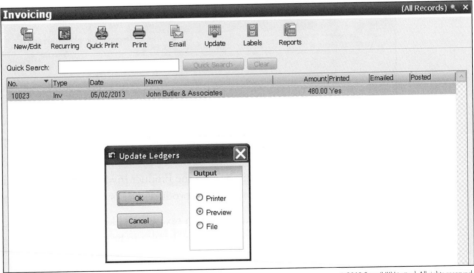

use of invoicing without sales order processing

Some businesses may choose not to use the SALES ORDER PROCESSING module. The INVOICING module can be used independently of SALES ORDER PROCESSING, directly with the PRODUCTS module (product details are updated as they are sold on the sales invoice) or without reference to products.

SERVICE INVOICES

Service invoices are issued for services provided by a business rather than for products sold. Service invoices do not require product codes. They may be accessed by clicking on New/Edit on the INVOICING menu bar. In the Format box, click on the drop-down arrow and choose 'Service'. A completed input screen looks like this:

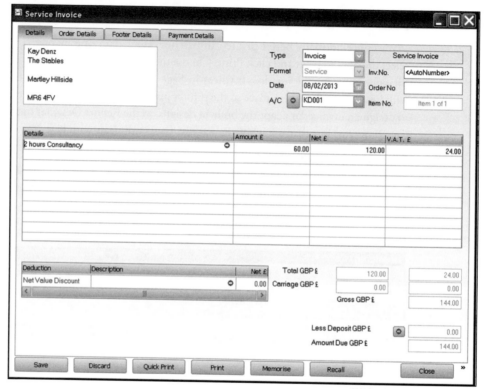

The procedure is much the same as with the Product Invoice except that the details and price have to be entered manually, because no product code is entered. Note the following:

Details   You can enter as much text as you like in this box. By clicking the arrow in the Details box more details can be checked or added, eg nominal code, quantity and price.

Amount   If the price has not yet been entered you enter the net amount here, ie the amount before VAT is added on and before discounts are calculated.

VAT   This is automatically calculated, based on the tax code entered. The tax code can be checked if you click on the arrow in the Details line.

Nominal code   The Nominal account code to which the invoice is posted (eg Computer Consultancy Account) can also be checked and amended by clicking on the arrow in the Details line.

The Edit Item Line screen appears as follows:

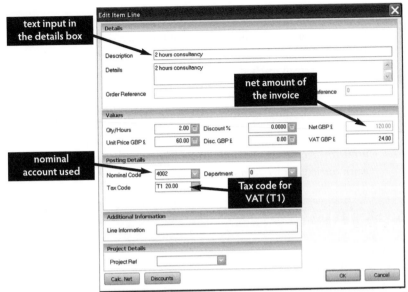

service item product codes

It is possible to create product codes for "non-stock" or "service" items where this suits the business. For example, a gardening business may use a non-stock product code for its services, eg mowing a lawn or cutting a hedge where pre-loaded text and pricing information is automatically inserted when the code is entered on the sales order or sales invoice. A non-stock product record is set up in the PRODUCTS module with the "Item Type" specified as 'Non-Stock' or 'Service' item.

'memorising' invoices

If you repeatedly invoice the same service or product at the same price you can save the details as a 'skeleton' invoice by clicking on the Memorise button at the bottom of the invoice screen and providing a file name and description. If you need to bring up these same details again for another invoice, click the Recall button and select the file you need.

printing and updating – service invoices

The procedure for printing service invoices and updating the ledgers is exactly the same as for a product invoice, as explained on page 103. It is advisable also to print out a report for all invoices produced, either when updating the ledgers in INVOICING or as a Day Books: Customer Invoice (Detailed) Report in CUSTOMERS.

CREDIT NOTE PRODUCTION

Exactly the same procedure is followed for processing and printing Product and Service credit notes. These are accessed by amending the options in the Type and Format boxes of the New/Edit screen reached from the INVOICING menu bar.

A credit note processed in the INVOICING module for a product returned will automatically update the product record.

The Case Study which follows shows how Pronto Supplies Limited decides to process and print its invoices on the computer, starting with service invoices for computer consultancy work carried out by Tom Cox.

CASE STUDY

PRONTO SUPPLIES LIMITED:
PROCESSING SALES ORDERS, SALES INVOICES AND CREDIT NOTES

It is 4 February.

Tom already has some numbers running for invoices and credit notes so he needs to adjust the automatic numbering in Sage before entering any more transactions.

He goes to Settings/Invoice & Order Defaults/Options tab and enters 10023 as the starting number for invoices, 551 for credits, 1000 for sales orders and 2000 for purchase orders.

Before saving he goes to the General tab and ensures that the 'Lock Autonumber on Invoicing/SOP/POP' is checked.

Now he clicks OK.

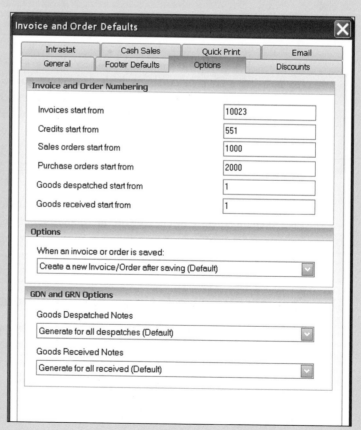

Tom has the following sales order to process. He opens CUSTOMERS and selects Sales Order List from the Links pane.

Order date	Customer	Customer order no.	Product code	Details
4 02 13	John Butler & Associates	DD472	H201	4 x Monitor 17 inch

After entering the order, Tom selects it, allocates and despatches the goods. He checks that the details are now showing in the INVOICING module. He highlights the invoice and clicks on New/Edit (or double-clicks the invoice) and changes the date of the invoice to 5 February. He then prints the invoice and updates the ledgers.

Pronto Supplies Limited
Unit 17 Severnvale Estate
Broadwater Road
Mereford
Wyvern
MR1 6TF
VAT Reg No: 404 7106 52

Invoice   Page   1

John Butler & Associates   10023
24 Shaw Street
Mereford   05/02/2013
MR4 6KJ
                                                            DD472

VAT Reg No: JB001

Quantity	Details	Unit Price	Net Amount	VAT Rate	VAT
4.00	Monitor 17 inch	100.00	400.00	20.00	80.00

Total Net Amount	400.00
Carriage Net	0.00
Total VAT Amount	80.00
Invoice Total	480.00

Pronto Supplies Limited
Update Ledgers

Inv	Type	Tran	Date	A/C	N/C	Stock Code	Details	Quantity	Net	Tax	Gross
10023	SI	48	05/02/2013	JB001	4000	H201	Monitor 17 inch	4.00	400.00	80.00	480.00
							Total for Invoice 10023		400.00	80.00	480.00
							Grand Total for All:		400.00	80.00	480.00

Tom has two more product sales orders to process. He enters the order details as shown below.

Order date	Customer	Customer order no.	Product code	Details
4 02 13	Charisma Design	9756	AP300	1 x Power lead 3 mtr
4 02 13	Crowmatic Ltd	12/793	S100	1 x Macroworx software Version 9

He allocates and despatches the goods and then processes two sales invoices for them dated 6 February.

On 8 February, Tom needs to process a service sales invoice and two credit notes.

Using the Service option in INVOICING, he prepares the following invoice, remembering to check that the nominal code of 4002 for consultancy is used:

Invoice date	Customer	Customer order no.	Details
8 02 13	Kay Denz	Verbal	2 hours consultancy @ £60 per hour

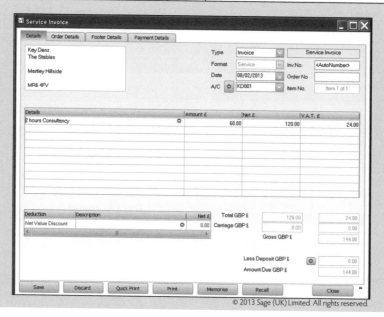

He has issued credit notes as follows. He enters these via INVOICING, choosing the credit note option in the Type box. He enters the reason for the return in the Comment 1 box reached by clicking the arrow in the Description field. In both cases the goods are returned to stock.

Date	Customer	Credit note no	Product code	Details	Reason
6 02 13	David Boossey	551	S100	1 x Macroworx software Version 9	Not required
6 02 13	L Garr & Co	552	AP302	2 packs Zap USB flash memory drive	Goods returned

Pronto Supplies Limited
Unit 17 Severnvale Estate
Broadwater Road
Mereford
Wyvern
MR1 6TF
VAT Reg No: 404 7106 52

Credit Note   Page   1

David Boossey   551
17 Harebell Road
Mereford Green   06/02/2013
MR6 4NB

VAT Reg No: 404 7106 52   DB001

Quantity	Details	Unit Price	Net Amount	VAT Rate	VAT
1.00	Macroworx software Version 9 Not required	450.00	450.00	20.00	90.00

Total Net Amount	450.00
Carriage Net	0.00
Total VAT Amount	90.00
Invoice Total	540.00

Tom can now print the service invoice and credit notes, and update the ledgers by selecting all three documents and clicking Update.

Pronto Supplies Limited
Update Ledgers

Inv	Type	Tran	Date	A/C	N/C	Stock Code	Details	Quantity	Net	Tax	Gross
551	SC	51	06/02/2013	DB001	4001	S100	Macroworx software Version 9	1.00	-450.00	-90.00	-540.00
							Total for Invoice 551		-450.00	-90.00	-540.00
552	SC	52	06/02/2013	LG001	4000	AP302	Zap USB flash memory drive	2.00	-40.00	-8.00	-48.00
							Total for Invoice 552		-40.00	-8.00	-48.00
10026	SI	53	08/02/2013	KD001	4002		2 hours Consultancy		120.00	24.00	144.00
							Total for Invoice 10026		120.00	24.00	144.00
							Grand Total for All:		-370.00	-74.00	-444.00

Finally Tom prints Day Books: Customer Invoices (Detailed) to record the invoices, and Day Books: Customer Credits (Detailed) to record the credit notes that have been processed and posted to customer accounts.

Pronto Supplies Limited
Day Books: Customer Invoices (Detailed)

Date From: 05/02/2013
Date To: 08/02/2013

Transaction From: 1
Transaction To: 99,999,999

Dept From: 0
Dept To: 999

Customer From:
Customer To: ZZZZZZZZ

N/C From:
N/C To: 99999999

Tran No.	Type	Date	A/C Ref	N/C	Inv Ref	Dept.	Details	Net Amount	Tax Amount	T/C	Gross Amount	V	B
50	SI	05/02/2013	JB001	4000	10023	0	Monitor 17 inch	400.00	80.00	T1	480.00	N	-
51	SI	06/02/2013	CH001	4000	10024	0	Power lead 3 mtr	16.00	3.20	T1	19.20	N	-
52	SI	06/02/2013	CR001	4001	10025	0	Macroworx software Version 9	450.00	90.00	T1	540.00	N	-
53	SI	08/02/2013	KD001	4002	10026	0	2 hours consultancy	120.00	24.00	T1	144.00	N	-
							Totals:	986.00	197.20		1,183.20		

Pronto Supplies Limited
Day Books: Customer Credits (Detailed)

Date From: 06/02/2013
Date To: 06/02/2013

Transaction From: 1
Transaction To: 99,999,999

Dept From: 0
Dept To: 999

Customer From:
Customer To: ZZZZZZZZ

N/C From:
N/C To: 99999999

Tran No.	Type	Date	A/C Ref	N/C	Inv Ref	Dept.	Details	Net Amount	Tax Amount	T/C	Gross Amount	V	B
48	SC	06/02/2013	DB001	4001	551	0	Macroworx software Version 9	450.00	90.00	T1	540.00	N	-
49	SC	06/02/2013	LG001	4000	552	0	Zap USB flash memory drive	40.00	8.00	T1	48.00	N	-
							Totals:	490.00	98.00		588.00		

PURCHASE ORDER PROCESSING

PURCHASE ORDER PROCESSING can be used for ordering and re-ordering stock. In order to use this module efficiently, re-order levels and supplier names must be entered on Product records. The example below shows the addition of a re-order level of 2 and the supplier code DE001 for Delco PLC for product ref H200.

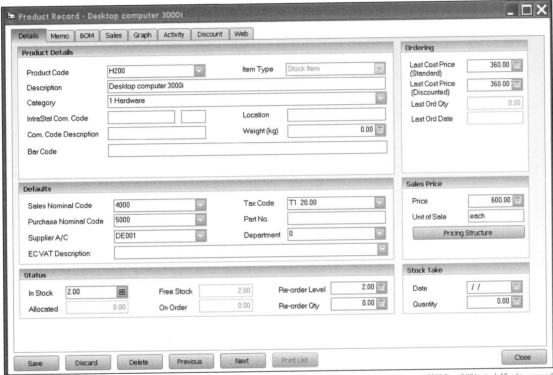

This product has reached its re-order level so an order is placed with Delco PLC for 10 more as follows.

PURCHASE ORDER PROCESSING is reached through opening SUPPLIERS and clicking Purchase Order List in the Links pane. Now click New/Edit. A purchase order form appears. The form resembles the sales order form and is completed in a similar way.

Enter the following details:

- Date of order
- Supplier account
- Product code
- Quantity required
- Other fields will be automatically completed

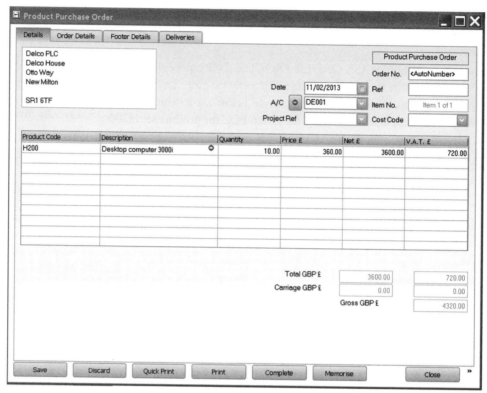

When the form is complete, click Save. If the credit limit set in the supplier account is now exceeded a warning message will appear asking for confirmation as to whether to go ahead with the order or not. This built-in check in Sage applies to the processing of sales and purchase orders and will take the user to the Customer or Supplier account to amend the credit limit if appropriate.

The order will appear in the PURCHASE ORDER PROCESSING screen list.

To place the purchase order, highlight it and click Order on the module toolbar. An option to print the order is generated. The order is now marked On Order on the screen.

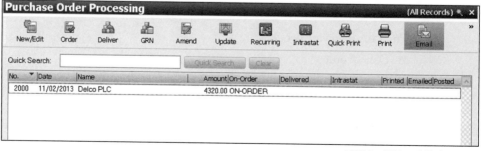

The product record now shows the ordered quantity in the On Order box.

When the goods are received from the supplier the purchase order and stock record are updated by highlighting the purchase order and clicking Deliver and Yes. Sage will use the program date as the delivery date. There is an option to print a Goods Received Note at this point. The order now shows as Complete in the PURCHASE ORDER PROCESSING screen.

The product record is automatically updated and now shows the increased stock level.

If only part of the order is delivered, the procedure is to click Amend (instead of Deliver). Enter the quantity actually delivered in This Delivery and then click Deliver.

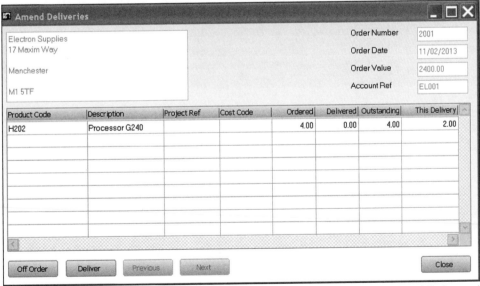

The screen will indicate Part to show that the delivery is not complete. When the balance of the order is received the remaining stock can be entered by either clicking Deliver on the module toolbar or again going through the Amend option.

using purchase orders to produce purchase invoices

Supplier invoices received against purchase orders would normally be entered via batch invoices in Sage. By using the details already entered in PURCHASE ORDER PROCESSING and linking them to the accounting records, time can be saved when entering a purchase invoice received.

Highlight the purchase order in the PURCHASE ORDER PROCESSING screen for which a purchase invoice has been received. Click Update and then update again. This brings up the batch supplier invoices screen. The date of the invoice and the reference number must be amended to match the invoice but otherwise the details should match.

In the examples below Delco PLC's invoice no 11365 dated 20 Feb has been received against Purchase Order 2000 above.

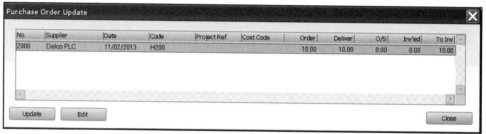

Purchase credit notes are not entered through PURCHASE ORDER PROCESSING.

report options

A range of report options are available for different stages of SALES ORDER PROCESSING, INVOICING and PURCHASE ORDER PROCESSING. Examples will be used in the Case Study that follows and in the tasks at the end of the chapter.

CASE STUDY

PRONTO SUPPLIES LIMITED: PURCHASE ORDER PROCESSING

It is 11 February 2013. Tom is aware that stocks are running low of some items. He adds the following information to his product records to help him control and monitor his stocks.

Product code	Re-order level	Supplier
H200	2	Delco PLC
H202	3	Electron Supplies
S100	5	MacCity

He runs a re-order report: Reports/Stock Control/Product Re-Order Levels

Date: 22/06/2012		**Pronto Supplies Limited**				**Page:** 1	
Time: 09:52:58		**Product Re-Order Levels**					
Product From:					Category From:	1	
Product To: ZZZZZZZZZZZZ					Category To:	999	
Code & Supplier	Product Description	Quantity In Stock	Quantity Allocated	Quantity On Order	Reorder Level	Last Purchase Quantity	Purchase Price
H200 DE001	Desktop computer 3000i	2.00	0.00	0.00	2.00	0.00	360.00
H202 EL001	Processor G240	2.00	0.00	0.00	3.00	0.00	500.00
S100 MA001	Macroworx software Version 9	5.00	0.00	0.00	5.00	0.00	230.00

He needs to replenish all these items so he processes the following purchase orders. Before he does this he checks that his first Purchase Order number is set at 2000 in Settings/Invoice & Order defaults/Options.

Product code	Order quantity	Supplier
H200	10	Delco PLC
H202	4	Electron Supplies
S100	16	MacCity

Tom highlights all the orders in the PURCHASE ORDER PROCESSING screen and clicks Order to place them. He could print the orders at this time if needed. The orders show as On Order and the relevant product records will be updated to show the items ordered.

Now he prints an outstanding Purchase Order report available from the Report options in PURCHASE ORDER PROCESSING.

Pronto Supplies Limited
Outstanding Purchase Orders

Order From:	1
Order To:	9,999,999

Date From:	01/01/1980
Date To:	31/12/2019

Supplier From:	
Supplier To:	ZZZZZZZZ

Supplier A/C:	DE001
Supplier Name:	Delco PLC
Supplier Address:	Delco House
	Otto Way
	New Milton
	SR1 6TF

Order No:	2000
Order Date:	11/02/2013
Due Delivery:	
Notes:	

Telephone Number: 01722 295875   Taken By: MANAGER

Product Code:	Product Description	Comment	Total Quantity	Outstanding	Disc (%)	Price
H200	Desktop computer 3000i		10.00	10.00	0.00	3,600.00
Carriage:	0.00			Order Value:		3,600.00

Supplier A/C:	EL001
Supplier Name:	Electron Supplies
Supplier Address:	17 Maxim Way
	Manchester
	M1 5TF

Order No:	2001
Order Date:	11/02/2013
Due Delivery:	
Notes:	

Telephone Number: 0161 628 2151   Taken By: MANAGER

Product Code:	Product Description	Comment	Total Quantity	Outstanding	Disc (%)	Price
H202	Processor G240		4.00	4.00	0.00	2,000.00
Carriage:	0.00			Order Value:		2,000.00

Supplier A/C:	MA001
Supplier Name:	MacCity
Supplier Address:	Unit 15 Elmwood Trading Estate
	Roughway
	RM2 9TG

Order No:	2002
Order Date:	11/02/2013
Due Delivery:	
Notes:	

Telephone Number: 01899 949233   Taken By: MANAGER

Product Code:	Product Description	Comment	Total Quantity	Outstanding	Disc (%)	Price
S100	Macroworx software Version 9		16.00	16.00	0.00	3,680.00
Carriage:	0.00			Order Value:		3,680.00
				Total Order Value:		9,280.00

The goods are delivered over the next few days and the screen updated:

20 Feb

Order no 2000 Delco PLC delivered in full.

Tom highlights the order and clicks Deliver and Yes to complete the order. The stock record is updated to include the new stock.

Status

In Stock	12.00	Free Stock	12.00
Allocated	0.00	On Order	0.00

Re-order Level	2.00
Re-order Qty	0.00

Stock Take

Date	/ /
Quantity	0.00

21 Feb

Order no 2001 Electron Supplies only 2 delivered.

Tom clicks Amend and enters 2 in This Delivery and then clicks Deliver.

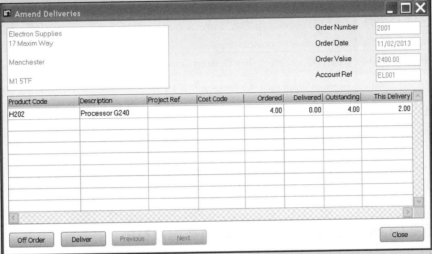

The screen now shows Part against this order.

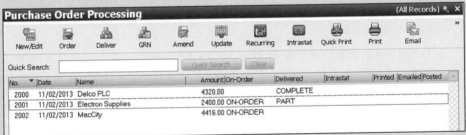

22 Feb

Order no 2002 MacCity delivered in full.

25 Feb

Order 2001 Electron Supplies, balance of 2 delivered.

Tom highlights the order and clicks Deliver to complete the order.

Now all orders show as complete on the PURCHASE ORDER PROCESSING screen.

Purchase invoices as shown below are received and Tom uses PURCHASE ORDER PROCESSING to enter these in Sage. He highlights all the orders and clicks Update then update again to bring up the batch supplier invoice screen. Here he amends the pre-filled boxes to match the invoices shown below.

Date	Invoice ref	Order no	Supplier	Details	Net amount	VAT
20 02 13	11365	2000	Delco PLC	10 x Desktop Computer 3000i	3,600.00	720.00
25 02 13	8576	2001	Electron Supplies	4 x Processor G240	2,000.00	400.00
25 02 13	2947	2002	MacCity	16 x Macroworx Software Version 9	3,680.00	736.00

DELETING COMPLETED TRANSACTIONS

From time to time it may be necessary to clear the screen of completed transactions in SALES ORDER PROCESSING, INVOICING and PURCHASE ORDER PROCESSING. This avoids the user having to scroll down the page to process new transactions. There are two ways of doing this:

The first is to select the transactions that are no longer needed and click Delete. This will remove the transactions permanently from the system so that they can no longer be checked or accessed. This should only be done if all relevant updating has been done, eg sales invoice created and updated to the main accounts.

The second is to use the Search facility to isolate only the most recent transactions. This will allow only desired transactions to show on-screen but previous transactions can be viewed if needed by changing the criteria. The example given is for modification of the SALES ORDER PROCESSING screen in Demo Data (File/Open/Open Demo Data) but the method can be used wherever the Search facility appears in Sage.

In the SALES ORDER PROCESSING screen, click the Search button. Complete the Search window as shown at the top of the next page. This tells Sage to show only the sales orders that have a number of 10 or higher.

Click Apply and close the Search screen. Note that in the top right of the screen on the blue bar, the number of records displayed is given. If you click on the magnifying glass next to this number the screen will revert to displaying all orders. The Search criteria are saved so that when you click Search again, the first option is to repeat the same search as before. You can amend or discard this to suit your purposes.

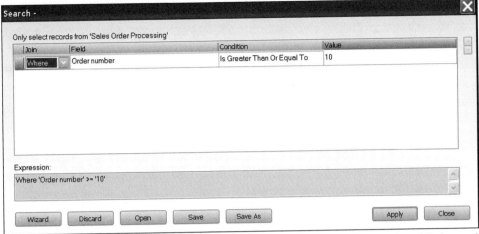

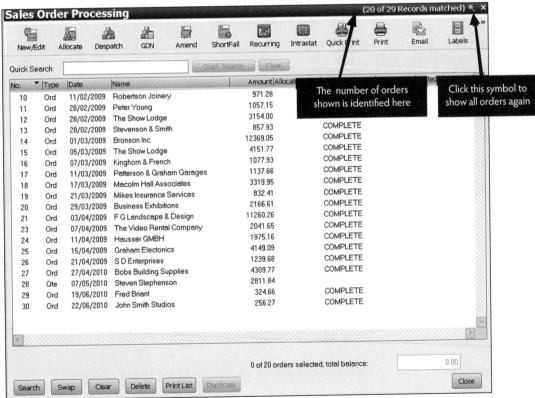

CHAPTER SUMMARY

- Product records can be set up in Sage using a unique code for each product. The product record includes product description, pricing and ordering information.

- The Sales Order Processing module is used to enter customer orders for stock products. Delivery notes can be printed.

- The Invoicing module is automatically updated with details of completed sales orders in the Sales Order Processing module. It can also be used independently of Sales Order Processing, and for non-stock or service items.

- Printing of sales invoices for sending to customers allows automatic updating of customer accounts.

- The Purchase Order Processing module is used for controlling the ordering of stock in conjunction with the Product records. Supplier accounts can be updated with details of the stock purchase invoices received using the data in Purchase Order Processing.

- A variety of useful reports and printing options are available across the order processing and invoicing modules.

- Completed transactions can be removed from the screen by either deleting them or by applying search criteria.

KEY TERMS

product code	A reference code made up of letters and/or numbers which is specific to each stock item
sales order	A document detailing customer order information
product invoice	An invoice charging for actual goods (rather than a service provided)
service invoice	An invoice charging for a service provided (rather than goods)
purchase order	A document detailing supplier order details
ledger update	Posting of invoice details to accounting records

EXERCISES

PRONTO SUPPLIES INPUTTING TASKS

Task 1

Set the program date to 1 February 2013.

Set up the following product categories in Configuration Editor:

1   Hardware

2   Software

3   Accessories and peripherals

Task 2

Set up records for the following products in the Products module using the product codes given:

Product code	Description	Category	Nominal code	Opening balance	Cost price	Sales Price
AP300	Power lead 3 mtr	3	4000	6	9.50	16.00 each
AP301	Zap external drive	3	4000	5	52.00	90.00 each
AP302	Zap USB flash memory drive	3	4000	9	11.00	20.00 pack 5
H200	Desktop computer 3000i	1	4000	2	360.00	600.00 each
H201	Monitor 17 inch	1	4000	7	65.00	100.00 each
H202	Processor G240	1	4000	2	500.00	799.00 each
H203	Printer EF102 Multi	1	4000	3	420.00	600.00 each
S100	Macroworx software Version 9	2	4001	5	230.00	450.00 each

Run a Product Details Report. Check your answer against the report on pages 275-276.

Task 3

Set up document numbering options as shown in the Case Study on page 106.

Task 4

Set the program date as appropriate for the data being processed.

Create and despatch sales orders and sales invoices as follows.

Order date	Customer	Customer order no.	Product code	Details	Invoice date
4 02 13	John Butler & Associates	DD472	H201	4 x Monitor 17 inch	5 02 13
4 02 13	Charisma Design	9756	AP300	1 x Power lead 3 mtr	6 02 13
4 02 13	Crowmatic Ltd	12/793	S100	1 x Macroworx software Version 9	6 02 13

Print a Sales Order List (in Sales Order Details Reports options) and check it against the report on page 276.

Task 5

Process a service sales invoice as follows:

Invoice date	Customer	Customer order no.	Details
8 02 13	Kay Denz	Verbal	2 hours consultancy @ £60 per hour

Task 6

Process the two sales credit notes shown below using the Invoicing module. Enter the reason for the return in the Comment 1 box. In both cases the goods are to be returned to stock.

Date	Customer	Credit note no	Product code	Details	Reason
6 02 13	David Boossey	551	S100	1 x Macroworx software Version 9	Not required
6 02 13	L Garr & Co	552	AP302	2 packs Zap USB flash memory drive	Goods returned

Print or preview the invoices and credits in tasks 4-6 above and then update the ledgers. Check the Update Ledgers Report against the one on page 276.

Print or preview Day Books: Customer Invoices (Detailed) Report and Day Books: Customer Credits (Detailed) Report and check them against those on page 277.

Task 7

Amend customer trade discount for John Butler & Associates and L Garr & Co, and cash discount for Kay Denz with effect from 11 February. Details are shown in the Case Study on page 81.

Task 8

It is 11 February 2013. Update the product records with the following additional re-order level and supplier information:

Product code	Re-order level	Supplier
H200	2	Delco PLC
H202	3	Electron Supplies
S100	5	MacCity

Run a re-order report: Reports/Stock Control/Product re-order levels and check it against the one on page 277.

Task 9

Process purchase orders on 11 February and purchase invoices as shown below. The delivery dates are in the Case Study starting on page 115.

Product code	Order quantity	Supplier
H200	10	Delco PLC
H202	4	Electron Supplies
S100	16	MacCity

Date	Invoice ref	Order no	Supplier	Details	Net amount	VAT
20 02 13	11365	2000	Delco PLC	10 x Desktop Computer 3000i	3,600.00	720.00
25 02 13	8576	2001	Electron Supplies	4 x Processor G240	2,000.00	400.00
25 02 13	2947	2002	MacCity	16 x Macroworx Software Version 9	3,680.00	736.00

Print a Purchase Order List and a Day Books: Supplier Invoices (Detailed) Report. Check them against the ones on page 278.

Task 10

Enter the following purchase credit note details. These are entered through SUPPLIERS in batch form, not through PURCHASE ORDER PROCESSING.

Date	Name	Number	Details	Net amount	VAT
6 02 13	Delco PLC	7223	1 x Pro 704 Computer	480.00	96.00
8 02 13	MacCity	552	1 x 10 Optical Mouse	38.00	7.60

Task 11

Now process the following sales invoices and credit notes. You can use SALES ORDER PROCESSING to process sales orders first, or you can produce the sales invoices directly from the Sales Invoicing module. The credit notes relate to goods returned to stock.

Account	Invoice date	Number	Details	Net	VAT
David Boossey	11 02 13	10027	1 x Printer EF102 Multi	600.00	120.00
L Garr & Co	12 02 13	10028	2 x Zap external drive	162.00	32.40
Kay Denz	13 02 13	10029	1 x Macroworx software V9	450.00	* 87.30
Charisma Design	15 02 13	10030	2 x Monitor 17 inch	200.00	40.00
John Butler & Associates	15 02 13	10031	2 hours consultancy @ £60 less 10% trade discount	108.00	21.60

*The reduced VAT is due to the settlement discount now offered

Account	Invoice date	Number	Details	Net	VAT
Charisma Design	12 02 13	553	1 x Power lead 3 mtr	16.00	3.20
Crowmatic Ltd	13 02 13	554	1 x Zap USB flash memory drive	20.00	4.00

Preview or print the invoices and credit notes, then update the ledgers.

Task 12

The following invoice has been received for new office equipment purchased from Delco PLC. Process a non-stock purchase invoice and be careful to code the items with the appropriate nominal code, ie 0030. Note that the VAT is reduced due to the settlement discount offered.

INVOICE

DELCO PLC

Delco House, Otto Way, New Milton SR1 6TF
Tel 01722 295875 Fax 01722 295611 Email sales@delco.co.uk
VAT Reg GB 0745 4672 76

invoice to

Pronto Supplies Limited Unit 17 Severnvale Estate Broadwater Road Mereford MR1 6TF	invoice no 11377 account 3993 date 25 02 13

product code	description	quantity	price (£)	unit	net	VAT
X70	Laptop X70	1	400.00	each	400.00	78.00
P28	Laser multi-printer P28	1	360.00	each	360.00	70.20

goods total	760.00
VAT	148.20
TOTAL	908.20

terms
2.5% settlement discount for payment
within 14 days of invoice date

Task 13

Finally print the following reports and compare them to the ones on pages 278-281:

Product Movement Report (Products/Reports/Product Analysis Reports/Product Movement In/Out)

Product Activity Report (Products/Reports/Product Analysis Reports/Product Activity)

Product Audit Trail (Products/Reports/Product Analysis Reports/Product Audit Trail)

Trial Balance for February 2013

Reminder! Have you made a back-up?

9 CUSTOMER AND SUPPLIER PAYMENTS

Chapter introduction

- So far in this book we have set up accounts for customers and suppliers and entered details of financial documents. But we have not covered the way in which the accounting system records the payment of money by customers to the business or by the business to suppliers.

- The bank account is central to any accounting system as the payment of money is vital to all business transactions.

- The bank account will be used not only for payments by customers and to suppliers (credit transactions), but also for transactions for which settlement is made straightaway (cash transactions), for example payment of telephone bills and wages.

- A computer accounting system may maintain more than one 'bank' account in its Nominal Ledger. For example, it may also keep a petty cash account for purchases made from the office petty cash tin and a credit card account for purchases made with the company credit card.

- This chapter concentrates on the use of the bank account for credit transactions, ie when a business receives payment of its customers' invoices and when it makes payments of its suppliers' invoices.

  The 'cash' transactions mentioned above are covered in detail in the next two chapters.

THE BANK ACCOUNTS IN COMPUTER ACCOUNTING

The bank accounts and all the functions associated with them are found in Sage by clicking on the BANK button on the vertical toolbar.

The BANK screen then appears as shown below.

Study the screen below and read the notes that follow. The most important icons are explained by the text with the arrows.

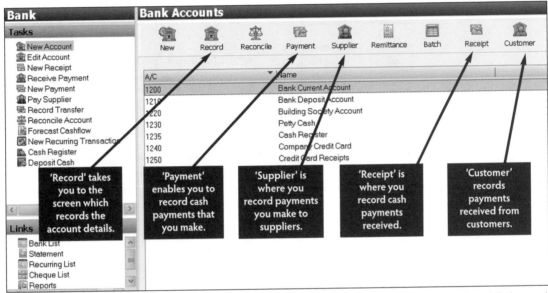

types of bank account

The accounts listed above come from the default list in the Chart of Accounts (see page 57 if you need reminding about this). The business does not have to adopt all the accounts listed here, but may use some of them if it needs them:

- **bank current account** records all payments in and out of the bank account used for everyday purposes – it is the most commonly used account

- **bank deposit account** and **building society account** can be used if the business maintains interest-paying accounts for savings and money that is not needed in the short term

- **petty cash account** can be used if the business keeps a petty cash tin in the office for small business purchases such as stationery and stamps

- **cash register** can be used for recording takings in a retail business

- **company credit card account** can be used if the business issues credit cards to its employees to enable them to pay for expenses

- **credit card receipts account** can be used if the business receives a significant number of credit or debit card payments from its customers

cash or credit payments?

A number of icons on the menu bar record payments which are either:

■ **cash payments** – ie made straightaway without the need for invoices or credit notes

■ **credit payments** – ie made in settlement of invoices

The problem is, which is which?

The rule is:

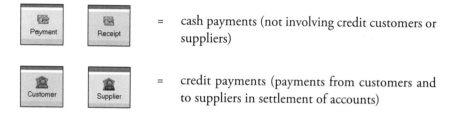

= cash payments (not involving credit customers or suppliers)

= credit payments (payments from customers and to suppliers in settlement of accounts)

bank account details

It must be stressed that if a Sage computer account number is listed on the BANK screen it does not have to be used. It is there so that it can be used if the business needs it. The Bank Current Account (here number 1200), for example, is always going to be used, assuming businesses always have bank current accounts!

When a business is setting up its bank accounts it should click on RECORD on the BANK screen to produce the bank account DETAILS screen . . .

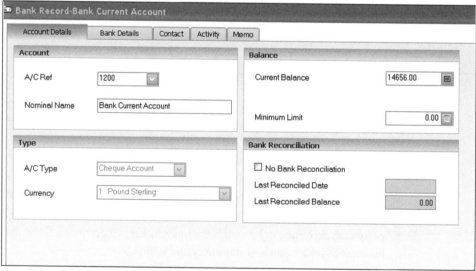

This screen enables the business to input details of the account, the bank and bank contact and to see the activity on the account.

RECORDING PAYMENTS FROM CUSTOMERS

how do payments arrive?

When a payment arrives from a customer who has bought on credit it will normally arrive at the business in one of two ways:

- A cheque and **remittance advice**. A remittance advice is a document stating what the payment relates to – eg which invoices and credit notes.

- A **BACS payment**. A BACS (Bankers Automated Clearing Services) payment is a payment sent directly between the banks' computers and does not involve a cheque. Information relating to the BACS payment may be received in the form of a BACS remittance advice or from the business bank statement.

Examples of cheque and BACS remittance advices are shown below:

TO		**REMITTANCE ADVICE**	FROM	
Pronto Supplies Ltd Unit 17 Severnvale Estate Broadwater Road Mereford MR1 6TF			**Compsync** **4 Friar Street** **Broadfield** **BR1 3RF** Tel 01908 761234 Fax 01908 761987	
Account PS765		6 November 2013		
date	your reference	our reference	payment amount	
01 10 13 10 10 13	INVOICE 787923 CREDIT NOTE 12157	47609 47609	277.30 (27.73)	
		CHEQUE TOTAL	249.57	

BACS REMITTANCE ADVICE			FROM: Excelsior Services 17 Gatley Way Bristol BS1 9GH
TO Pronto Supplies Ltd Unit 17 Severnvale Estate, Broadwater Rd, Mereford MR1 6TF			06 12 13
Your ref	Our ref		Amount
13982	3323	BACS TRANSFER	465.00
			TOTAL 465.00

THIS HAS BEEN PAID BY BACS CREDIT TRANSFER DIRECTLY INTO YOUR BANK ACCOUNT AT ALBION BANK NO 11719881 SORT CODE 90 47 17

customer payments and the accounting system

An incoming payment from a customer settling one or more invoices (less any credit notes) needs to be recorded in the accounting system:

■ the balance in the bank account will increase (a debit in double-entry accounting)

■ the balance in the customer's account (and the Debtors Control Account) will decrease because the customer will owe less (a credit in double-entry accounting)

In computer accounting the payment is input once and the two entries will be automatically made from the same screen.

the practicalities

The business will normally input a number of payments at one time on a regular basis, eg every week, using the remittance advice and/or the bank statement as the source document.

The appropriate bank account should first be selected on the BANK screen and then the CUSTOMER icon selected to access the Customer Receipt input screen:

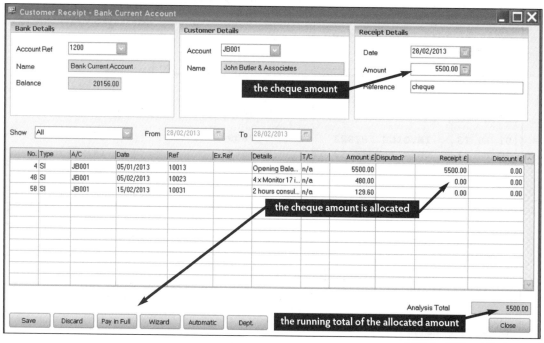

processing the payments received

The procedure for recording the customer payment on this screen is to:

1 input the customer account reference – this will bring up on-screen the account name and all the outstanding amounts due on invoices

2 input a reference if required – for example you might type 'cheque' or 'BACS' or the numerical reference relating to the payment

3 input the amount of the payment in the Amount box

4 click on the 'Receipt' box of the invoice that is being paid

5 click on the 'Pay in Full' button at the bottom

6 if cash/settlement discount has been deducted from the payment, enter the net amount received in the Receipt box and the discount taken in the Discount box (see page 80 for a full explanation of how to enter settlement discounts)

7 if there is more than one invoice being paid click on the items being paid as appropriate; the Analysis Total box at the bottom will show a running total of the money allocated

8 if there is a long list of invoices and a payment to cover them, click on 'Automatic' at the bottom and the computer will allocate the payment down the invoice list until it runs out

9 if a credit note (code 'SC') has been taken account of in the net payment, this should be dealt with first – see page 134-135 for a full explanation

10 check that what you have done is correct and SAVE; details to check are:

  – customer, amount, invoices being paid and amount received

  – the amounts in the Amount box and the Analysis Total box should be
    the same (but see next point)

11 if the amount received by way of payment is greater than the amount allocated to outstanding invoices the extra payment will show as a 'Payment on Account' after you have saved – see page 136 for a full explanation

12 if the amount received by way of payment is less than the amount of the invoice(s) it is settling, the amount received will be allocated to the appropriate invoice(s) and the unpaid amount will show as outstanding on the customer's account

13 you should print out a Day Books: Customer Receipts (Summary) for these transactions from REPORTS, Customer Reports in BANK to check that the total of the cheques (or BACS payments) received equals the total input

RECORDING PAYMENTS TO SUPPLIERS

what documents are involved?

A business often pays its suppliers after it receives a **statement** setting out the amounts due from invoices and any deductions made following the issue of credit notes. This is not a hard and fast rule, however, and it is quite in order to pay individual invoices as and when they are received.

Payment may be made by cheque, although payments are increasingly processed electronically by BACS transfer between the banks' computers. Payment is normally made in full, but occasionally a part payment may be made. A typical payment cheque, together with a completed counterfoil (cheque stub) is shown on the next page.

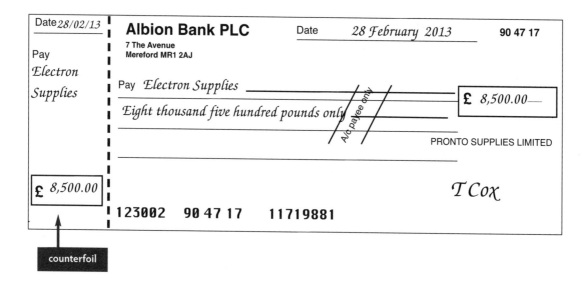

The business will send a remittance advice (see page 129) to the supplier with the cheque, or, if a BACS payment is being made, on its own.

supplier payments and the accounting system

Payment to a supplier settling one or more invoices (less any credit notes) needs to be recorded in the accounting system:

■ the balance in the bank account will decrease (a credit in double-entry accounting)

■ the balance in the supplier's account (and the Creditors Control Account) will decrease because the supplier will be owed less (a debit in double-entry accounting)

In computer accounting the payment is input once and the two entries will be automatically made from the same screen.

processing the payments

As with customer receipts, the business will normally input a number of payments at one time on a regular basis, for example just after the cheques have been written out, or the BACS payment instructions prepared.

The payments are input in Sage from the SUPPLIER icon on the BANK screen – after the appropriate bank account has been selected.

The procedure for recording the supplier payment is to:

1   input the supplier reference in the box next to the word 'Payee' on the 'cheque' – this will bring up on-screen the account name and all the outstanding amounts due on invoices

2   input the cheque number on the cheque and alter the date if the cheque date is different

3   input the amount of the payment in the amount box on the cheque; if it is a part payment the same procedure will be followed

4   click on the Payment box of the invoice that is being paid – here it is the first one – and click on the 'Pay in full' icon at the bottom; if there is more than one invoice being paid click on the items being paid as appropriate; any part payment will be allocated to the appropriate invoice(s) in the same way

5   check that what you have done is correct (ie supplier, amount, invoices being paid) and SAVE (see below if you wish to print out a remittance advice)

6   print out a Day Books: Supplier Payments (Summary) from REPORTS, Supplier Reports in BANK to check that the total of the cheques (or BACS payments) issued equals the total input on the computer

Note that when processing supplier payments you may, as with customer payments, have to adjust for credit notes, overpayments, underpayments and settlement discount. These are covered in detail on pages 134-136. The treatment of cash/settlement discount is dealt with on pages 79-80.

A supplier payment screen is shown below.

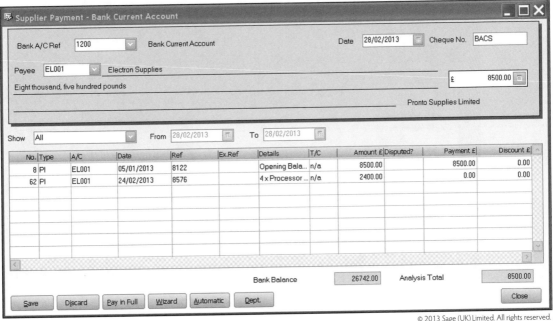

printing remittance advices and cheques

Remittance advices and cheques may be printed once a payment has been processed in Sage.

To print a remittance advice, click on Remittance on the Bank toolbar. Select the transaction or transactions for which the remittance advice is required, click Print and then choose one of the remittance options and click Run. From the Preview screen there is an option to email the document direct to a supplier.

To print cheques (with remittance advice attached), click on Cheques on the Bank toolbar. Pre-printed cheques to use with Sage must be specially ordered.

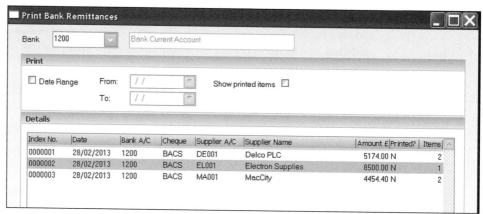

An extract from the printed remittance advice is shown below.

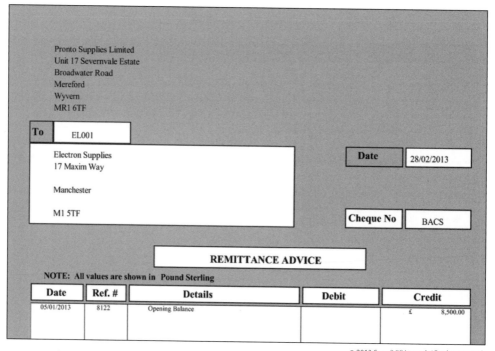

DEALING WITH CREDIT NOTES

When inputting payments from customers and to suppliers in a program like Sage, you may encounter the situation where the amount received (or paid out) is not the same as the amount of the invoice being settled.

For example, if a customer is issued with an invoice for £1,000 and then issued with a credit note for £100 because some of the goods are faulty, the customer will only owe – and pay – £900. The computer screen, however, will show this £900 as two separate lines: an invoice for

£1,000 and a credit note for £100. If the £900 cheque received is allocated against the £1,000, the computer will think a balance of £100 still needs to be paid against this invoice, even though the account balance is nil.

the solution

The credit note needs to be allocated to the balance of the invoice. This is done by:

- clicking on the Receipt box on the credit note line
- clicking on 'Pay in Full' so that the analysis total shows a minus amount
- clicking on the Receipt box on the invoice line and then 'Pay in Full' so that the analysis box shows the payment amount

This procedure can be carried out during or after the payments received routine. In the example below a credit note for £540 is being set off against an invoice for £3,400, the amount received being £2,860.

Note that the procedure for allocating supplier credit notes to supplier invoices works on exactly the same principle.

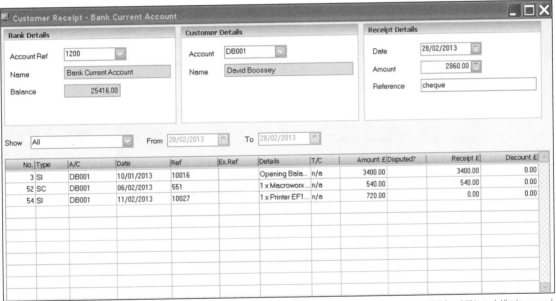

DEALING WITH PAYMENTS THAT ARE TOO HIGH OR TOO LOW

Sometimes a customer will send an amount which does not tally with the amount that appears on the customer's statement and the amount on the computer records. For example:

- the customer sends a part payment of an invoice because he or she is short of money, or thinks a credit note is due
- the customer sends too much money, ignoring a credit note that has been issued

the solution – underpayment

The amount that has been received is allocated against the relevant invoice. The amount that is still owing will show on the customer's account.

the solution – overpayment

The amount that has been received is allocated against all the relevant invoices. The extra amount that is received will show as a 'Payment on Account' which will be available to allocate against future invoices.

In the example below, D Boossey paid his account with a cheque for £4,120 at the end of the month. He did not make an adjustment for a credit note for £540 he had received and so he overpaid by this amount. Sage asks if an overpayment should be entered as a payment on account. Note the 'payment on account' on the second screen which shows how his account appears following the payment.

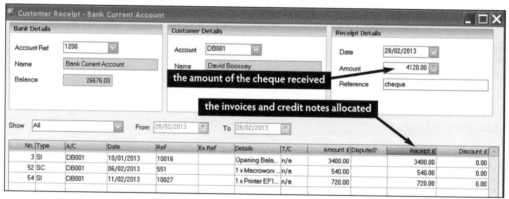

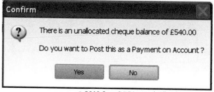

dealing with settlement discount

When settlement discount has been deducted from a customer or supplier payment, the amount of the discount taken is entered in the Discount column in the payment screen. The net (actual) amount of the payment is entered at the top of the screen in the Amount box. This amount is also entered in the Receipt column of the invoice line if only one invoice is being paid; if more than one invoice is being paid then the relevant discounts and net amounts are entered against each invoice (or one total discount sum can be entered against any one invoice being paid).

In the screenshot below a customer payment of £523.80 has been received. This relates to an original invoice value of £537.30 where £13.50 settlement discount has been deducted.

More information about discounts can be found on pages 79-80.

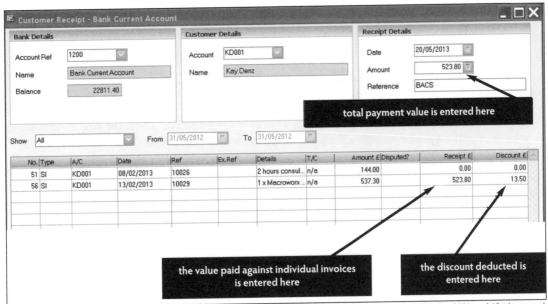

SET-OFF PAYMENTS/CONTRA ENTRIES

Where a business trades with another as both a customer and a supplier, the two parties may agree to settle their respective accounts using set-off rather than making payments to each other. In Sage this is referred to as 'contra entry'.

In the example below, Pronto Supplies trades with Charisma Design as both a customer and a supplier. They agree to set off the amount owed to Charisma Design (£1,200.00) against the amount owing to them.

The contra entry screen is found in the Tools menu at the top of the screen.

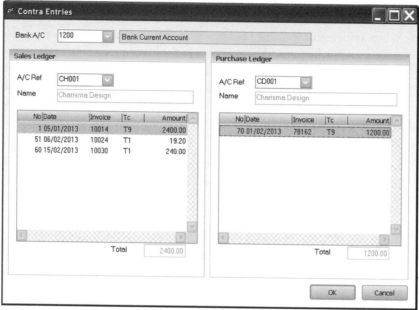

As the two accounts involved do not have the same balance, a warning screen alerts the user and suggests a possible solution. The answer in this case is Yes.

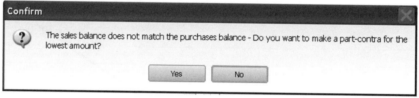

We will now look at the way in which Tom Cox's business, Pronto Supplies Limited, inputs its payments from customers and payments to suppliers on the computer.

CASE STUDY

PRONTO SUPPLIES LIMITED:
PROCESSING PAYMENTS FROM CUSTOMERS AND TO SUPPLIERS

It is 28 February 2013. Tom has received a number of payments (with remittance advices) from his customers in settlement of their accounts.

Tom also has a list of supplier invoices to pay, the money being due at the end of the month.

receipts from customers

The list of payments received is shown below.

John Butler & Associates	£5,500.00	Cheque
Charisma Design	£2,400.00	Cheque
David Boossey	£2,860.00	Cheque
Kay Denz	£6,500.00	BACS
L Garr & Co	£8,500.00	BACS
Total of payments received	£25,760.00	

Tom notes that the cheque from David Boossey includes an adjustment made for a credit note issued on 6 February.

These payments are entered into the computer accounting system under CUSTOMERS in the BANK section as shown on the screen below. This illustrates the John Butler & Associates cheque being input.

When entering the cheque received from David Boossey, Tom takes account of the credit note by clicking first in the Receipt box on the credit note line and then 'Pay in Full', before allocating the amount to the line of the amount originally due.

Tom then prints out a report 'Day Books: Customer Receipts (Summary)' from REPORTS, Customer Reports in BANK. This shows the transactions he has processed and is shown on the next page. He checks the total on the report against the batch total of the payments (or remittance advices) he has received.

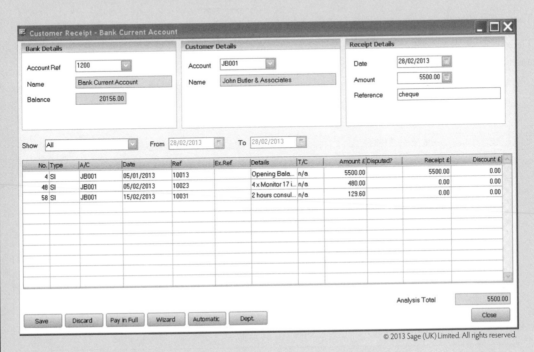

Pronto Supplies Limited

Day Books: Customer Receipts (Summary)

Date From:	28/02/2013						Bank From:	1200	
DateTo:	28/02/2013						Bank To:	1200	
Transaction From:	1						Customer From :		
Transaction To:	99,999,999						Customer To:	ZZZZZZZZ.	

Bank 1200 **Currency** Pound Sterling

No	Type	Date	Account	Ref	Details	Net £	Tax £	Gross £	B	Bank Rec.
68	SR	28/02/2013	JB001	cheque	Sales Receipt	5,500.00	0.00	5,500.00	N	
69	SR	28/02/2013	CH001	cheque	Sales Receipt	2,400.00	0.00	2,400.00	N	
70	SR	28/02/2013	DB001	cheque	Sales Receipt	2,860.00	0.00	2,860.00	N	
71	SR	28/02/2013	KD001	BACS	Sales Receipt	6,500.00	0.00	6,500.00	N	
72	SR	28/02/2013	LG001	BACS	Sales Receipt	8,500.00	0.00	8,500.00	N	
					Totals £	**25,760.00**	**0.00**	**25,760.00**		

payments to suppliers

Tom has made a list of the amounts he owes to his suppliers for goods sent to Pronto Supplies Limited in January.

The documents he has for this are his original purchase orders, invoices received and any credit notes issued by his suppliers.

The data is now ready for input. The details are:

Delco PLC	£5,174.00	BACS
Electron Supplies	£8,500.00	BACS
MacCity	£4,454.40	BACS
Total of payments made	£18,128.40	

Tom notes that the payments to Delco PLC and MacCity include adjustments for credit notes issued.

These payments are entered into the computer accounting system under SUPPLIERS in the BANK section as shown below. Tom will also send remittance advices.

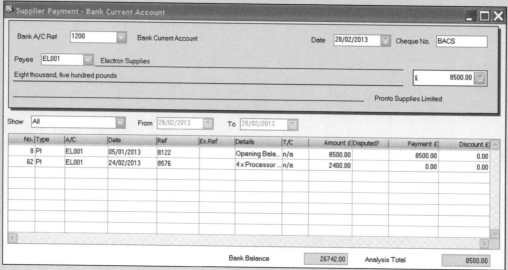

Tom then prints out a report Day Books: Supplier Payments (Summary) from REPORTS, Supplier Reports in BANK. This shows the transactions he has processed. He checks the total on the report against the total of the payments he has issued.

Pronto Supplies Limited

Day Books: Supplier Payments (Summary)

Date From:	28/02/2013								Bank From:	1200	
DateTo:	28/02/2013								Bank To:	1200	
Transaction From:	1								Supplier From:		
Transaction To:	99,999,999								Supplier To:	ZZZZZZZZ	

Bank	1200			Currency	Pound Sterling						
No	Type	Date	Supplier	Ref	Details	Net £	Tax £	Gross £	B	Bank Rec.
73	PP	28/02/2013	DE001	BACS	Purchase Payment	5,174.00	0.00	5,174.00	N	
74	PP	28/02/2013	EL001	BACS	Purchase Payment	8,500.00	0.00	8,500.00	N	
75	PP	28/02/2013	MA001	BACS	Purchase Payment	4,454.40	0.00	4,454.40	N	
					Totals £	18,128.40	0.00	18,128.40		

CHAPTER SUMMARY

■ The bank account is a central account in the operation of any business as so many transactions pass through it.

■ A business can set up not only the bank current account in the computer accounting system, but also a number of other 'money' accounts. These, which include petty cash account and credit card accounts, enable the business to keep track of the processing of money in a variety of forms.

■ Payments received from customers who have bought on credit can be processed through the computer accounting system. The accounting system is adjusted in each case by an increase in the bank current account and a reduction of the customer's account balance in the Sales Ledger.

■ Payments to suppliers from whom the business has bought on credit can also be processed on the computer and remittance advices printed if required. The accounting entries in this case are a decrease in the bank current account and a reduction in the supplier's account balance in the Purchases Ledger.

■ The payment amount in each case (customer or supplier) will relate to invoices and any credit notes issued. Any overpayment or underpayment will be logged on the relevant Sage account.

- Sometimes the customer or supplier payment amount will be reduced because settlement (cash) discount has been deducted. Any discount of this type will be entered in a discount column in Sage.

- It is essential to check the input of payments from customers and to suppliers by obtaining a printout such as a Day Book Report from the computer.

- Set-off or contra entries may be used to settle accounts between businesses that owe each other money.

KEY TERMS

current account	the 'everyday' bank account which handles routine receipts and payments
cash payments	payments made straightaway
credit payments	payments made at a later date following the issue of an invoice to a customer or by a supplier
remittance advice	a document that tells a business that a payment is being made

EXERCISES

PRONTO SUPPLIES INPUTTING TASKS

Task 1

Set the program date to 28 February 2013. Enter the following customer payments into BANK (CUSTOMERS). Check your total before saving and print out a Day Books: Customer Receipts (Summary) Report to confirm the accuracy of your input (see page 282).

Note: the cheque from David Boossey includes an adjustment made for a credit note, which will have to be allocated as described in the Case Study (see page 138).

John Butler & Associates	£5,500.00	Cheque
Charisma Design	£2,400.00	Cheque
David Boossey	£2,860.00	Cheque
Kay Denz	£6,500.00	BACS
L Garr & Co	£8,500.00	BACS
Total of payments received	£25,760.00	

Task 2

Enter into the computer the three BACS payments listed below that Tom is paying to suppliers.

In the case of Delco PLC and MacCity, ensure that you adjust the account for credit notes issued.

Check your total before saving and print out a Day Books: Supplier Payments (Summary) Report to confirm the accuracy of your input (see page 282).

If you are able to, print out remittance advices.

Delco PLC	£5,174.00
Electron Supplies	£8,500.00
MacCity	£4,454.40
Total of payments made	£18,128.40

Task 3

Enter a BACS payment received on 20 February from Kay Denz for £523.80. This pays invoice 10029 less £13.50 settlement discount.

Task 4

Print out a Trial Balance for Pronto Supplies as at 28 February 2013 from the FINANCIALS module and check it against the Trial Balance on page 283.

Compare this new Trial Balance with the Trial Balance produced at the end of the last chapter.

10 CASH RECEIPTS AND PAYMENTS

Chapter introduction

- The last chapter explained how payments settling invoices are recorded in a computer accounting system. These payments received from customers and made to suppliers settle up 'credit sales' where invoices are issued when the sale is made and payment is made later.

- A business will also process a substantial number of varied 'cash payments' where the money is transferred at the same time as the transaction. Note that 'cash' does not just mean notes and coins in this context; it means immediate payment.

  Examples of these payments (and receipts) include:

  - money received from sales – over the counter sales or online sales

  - money spent on purchases – buying stock and material for use in the business

  - running expenses paid – wages, power bills, rent

  - items bought for permanent use in the business – fixed assets not bought on credit

  - loans made to the business

  - money (capital) put into the business by the owner(s)

- A computer accounting system will record these 'cash' items in a different way from the 'credit' items seen in the last chapter. In a Sage system they are processed through the PAYMENT or RECEIPT icons on the BANK menu bar.

- The transactions mentioned so far involve payments which are made straight through the bank current account. A business may also use other funds for making payments and receiving money. These are covered in the next chapter.

THE BANK ACCOUNTS

The last chapter started by looking at the different bank accounts that a Sage system will allow a business to set up. Whereas the last chapter concentrated on the use of the Bank Current Account for payments made on credit, this chapter examines the way in which cash payments (immediate payments) are recorded in the Bank Current Account of a computer accounting system.

The BANK screen shown below (the default accounts screen) explains the icons that you will be using in this chapter.

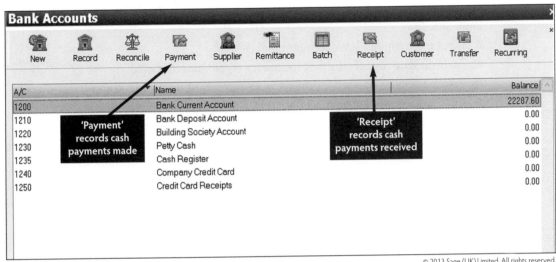

CASH RECEIPTS

Cash sales made by a business are usually sales made at a checkout or through an online shop. 'Cash' here means 'immediate payment'.

Receipts from 'cash' sales can be made by cash (notes and coins), cheque or debit or credit card. The important point here is that the business should ensure the money reaches the bank current account as soon as possible, so that it can be used to meet payments the business may have made or may have to make.

The input screen for cash sales is reached from the RECEIPT icon on the BANK menu bar. Where the money has been paid straight into the bank current account, it would look like this:

Bank	Date	Ref	N/C	Dept	Project Ref	Details	Net	T/C	Tax
1200	08/02/2013	10736	4000	0		Hardware sal...	12500.00	T1	2500.00
1200	08/02/2013	10737	4001	0		Software sales	4680.00	T1	936.00
1200	15/02/2013	10738	4000	0		Hardware sal...	15840.00	T1	3168.00
1200	15/02/2013	10739	4001	0		Software sales	3680.00	T1	736.00
1200	22/02/2013	10740	4000	0		Hardware sal...	17800.00	T1	3560.00
1200	22/02/2013	10741	4001	0		Software sales	4800.00	T1	960.00

Bank: Bank Current Account
N/C: Computer software sales
Tax Rate: 20.00
Total: 71160.00

inputting bank receipts

Cash sale values may be input from sales listing sheets, till rolls or from bank paying-in slips if paid straight into the bank. These receipts are known in Sage as Bank Receipts and are input as follows:

- input the computer bank account number
- enter the date (usually the date the money is paid into the bank)
- enter a reference (this can be the reference number of the paying-in slip)
- input the appropriate nominal code (N/C) for the type of sales involved
- enter a description of the payment (eg 'hardware sales') under 'Details'
- enter the net amount of the sales (ie the sales amount excluding VAT) and then click on T1 if the goods are standard rated for VAT – the computer will then automatically calculate the VAT amount for you and show it in the right-hand column
- check that the VAT amount shown agrees with your figure and change it on-screen if it does not – there may be a rounding difference
- check the input details and totals and then SAVE

Money from cash sales may be retained within the business in a cash account, or split between money retained and money paid into the bank. In the example below, cash sales of £1,200 have been split: £800 to the bank current account and £400 to the Cash Register account. See page 165 for more information about the Cash Register account.

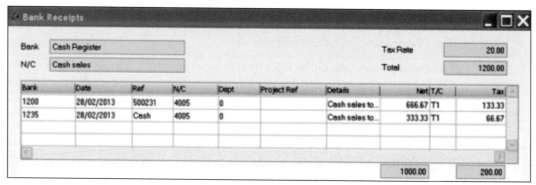

a note on VAT

The rates of VAT (**tax codes**) that you are most likely to come across are:

T1   standard rate (20% at the time of writing)

T2   exempt from VAT – eg postage stamps, insurance

T5   reduced-rate, eg domestic heating

T0   zero-rated, ie VAT could be charged but it is zero at the moment – eg books, some food and some children's clothes

T9   transactions not involving VAT

If you only have a VAT inclusive figure and do not know what the VAT amount is, enter the total figure in the 'Net' column and click on 'Calc. Net' at the bottom of the screen. The computer then automatically calculates and shows the net amount and the VAT (see illustrations opposite).

other cash receipts

You can also enter other cash (= not credit) receipts using the same Bank Receipts screen. Examples include:

- money invested by the owner(s) of the business – capital
- loans and grants from outside bodies
- income from other sources such as rent received, bank interest, commission received, or sales of fixed assets
- insurance claim receipts

This money is likely to be received in the form of a cheque or bank transfer and will need to be recorded as such.

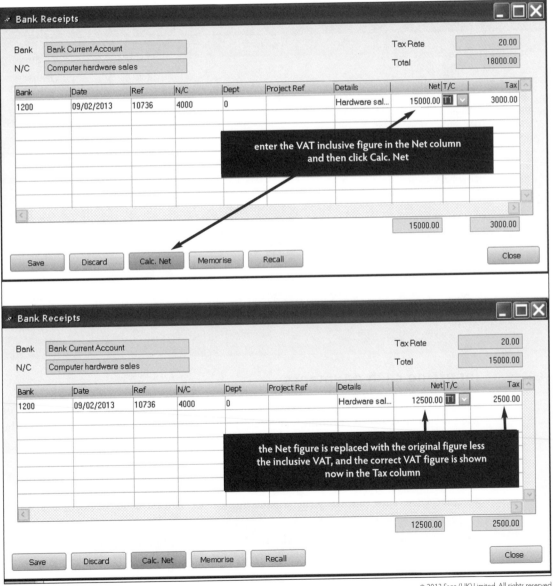

CASH PAYMENTS

Most credit payments made by businesses, as we saw in the last chapter, are to suppliers for goods and services provided and paid for on invoice. But businesses also have to make payments on a day-to-day cash basis (immediate payment) for running costs and expenses such as wages, telephone bills, owner drawings and sundry (miscellaneous) expenses. Cash payments may also be made to suppliers where no credit terms have been agreed.

These payments are input from the screen reached by clicking on the PAYMENT icon on the BANK menu bar. Study the example shown below: a telephone bill and wages have been paid from the Bank Current Account.

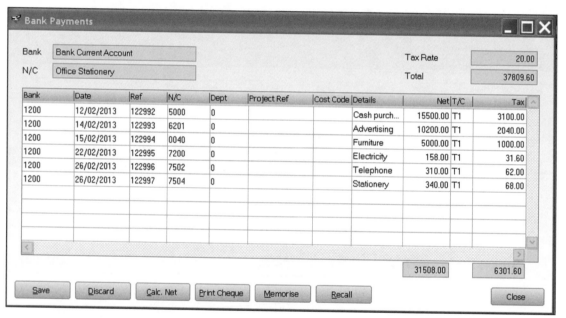

inputting cash payments

Cash payments can be input from the handwritten business **cash book** (if one is used), or from the cheques issued and bills being paid (which should show any VAT element). The procedure for inputting is:

- input the computer bank account number
- enter the date (the date the payment is made)
- enter a reference (normally the cheque number or 'BACS' if the payment is a BACS payment)
- input the appropriate nominal code (N/C) for the type of payment involved
- enter a brief description of the nature of the payment (eg 'Telephone') under 'Details'

■ enter the net amount of the payment (ie the amount excluding VAT) and then click on T1 if the product is standard rated for VAT – the computer will then automatically calculate the VAT amount for you and show it in the right-hand column

■ check that the VAT amount shown agrees with your figure and change it on-screen if it does not – there may be a rounding difference

a note on VAT

The VAT rates used here are:

T1	the telephone bill is standard rated
T9	wages do not involve VAT

The code for a zero-rated item would have been T0. The code for a VAT exempt item would have been T2, and for a reduced-rate item, T5.

If you do not know what the VAT amount is included in a payment figure, enter the total figure in the 'Net' column and click on 'Calc. Net' at the bottom of the screen. The computer will then automatically calculate the VAT and adjust the Net figure accordingly. For example, a VAT-inclusive, standard-rated figure of £120 would be split £100 net and £20 VAT, or a reduced-rate (5%) figure of £105 would split £100 net and £5 VAT.

checking the input data

It is important to check your input for each item against the source data for the input. You will see that the screen on the previous page has running total boxes below the Net and Tax columns. There is also a Total (Net plus Tax) box at the top. These boxes will all update as you enter the transactions.

If you are entering the data for a number of transactions you should add up the three 'batch' totals (Net, VAT and Total) and check them against the screen figures in the total boxes when you have finished your data entry.

As a final check you should print out a Day Books report (see extract below) from Reports in BANK and check the entries against your handwritten records (your cash book, for example).

Pronto Supplies Limited

Day Books: Bank Payments (Detailed)

Bank:	1200		**Currency:**	Pound Sterling									
No	**Type**	**N/C**	**Date**	**Ref**	**Details**	**Dept**	**Net £**	**Tax**	**£ T/C**	**Gross £**	**V**	**B**
84	BP	5000	12/02/2013	122992	Cash purchases	0	15,500.00	3,100.00 T1		18,600.00	N	N
85	BP	6201	14/02/2013	122993	Advertising	0	10,200.00	2,040.00 T1		12,240.00	N	N
86	BP	0040	15/02/2013	122994	Furniture	0	5,000.00	1,000.00 T1		6,000.00	N	N
87	BP	7200	22/02/2013	122995	Electricity	0	158.00	31.60 T1		189.60	N	N
88	BP	7550	26/02/2013	122996	Telephone	0	310.00	62.00 T1		372.00	N	N
89	BP	7502	26/02/2013	122997	Stationery	0	340.00	68.00 T1		408.00	N	N
						Totals £	31,508.00	6,301.60		37,809.60		

CASE STUDY

PRONTO SUPPLIES LIMITED: CASH RECEIPTS AND PAYMENTS

It is 28 February 2013 and Tom has completed and checked his input of customer receipts and supplier payments (see pages 138 to 141).

He now has to input the various cash receipts and payments received and made during the month.

cash receipts

Pronto Supplies Limited paid takings of cash sales into the bank current account three times during the month. The amounts recorded in the cash book are shown below. The reference quoted is the paying-in slip reference.

Date	Details	Net amount (£)	VAT (£)	ref.
8 Feb 2013	Hardware sales	12,500.00	2,500.00	10736
8 Feb 2013	Software sales	4,680.00	936.00	10737
15 Feb 2013	Hardware sales	15,840.00	3,168.00	10738
15 Feb 2013	Software sales	3,680.00	736.00	10739
22 Feb 2013	Hardware sales	17,800.00	3,560.00	10740
22 Feb 2013	Software sales	4,800.00	960.00	10741
	Totals	59,300.00	11,860.00	

These sales receipts are entered into the computer accounting system on the RECEIPTS screen reached from the BANK menu bar. Note that the Bank Current Account and the appropriate nominal sales code (N/C) are used each time.

Tom can use some helpful features when inputting. When in a line and wanting to copy the box above (eg the bank account number or the date) he presses F6; when wanting to raise the number in the box by one (eg reference number) he presses Shift F6.

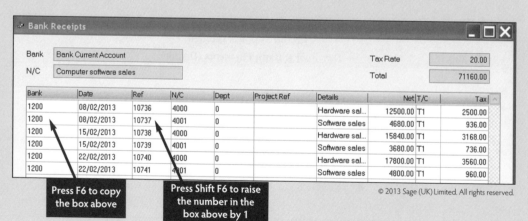

Press F6 to copy the box above

Press Shift F6 to raise the number in the box above by 1

Tom then checks his listing totals against the on-screen totals for accuracy and clicks SAVE. He then prints out a report 'Day Books: Bank Receipts (Detailed)' as a paper-based record of the transactions he has processed. This is shown below. He again checks the totals on the report against the totals on his original listing.

Pronto Supplies Limited

Day Books: Bank Receipts (Detailed)

Date From:	01/01/1980								N/C From:		
DateTo:	31/12/2019										
Transaction From:	1								N/C To:	99999999	
Transaction To:	99,999,999										
Dept From:	0										
Dept To:	999										

Bank:	1200		Currency:	Pound Sterling							
No	**Type**	**N/C**	**Date**	**Ref**	**Details**	**Dept**	**Net £**	**Tax £ T/C**	**Gross £ V B**		
78	BR	4000	08/02/2013	10736	Hardware sales	0	12,500.00	2,500.00 T1	15,000.00 N N		
79	BR	4001	08/02/2013	10737	Software sales	0	4,680.00	936.00 T1	5,616.00 N N		
80	BR	4000	15/02/2013	10738	Hardware sales	0	15,840.00	3,168.00 T1	19,008.00 N N		
81	BR	4001	15/02/2013	10739	Software sales	0	3,680.00	736.00 T1	4,416.00 N N		
82	BR	4000	22/02/2013	10740	Hardware sales	0	17,800.00	3,560.00 T1	21,360.00 N N		
83	BR	4001	22/02/2013	10741	Software sales	0	4,800.00	960.00 T1	5,760.00 N N		
						Totals £	59,300.00	11,860.00	71,160.00		

cash payments

Tom sees from the company cash book that Pronto Supplies Limited has made a number of cash payments during the month for a variety of purposes. They are listed below. They include:

■ normal day-to-day running expenses paid on a cash basis

■ the purchase of furniture for £5,000 (a fixed asset) on 15 February

Date	Details	Net amount (£)	VAT (£)	chq no
12 Feb 2013	Cash purchases	15,500.00	3,100.00	122992
14 Feb 2013	Advertising	10,200.00	2,040.00	122993
15 Feb 2013	Furniture	5,000.00	1,000.00	122994
22 Feb 2013	Electricity	158.00	31.60	122995
26 Feb 2013	Telephone	310.00	62.00	122996
26 Feb 2013	Stationery	340.00	68.00	122997
	Totals	31,508.00	6,301.60	

These payments are entered into the computer accounting system on the PAYMENTS screen reached from the BANK menu bar. Note that the Bank Current Account and the appropriate nominal code (N/C) is used each time. The reference in each case is the relevant cheque number or BACS.

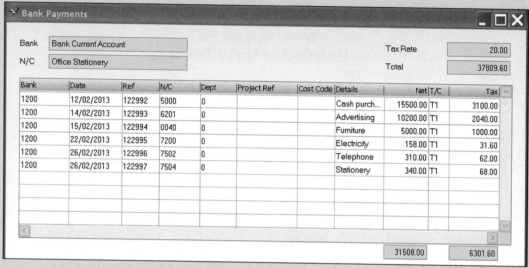

If Tom wants to insert or delete lines when entering data, he can press F7 to insert a blank line between two lines already entered, or F8 to delete a line already entered.

Tom then checks his listing totals against the on-screen totals for accuracy and clicks SAVE. He prints out a report Day Books: Bank Payments (Detailed) as a record of the transactions he has processed. This is shown below. He compares the totals on the report against the totals on his original listing as a final check of input accuracy.

Pronto Supplies Limited
Day Books: Bank Payments (Detailed)

| Date From: | 01/01/1980 |
| Date To: | 31/12/2019 |

| Transaction From: | 1 | | | N/C From: | |
| Transaction To: | 99,999,999 | | | N/C To: | 99999999 |

| Dept From: | 0 |
| Dept To: | 999 |

Bank: 1200   **Currency:** Pound Sterling

No	Type	N/C	Date	Ref	Details	Dept	Net £	Tax £	T/C	Gross £	V	B	Bank Date
84	BP	5000	12/02/2013	122992	Cash purchases	0	15,500.00	3,100.00	T1	18,600.00	N	N	
85	BP	6201	14/02/2013	122993	Advertising	0	10,200.00	2,040.00	T1	12,240.00	N	N	
86	BP	0040	15/02/2013	122994	Furniture	0	5,000.00	1,000.00	T1	6,000.00	N	N	
87	BP	7200	22/02/2013	122995	Electricity	0	158.00	31.60	T1	189.60	N	N	
88	BP	7550	26/02/2013	122996	Telephone	0	310.00	62.00	T1	372.00	N	N	
89	BP	7502	26/02/2013	122997	Stationery	0	340.00	68.00	T1	408.00	N	N	
					Totals £		**31,508.00**	**6,301.60**		**37,809.60**			

RECEIPTS AND PAYMENTS AND THE ACCOUNTING SYSTEM

It is important to appreciate how the cash receipts and payments in this chapter relate to the accounting system of a business, particularly if you are also studying double-entry bookkeeping.

Remember that transactions involve debits and credits and that the debit amount always equals the credit amount. Because of the VAT included in many sales and purchases, these transactions may involve three entries:

- the amount posted to the bank account (the full amount)
- the 'net' amount (the amount before VAT is added on) posted to the sales account or purchases (or expense) account
- any VAT involved in the transaction being posted to sales or purchases VAT account

The whole cash payment system is summarised in the linked diagram below. This shows how the money comes into and out of the bank account and illustrates how the double-entry bookkeeping works. If you are not studying double-entry, just concentrate on the types of receipts and payments and study how they are input.

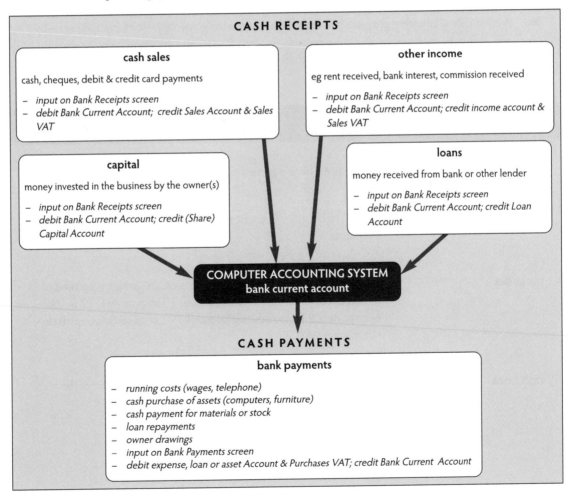

CASH RECEIPTS

cash sales

cash, cheques, debit & credit card payments

- *input on Bank Receipts screen*
- *debit Bank Current Account; credit Sales Account & Sales VAT*

other income

eg rent received, bank interest, commission received

- *input on Bank Receipts screen*
- *debit Bank Current Account; credit income account & Sales VAT*

capital

money invested in the business by the owner(s)

- *input on Bank Receipts screen*
- *debit Bank Current Account; credit (Share) Capital Account*

loans

money received from bank or other lender

- *input on Bank Receipts screen*
- *debit Bank Current Account; credit Loan Account*

COMPUTER ACCOUNTING SYSTEM
bank current account

CASH PAYMENTS

bank payments

- *running costs (wages, telephone)*
- *cash purchase of assets (computers, furniture)*
- *cash payment for materials or stock*
- *loan repayments*
- *owner drawings*
- *input on Bank Payments screen*
- *debit expense, loan or asset Account & Purchases VAT; credit Bank Current Account*

CHAPTER SUMMARY

- Cash payments are payments which are immediate, unlike credit payments which are made at a later date.

- Cash receipts and payments include payment by cash, cheques, debit and credit cards and BACS.

- Businesses receive cash payments from a variety of sources: cash sales, loans, capital introduced by the owner(s) and other income such as rent of property, bank interest, commission received, sale of fixed assets and insurance claims.

- Businesses make cash payments for day-to-day running costs, purchases where no credit is given, loan repayments and owner drawings.

- A computer accounting program will record cash payments coming in – ie cash receipts – by adding the money to the bank account and by adjusting the appropriate other account (eg sales, loan, capital, income account) and the Sales VAT account (if there is any VAT involved).

- A computer accounting program will record cash payments going out – ie cash payments – by deducting the money from the bank account and by adjusting the appropriate other account (eg expense, asset purchase) and the Purchases VAT account (if there is any VAT involved).

KEY TERMS

cash sales	sales made where payment is immediate
current account	the 'everyday' bank account which handles routine receipts and payments
tax codes	a term used by Sage to refer to the rate of VAT which is applied to transactions; T1 refers to standard rate, T0 to zero rate, T2 to VAT exempt items, T5 to reduced rate and T9 to transactions which do not involve VAT
cash book	the manual record which records money paid in and out of the bank account

EXERCISES

PRONTO SUPPLIES INPUTTING TASKS

Task 1

Set the program date to 28 February 2013. Enter the following bank receipts into the computer. Check your totals before saving and print out a Day Books: Bank Receipts (Detailed) Report (date range 8 Feb to 22 Feb) to confirm the accuracy of your input (see page 283).

Date	Details	Net amount (£)	VAT (£)	ref.
8 Feb 2013	Hardware sales	12,500.00	2,500.00	10736
8 Feb 2013	Software sales	4,680.00	936.00	10737
15 Feb 2013	Hardware sales	15,840.00	3,168.00	10738
15 Feb 2013	Software sales	3,680.00	736.00	10739
22 Feb 2013	Hardware sales	17,800.00	3,560.00	10740
22 Feb 2013	Software sales	4,800.00	960.00	10741
	Totals	59,300.00	11,860.00	

Task 2

Keeping the program date as 28 February 2013, enter the following cash payments into the computer. Take care over the nominal accounts that you choose.

Check your totals before saving and print out a Day Books: Bank Payments (Detailed) Report, using an appropriate date range to confirm the accuracy of your input (see page 284).

Date	Details	Net amount (£)	VAT (£)	chq no
12 Feb 2013	Cash purchases*	15,500.00	3,100.00	122992
14 Feb 2013	Advertising	10,200.00	2,040.00	122993
15 Feb 2013	Furniture	5,000.00	1,000.00	122994
22 Feb 2013	Electricity	158.00	31.60	122995
26 Feb 2013	Telephone	310.00	62.00	122996
26 Feb 2013	Stationery	340.00	68.00	122997
	Totals	31,508.00	6,301.60	

*use 'Materials Purchased' account for this transaction, as the purchases are for stock

Task 3

Keep the program date as 28 February 2013.

Tom has won £5,000 on a Premium Bond. He decides to pay the cheque into the business as extra issued share capital under reference 10742, Code T9.

Make the necessary entries into the computer account. The nominal accounts used will be Ordinary Shares.

Task 4

Print out a Trial Balance as at 28 February 2013 to check the accuracy of your input to date. Check with the Trial Balance on page 284.

Reminder! Have you made a back-up?

11 BANK ACCOUNTS AND RECURRING ENTRIES

Chapter introduction

- The last chapter explained how cash payments made directly in and out of the bank current account are recorded in a computer accounting system. 'Cash payment' here means 'immediate payment'. It can involve cash, cheques, payments by debit and credit card and BACS.

- The computer program also enables a business to set up accounts on the system which record funds of money held by the business. These funds are classified by Sage as 'Bank' accounts, but the money is not held at the bank – it is held by the business and managed by the business. These accounts cover both cash payments and cash receipts.

- The 'Bank' accounts – which allow payments to be made – include:

    - petty cash account – a cash fund held under lock and key in the office, used for making small purchases and payments

    - credit card account – company credit cards issued to employees which enable the employees to pay expenses and for the business to be billed by the credit card company

    The money for these accounts will come from the bank current account and be recorded in Sage by a Bank Transfer.

- If a business – a shop for example – receives cash payments and then holds them on the premises for a length of time before paying them into the bank, it may use the Cash Register account to record the takings.

    When the money is eventually paid into the bank, the business will record a Bank Transfer from Cash Account in Sage to show the money being paid into the bank.

- Businesses will from time-to-time need to record regular payments made in and out of the bank current account. Examples include standing orders and direct debits for outgoing payments of insurance premiums and business rates and incoming receipts of rent from tenants.

    In Sage the Recurring Entries facility enables the business to set up the payments so that they can be recorded automatically each month in the accounts on the click of a button.

THE BANK ACCOUNTS IN COMPUTER ACCOUNTING

The bank accounts and all the functions associated with them are found in Sage by clicking on the BANK button in the vertical toolbar.

The accounts listed come from the default list in the Chart of Accounts. The business does not have to adopt all the accounts, but may use some of them if it needs them. It can also set up new accounts within the appropriate account number range by clicking on NEW on the menu bar and using the new account Wizard. A summary of the Sage bank accounts is on page 127.

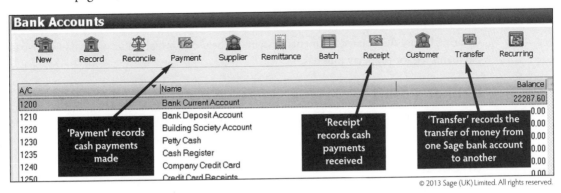

when is a bank account not a bank account?

The first three types of account shown on the above screen are actually maintained at the bank or building society. They are true 'bank' accounts. The other accounts – petty cash, cash register and credit card payment and receipts accounts – are not kept at the bank but within the business. They are the accounts Sage uses to record money funds within the business which originally came from the bank or will be paid into the bank.

transfers between accounts

A TRANSFER facility on the BANK menu bar records movements between the 'bank' accounts. The screen below shows a business paying a company credit card bill with a cheque for £1,276.85. The money comes out of the current account and wipes out all the payments made with the card and recorded on the Company Credit Card Account (see page 164).

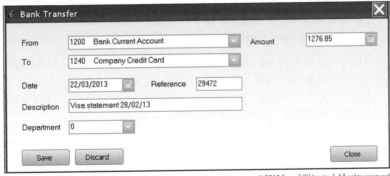

TYPES OF BANK TRANSACTIONS

We looked at cheque and BACS payments in Chapter 9. Businesses may use other types of bank transaction:

bank giro credit

A method of paying a bill where a pre-printed tear-off paper slip passes through the bank's clearing system together with payment (by cash or cheque) to reach the bank of the business being paid.

CHAPS

Clearing House Automated Payments System can be used for high value, same day inter-bank payments, eg for property purchase.

banker's draft

A cheque written out by the bank and purchased by a customer as a guaranteed form of payment.

direct debit

A type of BACS payment where the person or business paying the money authorises the supplier in advance to take money from their bank account. The value of the payment is controlled by the payee.

standing order

A type of BACS payment where the person or business paying the money sets up a regular series of payments from their bank to the supplier's bank. The value of the payment is controlled by the payer.

THE PETTY CASH ACCOUNT

what is a petty cash payment?

Petty cash is a float of cash – notes and coins – kept in an office, normally in a locked tin. It provides employees with the cash to make small purchases for the business, eg stationery, postage stamps and business taxi fares.

The petty cash is topped up with cash periodically. Some businesses operate an 'imprest' system, where the cash is topped up to a set limit, £100 for example. The amount of the top up will be the amount that has been spent: for example if £80 has been spent, the top up will be £80, restoring the imprest to £100.

The document used is the petty cash voucher (see below). When a payment is made, a petty cash voucher is completed and the appropriate evidence of payment is attached, for example:

- a till receipt from a shop or a Post Office receipt for stamps
- a rail or bus ticket or a receipt from a taxi firm

The cash can be paid out (or refunded) when the voucher is completed and authorised.

petty cash voucher			Number *807*	
			date	*15 May 2013*
description				amount
			£	p
Envelopes			*6*	*00*
		VAT	*1*	*20*
Receipt obtained			*7*	*20*
signature	*T Harris*			
authorised	*R Patel*			

petty cash and the accounting system

Petty cash is a fund of money kept in the business in the same way as the bank current account is a fund of money kept in the bank. A 'bank' account will be set up for petty cash which will handle all the transactions:

- payments of cash into petty cash from the bank current account

- payments out of petty cash to pay for small expense items

The Sage computer system has a default Petty Cash Account which it classes as a bank account, although, of course, the money is not in the bank. The computer sees it as a 'money fund'.

When cash is needed to top up the petty cash, the business will cash a cheque at the bank and then put the money in the cash tin. The computer program requires the business to input the transaction as a TRANSFER from the BANK menu bar. In the screen below, the business has cashed a £100 cheque at the bank (using cheque 122991) to provide the cash.

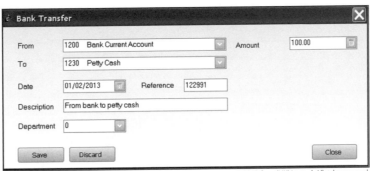

Payments out of Petty Cash Account are handled in exactly the same way on the computer as payments out of Bank Current Account. The PAYMENTS screen is reached through the BANK menu bar. The details are then input from the petty cash vouchers or the petty cash book in which they are recorded.

The screen below shows the input of the petty cash voucher for stationery shown on the previous page.

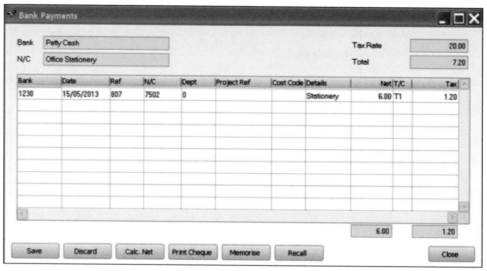

Points to remember are:

■ the bank account number used is the Petty Cash Account number

■ the reference is the petty cash voucher number

■ petty cash vouchers and their receipts will not always show the VAT amount – the VAT and net amount can be calculated on the computer by inputting the full amount under 'Net' and then clicking on 'Calc. Net' at the bottom of the screen (using T1 code to denote standard rate VAT)

■ when the details have been checked you should SAVE

■ the details can also be checked against a Cash Payments Day Book Report if required (accessed through Reports in BANK)

CASE STUDY

PRONTO SUPPLIES LIMITED: SETTING UP THE PETTY CASH SYSTEM

At the beginning of February Tom Cox set up a petty cash system at Pronto Supplies Limited. The situation at 28 February is as follows:

- Tom notes that he cashed cheque no 122991 for £100 at the bank on 1 February.

- The £100 cash was transferred to the petty cash tin on 1 February.

- The tin contains three vouchers for payments made during the month – these are shown below and on the next page. They are ready for entry in the petty cash book as part of the month-end routine.

  Voucher PC101 shows the VAT included in the total (standard rate: T1)

  Voucher PC102 does not have any VAT in it (postage stamps are exempt: T2)

  Voucher PC103 does not show the VAT included in the total (standard rate: T1) because it was not shown on the original receipt.

petty cash voucher		Number *PC101*	
		date	*7 Feb 2013*
description			**amount**
		£	p
Copy paper		36	00
	VAT	7	20
Receipt obtained		43	20
signature	*Nick Vellope*		
authorised	*Tom Cox*		

petty cash voucher		Number *PC102*	
		date	*14 Feb 2013*
description			**amount**
		£	p
Postage stamps		25	00
	VAT		
Receipt obtained		25	00
signature	*R Patel*		
authorised	*Tom Cox*		

petty cash voucher		Number *PC103*		
		date *20 Feb 2013*		
description		amount		
			£	p
Envelopes				
Receipt obtained (VAT included but not VAT *shown separately)*			19	20
signature	*B Radish*			
authorised	*Tom Cox*			

the transfer to petty cash

Tom Cox first inputs the £100 transfer from the Bank Current Account to the Petty Cash Account. The screen is illustrated below. Note the use of the cheque number as the reference.

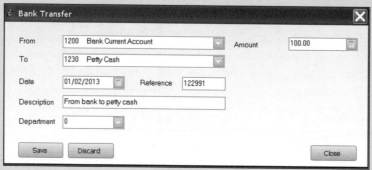

inputting the vouchers

The petty cash payments are entered into the computer accounting system on the PAYMENTS screen reached from the BANK menu bar.

Note that the bank Petty Cash Account number and the appropriate nominal code (N/C) is used each time.

The postage stamps nominal code was taken from the default nominal list.

The reference in each case is the relevant petty cash voucher number.

Postage stamps are VAT exempt. The VAT on the third petty cash voucher was not on the receipt but has been calculated on-screen by inputting the total amount of £19.20 in the 'Net' column and clicking on 'Calc. Net' at the bottom of the screen:

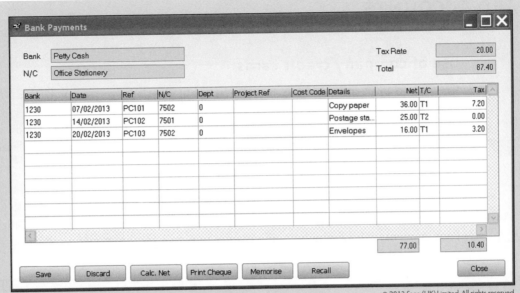

Tom then checks the batch total with the total of the vouchers and when he is happy that all the details are correct he will SAVE. The Day Book report will now show the petty cash payments. Note that the transaction code is 'CP' (second column from the left). This stands for 'Cash Payment'. This distinguishes the petty cash payments from payments from the bank current account (input through the same screen). These payments have the code 'BP' which stands for 'Bank Payment'.

Pronto Supplies Limited
Day Books: Cash Payments (Detailed)

Date From:	07/02/2013					Bank From:	1230
DateTo:	20/02/2013					Bank To:	1230
Transaction From:	1					N/C From:	
Transaction To:	99,999,999					N/C To:	99999999
Dept From:	0						
Dept To:	999						

Bank:	1230		Currency:	Pound Sterling									Bank Rec.
No	Type	N/C	Date	Ref	Details	Dept	Net £	Tax	£ T/C	Gross	£ V	B	Date
93	CP	7502	07/02/2013	PC101	Copy paper	0	36.00	7.20	T1	43.20	N	-	
94	CP	7501	14/02/2013	PC102	Postage stamps	0	25.00	0.00	T2	25.00	N	-	
95	CP	7502	20/02/2013	PC103	Envelopes	0	16.00	3.20	T1	19.20	N	-	
						Totals £	77.00	10.40		87.40			

CARD ACCOUNTS

use of company credit cards

Credit cards are often issued by an employer for use by their employees when they are out on business – for example a sales representative who needs to buy fuel for the company car and to take a client out to lunch. All expenses are billed to the company on the credit card statement and are checked by the management to make sure that the expenses are valid claims.

company credit card payments in the accounts

The business with a computer accounting system can make use of the Company Credit Card Account in the BANK function. This will be used to record all payments in Sage using the Bank Payment screen seen earlier in this chapter, but inputting the payments to the Company Credit Card Account.

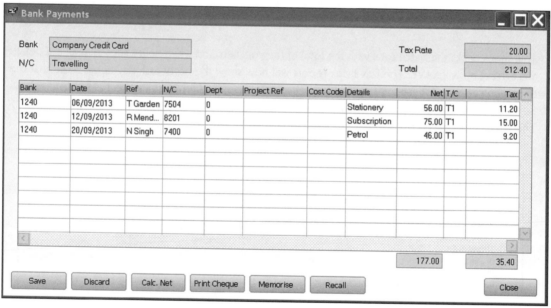

When the business pays the credit card bill the total amount will be input on the TRANSFER screen in the same way as the petty cash can be topped up to the imprest amount (see page 158).

credit/debit card receipt accounts

A business using computer accounting might also use the Credit Card Receipts account in BANK to record credit and debit card receipts. Totals will then be transferred to the current account in Sage (1200). Alternatively, these receipts can be entered directly into the current account. Totals should be reconciled with the advices from the card merchant.

USING A CASH RECEIPTS ACCOUNT

We have seen so far that cash receipts – for example the cash and cheques takings from a shop – are best paid into the bank current account as soon as possible. This reduces the risk of theft and means that the business has the use of the money earlier rather than later.

There may be a case, however, where a business keeps its cash takings on the premises for some time before paying in. This could happen when a week's takings of a shop, for example, are paid in the following Monday. The business here could use the Cash Register account in BANK to record the money fund kept on the premises. The procedure would be:

- check the Cash Register account settings in Settings/Bank Defaults, eg nominal codes for Sales and Cash Discrepancies. Note that entries in this account can be set to be VAT inclusive by ticking the box here

- designate the account as a Cash account in the Bank Records – Cash Register, A/C Type. No bank reconciliation is needed

- enter the totals of daily takings in RECEIPTS from the BANK menu – the totals could be taken from the various till listings or a summary

- using TRANSFER from the BANK menu, record the amounts as and when they are paid into the bank current account – the source document is the paying-in slip and the transfer is made from Cash Register Account to Bank Current Account

The RECEIPT and transfer screens are shown below and on the next page.

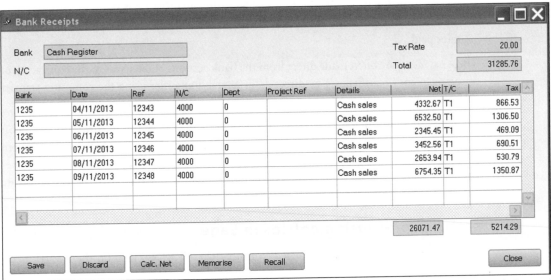

Here the takings for a week's trading (Monday to Saturday) by a shop are recorded on the BANK RECEIPTS screen. The money will be paid in on the following Monday and is held securely on the shop premises.

Here the shop takings for the week are being paid into the bank on a paying-in slip on Monday. The amount is transferred from Cash Receipts Account to Bank Current Account. The balance on the Cash Receipts Account should then revert to nil as all the money will have left the premises.

RECURRING PAYMENTS AND RECEIPTS

Recurring entries are payments or transfers which are made monthly or weekly or at other intervals. Businesses, for example:

- **receive** recurring payments, for example rent from an office owned
- **make** recurring payments, for example loan repayments, insurance premiums, rent and rates paid

These payments are often made direct from the bank account of the payer to the bank account of the recipient ('beneficiary') by direct debit or standing order using the computer transfer BACS system.

Payments due are often recorded on a document called a 'Standing order/Direct debit schedule'. If a business operates a manual accounting system these payments will be written individually in the cash book each time they are made or received – a laborious and time-consuming process. A business using a computer accounting system such as Sage can automate this procedure.

setting up recurring entries in Sage

The recurring entries routine is reached from the RECURRING icon on the BANK menu bar.

The recurring entries screen shows any existing entries already set up. If there are none, the screen will be blank.

To add a recurring entry, click the Add button at the bottom of the screen.

Now study the Case Study on the next three pages.

CASE STUDY

PRONTO SUPPLIES LIMITED:
SETTING UP RECURRING ENTRIES

setting up a recurring payment

Tom has set up a maintenance contract for his Xerax 566 colour printer/copier. He has to pay £19.80 plus VAT every month for the next 12 months and has completed a direct debit form so that the money can be taken directly from Pronto's bank current account.

The recurring entries routine is reached from the RECURRING icon on the BANK menu bar.

The recurring entries screen is blank because there are no existing recurring entries. To add a recurring entry, Tom clicks the Add button at the bottom of the screen and then inputs the details as follows:

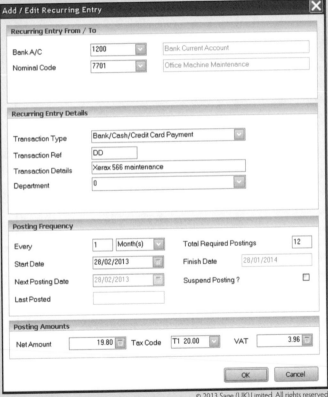

Note the following:

- ■ Tom indicates that the entry is a Bank/Cash/Credit Card Payment
- ■ he inputs the bank account and nominal account to be used (which is already set up on the Chart of Accounts)
- ■ the Transaction Reference entered is 'DD' (which stands for Direct Debit)
- ■ the Transaction Details explain what the payment is for

- the Posting Frequency is every 28th of the month
- the number of Total Required Postings is 12
- the Net Amount and VAT (tax) code T1 are entered to generate the VAT amount

setting up a recurring receipt

Pronto Supplies receives from the tenant of a small office at 10A High Street regular monthly rent payments of £456. Tom charges VAT on these payments. The payment is made by standing order to the bank current account.

Tom clicks the Add button at the bottom of the Recurring Entry screen and then inputs the details as follows:

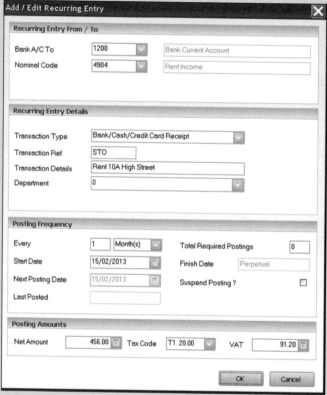

Note the following:

- Tom indicates that the entry is a Bank/Cash/Credit Card Receipt
- he inputs the bank account and nominal account to be used (which is already set up on the Chart of Accounts)
- the Transaction Reference is 'STO' (which stands for Standing Order)
- the Transaction Details explain what the payment is for
- the Posting Frequency is every 15th of the month and is 'perpetual' – ie until further notice
- the Net Amount and VAT (tax) code T1 are entered to generate the VAT amount

Tom's recurring entries are summarised on the RECURRING ENTRIES screen. The example below shows other payments that Pronto Supplies will be making. Note that the direct debit totalling £1000 per month for loan repayments is split between loan repayments (£850) and loan interest (£150) and entered on two lines to cater for the different nominal codes.

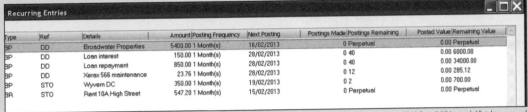

Recurring Entries

Type	Ref	Details	Amount	Posting Frequency	Next Posting	Postings Made	Postings Remaining	Posted Value	Remaining Value
BP	DD	Broadwater Properties	5400.00	1 Month(s)	16/02/2013	0	Perpetual	0.00	Perpetual
BP	DD	Loan interest	150.00	1 Month(s)	28/02/2013	0	40	0.00	6000.00
BP	DD	Loan repayment	850.00	1 Month(s)	28/02/2013	0	40	0.00	34000.00
BP	DD	Xerax 566 maintenance	23.76	1 Month(s)	28/02/2013	0	12	0.00	285.12
BP	STO	Wyvern DC	350.00	1 Month(s)	19/02/2013	0	2	0.00	700.00
BR	STO	Rent 10A High Street	547.20	1 Month(s)	15/02/2013	0	Perpetual	0.00	Perpetual

Tom can process all the payments up to the current date by clicking on the Process button. The program will only allow him to process each payment and receipt once in each month.

Process Recurring Entries

Show Due Entries Up To: 28/02/2013

Type	Account	Nominal	Due Date	Frequency	Ref	Dept	Details	Net	T/C	Tax
BR	1200	4904	15/02/2013	1 Month(s)	STO	0	Rent 10A High Street	456.00	T1	91.20
BP	1200	7100	16/02/2013	1 Month(s)	DD	0	Broadwater Propert...	4500.00	T1	900.00
BP	1200	7103	19/02/2013	1 Month(s)	STO	0	Wyvern DC	350.00	T2	0.00
BP	1200	7701	28/02/2013	1 Month(s)	DD	0	Xerax 566 maintena...	19.80	T1	3.96
BP	1200	2300	28/02/2013	1 Month(s)	DD	0	Loan repayment	850.00	T9	0.00
BP	1200	7903	28/02/2013	1 Month(s)	DD	0	Loan interest	150.00	T2	0.00

Post   Cancel

The recurring entries screen now shows the new status of the various postings.

Recurring Entries

Type	Ref	Details	Amount	Posting Frequency	Next Posting	Postings Made	Postings Remaining	Posted Value	Remaining Value
BP	DD	Broadwater Properties	5400.00	1 Month(s)	16/03/2013	1	Perpetual	5400.00	Perpetual
BP	DD	Loan interest	150.00	1 Month(s)	28/03/2013	1	39	150.00	5850.00
BP	DD	Loan repayment	850.00	1 Month(s)	28/03/2013	1	39	850.00	33150.00
BP	DD	Xerax 566 maintenance	23.76	1 Month(s)	28/03/2013	1	11	23.76	261.36
BP	STO	Wyvern DC	350.00	1 Month(s)	19/03/2013	1	1	350.00	350.00
BR	STO	Rent 10A High Street	547.20	1 Month(s)	15/03/2013	1	Perpetual	547.20	Perpetual

Note that the Sage program will remind Tom to process recurring entries when they are due by posting a message on the screen. Tom can decide at that point whether or not to process them.

CHAPTER SUMMARY

- Businesses can set up accounts on a computer accounting program for funds of money held by the business. These accounts are classified as 'bank' accounts, but the money is not held at the bank. The money for these accounts will come from the bank or will be paid into the bank and recorded in Sage by a Bank Transfer.

- Payment 'Bank' accounts – in addition to the ordinary Bank Current Account include:
  - Petty Cash Account – a cash fund held under lock and key in the office, used for making small purchases and payments
  - Credit Card Account – records payments by employees on company credit cards

  These two accounts will be 'topped up' regularly by a transfer from the Bank Current Account.

- 'Bank' accounts for receiving payments may also be set up, for example a Cash Register account or a Card Receipts account. These record money received from sales and held in the business. When the money is paid into the Bank Current Account a Bank Transfer will be made on the computer.

- Businesses use Recurring Entries on the computer accounting system to record regular payments made in and out of the Bank Current Account. These include standing orders and direct debits for outgoing payments and incoming receipts. The Recurring Entries facility enables the business to set up the payments so that they can be recorded automatically each month in the accounts on the click of a button.

KEY TERMS

petty cash	a float of cash kept in the office for making small purchases
petty cash account	an account used to record payments of small cash purchases from the office petty cash fund
petty cash voucher	the document which records and authorises a payment out of petty cash
company credit card account	an account used to record payments made on credit cards issued to employees to cover business expenses
cash register account	an account used to record cash received by a business where the money is kept for a time by the business before it is paid into the bank
credit card receipts	An account used to record credit and debit card receipts before transferring daily totals to the Bank current account

recurring entry	a bank payment or receipt which occurs on a regular basis and which is automated within the computer accounting program
Standing order/Direct debit schedule	a document which lists recurring payments and receipts with their due dates

EXERCISES

PRONTO SUPPLIES INPUTTING TASKS

Task 1

Set the program date as 28 February 2013.

On 1 February Tom cashed cheque 122991 for £100 at his bank to set up a petty cash system.

Carry out a bank transfer from Bank Current Account to Petty Cash Account for this amount.

Task 2

Keep the program date as 28 February 2013.

Tom has just authorised two more petty cash vouchers (shown here). Input these together with the three petty cash vouchers on pages 161 to 162 into Bank Payments, taking particular care with the VAT element on each one (postages are VAT exempt and packaging – nominal code 5003 – is standard-rated).

petty cash voucher   Number *PC104*

date   *28 Feb 2013*

description		amount	
		£	p
Postage stamps		5	00
	VAT		
Receipt obtained		5	00

signature   *R Cook*

petty cash voucher   Number *PC105*

date   *28 Feb 2013*

description		amount	
		£	p
Packing tape		4	00
	VAT		80
Receipt obtained		4	80

signature   *R Patel*

authorised   *Tom Cox*

Print out a Day Books: Cash Payments (Detailed) Report to confirm the accuracy of your input of the five vouchers (see page 285).

Hint: remember to select the Petty Cash Bank account on screen before running the report.

Task 3

Keep the program date as 28 February 2013.

Open the Cash Register account and designate it a 'cash' account. No bank reconciliation is required at present.

Tom sees that he has three days of cash takings in the office safe and so decides to enter these in the Cash Register account. Take care over selecting the correct Sales account number. The details are:

Date	Details	Net amount (£)	VAT (£)	ref.
26 Feb 2013	Hardware sales	5,000.00	1,000.00	10743
26 Feb 2013	Software sales	480.00	96.00	10743
27 Feb 2013	Hardware sales	1,200.00	240.00	10744
27 Feb 2013	Software sales	890.00	178.00	10744
28 Feb 2013	Hardware sales	600.00	120.00	10745
28 Feb 2013	Software sales	120.00	24.00	10745
	Totals	8,290.00	1,658.00	

Enter these transactions, check the totals, SAVE and print out a Day Books: Cash Receipts (Detailed) Report. Check with the printout on page 285.

Task 4

Keep the program date as 28 February 2013.

Create recurring entries for the payments and receipts on the schedule below.

You will need to ensure that your Nominal list includes the following accounts:

   7701   Office Machine Maintenance

   4904   Rent Income

   7100   Rent (paid out)

   7103   General Rates

   2300   Loans

   7903   Loan Interest Paid

When the recurring entries have been set up, process them for February.

<table>
<tr><td colspan="7">Pronto Supplies
Standing Order and Direct Debit Schedule</td></tr>
</table>

Start date	Type	To/from	Details	Value	Frequency	Total payments
15 02 13	STO receipt	F Morton	Rent 10A High St	£456.00 plus VAT	Monthly	Perpetual
16 02 13	DD payment	Broadwater Properties	Rent paid	£4500.00 plus VAT	Monthly	Perpetual
19 02 13	STO payment	Wyvern DC	Rates	£350.00 (VAT exempt)	Monthly	2
28 02 13	DD payment	Xerax Machines	Maintenance	£19.80 plus VAT	Monthly	12
28 02 13	DD payment	Albion Bank	Loan repayment	£850.00	Monthly	40
28 02 13	DD payment	Albion Bank	Loan interest	£150.00	Monthly	40

Task 5

Keep the program date as 28 February 2013. Print out from FINANCIALS the following reports:

(a)   an Audit Trail (summary version) of all the transactions on the computer so far (see pages 286-287)

(b)   a Trial Balance as at 28 February 2013 (this can be checked against the Trial Balance on page 288)

Check that all your input to date is accurate. These reports will be dealt with in the next chapter. Correction of errors will be dealt with in Chapter 13.

Reminder! Have you made a back-up?

12 REPORTS AND ROUTINES

Chapter introduction

- One of the major advantages of running a computer accounting system is that it will provide the business manager and administrative staff with a wide range of reports – on demand.

- These reports are produced regularly – sometimes at the end of the month – to enable the business to check the accuracy of its records, to ensure that customer and supplier payments are made on time, that other liabilities are settled when due, and to monitor performance against set targets.

- The reports that can be produced to help with checking the accuracy of the records include:

  - the trial balance – a full list of the Nominal account balances

  - the audit trail – a full numbered list of the transactions input on the computer in order of input

- The reports that can be produced to help with dealing with customers and suppliers include:

  - 'aged' analyses – separate lists of customers and suppliers which show what payments are due and when

  - activity reports – lists of transactions on individual accounts

  - account lists – lists of customers and suppliers with telephone numbers

  - label lists – names and addresses of customers and suppliers – suitable for mailing labels

  - customer statements – sent to each sales ledger customer, listing transactions and telling the customer the amount that is due

- A VAT return can be run at any time to monitor how much is owed to HMRC.

- A budget report can be produced to measure actual results against targets.

- A further regular checking routine is the bank reconciliation statement which agrees the bank statement with the accounting records of the business.

- The end of the month is also a good time to process recurring entries and other regular account transfers.

- The business in the Case Study – Pronto Supplies Limited – has reached the end of February and so will be used in this chapter to illustrate the various reports and routines and their uses.

- Retention of records legislation governs how long businesses must keep accounting records.

THE IMPORTANCE OF INFORMATION

information for management

The accounting system of any business – whether hand-written or computer-based – contains important information for management and provides an accurate basis for decision-making. The advantage of using a computer accounting system is that this information is available instantly.

The **trial balance** is a list of the Nominal account balances at a set date – which is often the last day of the month. The figures are set out in balancing debit and credit columns to prove the accuracy of the bookkeeping entries. If the column totals are not the same in a manual system, there is likely to be one or more errors in the double-entry bookkeeping. Computerised trial balances will normally balance.

The trial balance figures show how much money there is in the bank and provides management with details about sales and expense accounts, and how much is owed to outside organisations.

Activity on individual nominal accounts, eg sales, can be printed using a **nominal activity** report.

Managers can check on the performance of a business by contrasting actual results with budgeted results. Budgets (target values) are set before a period starts.

information for finance and administrative staff

The computer accounting program also enables finance and administrative staff to extract useful information, for example:

- The **audit trail** is a full list of the transactions input into the computer, presented in order of input. Accounts staff will use the audit trail to check the accuracy of the input and trace any discrepancies and errors.

- The analysis of customer accounts (the **aged debtor analysis**) tells credit control staff which customers need chasing for payment and which debts may need writing off. The computer can also print chase letters to customers chasing overdue accounts.

- The analysis of supplier accounts (the **aged creditor analysis**) tells accounts staff which bills and invoices need paying and when.

- The computer will also produce **activity reports** on individual customer and supplier accounts; these list all the transactions on each individual account and are useful to bring up on-screen when a customer telephones in with a query.

- Computer-produced **account lists** set out the names, account codes and telephone numbers of customers and suppliers. These are useful to sales and accounts staff when contacting customers and suppliers and when coding invoices and credit notes.

- The computer will also produce the names and addresses of customers and suppliers on **labels**, which is useful when doing a promotional mailing or a change of address notification.

- The amount owed to HMRC can be checked monthly or quarterly by running a VAT return.

We will now illustrate these procedures with a continuation of the Case Study.

CASE STUDY

PRONTO SUPPLIES LIMITED:
END-OF-MONTH REPORTS

It is 28 February 2013. Tom Cox has completed the input into his computer accounting system during the course of the month. Looking back he can see that he has:

- set up the company details and the Nominal ledger balances
- entered customer and supplier records and balances
- input customer and supplier invoices and credit notes processed during February
- input payments received from customers and sent to suppliers during February
- input cash receipts and payments for February
- set up a petty cash system and recurring entries for standing orders and direct debits

trial balance

Tom first extracts his Trial Balance as at the end of February. He does this by clicking on TRIAL on the FINANCIALS menu bar. His printout is shown below.

Pronto Supplies Limited
Period Trial Balance

To Period: Month 2, February 2013

N/C	Name	Debit	Credit
0020	Plant and Machinery	35,000.00	
0030	Office Equipment	15,760.00	
0040	Furniture and Fixtures	30,000.00	
1100	Debtors Control Account	5,610.00	
1200	Bank Current Account	54,835.24	
1230	Petty Cash	2.80	
1235	Cash Register	9,948.00	
2100	Creditors Control Account		12,044.20
2200	Sales Tax Control Account		31,922.50
2201	Purchase Tax Control Account	35,717.36	
2300	Loans		34,150.00
3000	Ordinary Shares		80,000.00
4000	Computer hardware sales		139,242.00
4001	Computer software sales		30,100.00
4002	Computer consultancy		2,628.00
4009	Discounts Allowed	13.50	
4904	Rent Income		456.00
5000	Materials Purchased	93,362.00	
5003	Packaging	4.00	
6201	Advertising	22,600.00	
7000	Gross Wages	16,230.00	
7100	Rent	9,000.00	
7103	General Rates	800.00	
7200	Electricity	308.00	
7501	Postage and Carriage	30.00	
7502	Office Stationery	567.00	
7550	Telephone and Fax	585.00	
7701	Office Machine Maintenance	19.80	
7903	Loan Interest Paid	150.00	
	Totals:	330,542.70	330,542.70

The trial balance shows the balances of the Nominal accounts. The debit column on the left equals the credit column on the right because in double-entry bookkeeping the total of debit entries should always equal the total of credit entries.

If in a manual accounting system the two column totals were not the same, there could be one or more errors in the bookkeeping entries. In a computer-based system the totals should always be the same because the computer generates equal debits and credits from every entry. If Tom's column totals were not the same it would mean that the computer data had become corrupted, which could be a major problem.

audit trail

As a further check (and also to satisfy his accountants) Tom prints out an audit trail which shows each transaction entered into the computer in order of input. This is done from the AUDIT icon on the FINANCIALS menu bar. An extract from a Summary Audit Trail is shown below. This should provide Tom with all the information he needs.

Pronto Supplies Limited
Audit Trail (Summary)

| Date From: | 01/01/1980 | | | | | | | | | | Customer From: | |
| Date To: | 31/12/2019 | | | | | | | | | | Customer To: | |

Transaction From: 1
Transaction To: 99,999,999
Supplier From:
Supplier To:

Dept From: 0
Dept To: 999
N/C From:
N/C To:

Exclude Deleted Tran: No

No	Type	Date	A/C	N/C	Dept	Ref	Details	Net	Tax	T/C	Pd	Paid	V
1	SI	31/01/2013	JB001	9998	0	10013	Opening Balance	5,500.00	0.00	T9	Y	5,500.00	-
2	SI	05/01/2013	CH001	9998	0	10014	Opening Balance	2,400.00	0.00	T9	Y	2,400.00	-
3	SI	09/01/2013	CR001	9998	0	10015	Opening Balance	3,234.00	0.00	T9	N	0.00	-
4	SI	10/01/2013	DB001	9998	0	10016	Opening Balance	3,400.00	0.00	T9	Y	3,400.00	-
5	SI	10/01/2013	KD001	9998	0	10017	Opening Balance	6,500.00	0.00	T9	Y	6,500.00	-
6	SI	17/01/2013	LG001	9998	0	10019	Opening Balance	8,500.00	0.00	T9	Y	8,500.00	-
7	PI	04/01/2013	DE001	9998	0	4563	Opening Balance	5,750.00	0.00	T9	Y	5,750.00	-
8	PI	05/01/2013	EL001	9998	0	8122	Opening Balance	8,500.00	0.00	T9	Y	8,500.00	-
9	PI	09/01/2013	MA001	9998	0	9252	Opening Balance	4,500.00	0.00	T9	Y	4,500.00	-
10	JD	31/01/2013	0020	0020	0	O/Bal	Opening Balance	35,000.00	0.00	T9	Y	35,000.00	-
11	JC	31/01/2013	9998	9998	0	O/Bal	Opening Balance	35,000.00	0.00	T9	Y	35,000.00	-
12	JD	31/01/2013	0030	0030	0	O/Bal	Opening Balance	15,000.00	0.00	T9	Y	15,000.00	-
13	JC	31/01/2013	9998	9998	0	O/Bal	Opening Balance	15,000.00	0.00	T9	Y	15,000.00	-
14	JD	31/01/2013	0040	0040	0	O/Bal	Opening Balance	25,000.00	0.00	T9	Y	25,000.00	-
15	JC	31/01/2013	9998	9998	0	O/Bal	Opening Balance	25,000.00	0.00	T9	Y	25,000.00	-
16	JD	31/01/2013	1200	1200	0	O/Bal	Opening Balance	14,656.00	0.00	T9	Y	14,656.00	-
17	JC	31/01/2013	9998	9998	0	O/Bal	Opening Balance	14,656.00	0.00	T9	Y	14,656.00	-
18	JC	31/01/2013	2200	2200	0	O/Bal	Opening Balance	17,920.00	0.00	T9	Y	17,920.00	-
19	JD	31/01/2013	9998	9998	0	O/Bal	Opening Balance	17,920.00	0.00	T9	Y	17,920.00	-
20	JD	31/01/2013	2201	2201	0	O/Bal	Opening Balance	26,600.00	0.00	T9	Y	26,600.00	-
21	JC	31/01/2013	9998	9998	0	O/Bal	Opening Balance	26,600.00	0.00	T9	Y	26,600.00	-
22	JC	31/01/2013	2300	2300	0	O/Bal	Opening Balance	35,000.00	0.00	T9	Y	35,000.00	-
23	JD	31/01/2013	9998	9998	0	O/Bal	Opening Balance	35,000.00	0.00	T9	Y	35,000.00	-
24	JC	31/01/2013	3000	3000	0	O/Bal	Opening Balance	75,000.00	0.00	T9	Y	75,000.00	-
25	JD	31/01/2013	9998	9998	0	O/Bal	Opening Balance	75,000.00	0.00	T9	Y	75,000.00	-
26	JC	31/01/2013	4000	4000	0	O/Bal	Opening Balance	85,000.00	0.00	T9	Y	85,000.00	-
27	JD	31/01/2013	9998	9998	0	O/Bal	Opening Balance	85,000.00	0.00	T9	Y	85,000.00	-
28	JC	31/01/2013	4001	4001	0	O/Bal	Opening Balance	15,000.00	0.00	T9	Y	15,000.00	-
29	JD	31/01/2013	9998	9998	0	O/Bal	Opening Balance	15,000.00	0.00	T9	Y	15,000.00	-
30	JC	31/01/2013	4002	4002	0	O/Bal	Opening Balance	2,400.00	0.00	T9	Y	2,400.00	-

Every transaction input into the computer (within the time period stipulated) is shown on the audit trail. The columns of the audit trail show, from the left ...

- the unique number allocated by the computer to the transaction
- the nature of the transaction, for example SI = sales invoice, PI = purchase invoice
- the date of the transaction (which is not necessarily the date of input)
- the account into which the item is entered
- the Nominal account code relating to the transaction
- the transaction reference (eg invoice or cheque number) input at the time
- the description of the transaction
- the Department reference, normally only used in larger organisations
- the net amount, any VAT, VAT tax code and the gross ('paid') amount

Tom will need to keep the audit trail for future reference in case any errors or discrepancies come to light. His accountants may also need to see it if they have to verify his accounts.

nominal activity

Tom can check his monthly sales for each sales code. He selects code 4000 (Computer hardware sales) in the Nominal Ledger screen and then clicks on Reports. In Nominal Activity Reports he chooses Nominal Activity and enters the date range of 1-28 February. The report, shown below, shows total computer hardware sales of £54,242 for the month.

Pronto Supplies Limited
Nominal Activity

| Date From: | 01/02/2013 | | N/C From: | 4000 |
| Date To: | 28/02/2013 | | N/C To: | 4000 |

Transaction From: 1
Transaction To: 99,999,999

N/C: 4000   Name: Computer hardware sales   Account Balance: 139,242.00 CR

No	Type	Date	Account	Ref	Details	Dept	T/C	Value	Debit	Credit	V	B
48	SI	05/02/2013	JB001	10023	4 x Monitor 17 inch	0	T1	400.00		400.00	N	-
49	SI	06/02/2013	CH001	10024	1 x Power lead 3 mtr	0	T1	16.00		16.00	N	-
53	SC	06/02/2013	LG001	552	2 x Zap USB flash memory drive	0	T1	40.00	40.00		N	-
54	SI	11/02/2013	DB001	10027	1 x Printer EF102 Multi	0	T1	600.00		600.00	N	-
55	SI	12/02/2013	LG001	10028	2 x Zap external drive	0	T1	162.00		162.00	N	-
57	SI	15/02/2013	CH001	10030	2 x Monitor 17 inch	0	T1	200.00		200.00	N	-
59	SC	12/02/2013	CH001	553	1 x Power lead 3 mtr	0	T1	16.00	16.00		N	-
60	SC	13/02/2013	CR001	554	1 x Zap USB flash memory drive	0	T1	20.00	20.00		N	-
78	BR	08/02/2013	1200	10736	Hardware sales	0	T1	12,500.00		12,500.00	N	N
80	BR	15/02/2013	1200	10738	Hardware sales	0	T1	15,840.00		15,840.00	N	N
82	BR	22/02/2013	1200	10740	Hardware sales	0	T1	17,800.00		17,800.00	N	N
98	CR	26/02/2013	1235	10743	Hardware sales	0	T1	5,000.00		5,000.00	N	-
100	CR	27/02/2013	1235	10744	Hardware sales	0	T1	1,200.00		1,200.00	N	-
102	CR	28/02/2013	1235	10745	Hardware sales	0	T1	600.00		600.00	N	-

Totals: 76.00   54,318.00
History Balance: 54,242.00

aged debtors analysis

It is important to Tom that he knows that his customers who buy on credit pay up on time. The credit period is indicated to them on the bottom of each invoice. Tom allows his customers 30 days from the date of the invoice in which to pay.

An Aged Debtors Analysis shows the amount owing by each customer and splits it up according to the length of time it has been outstanding. The Aged Debtors Analysis can be printed from the REPORTS icon on the CUSTOMERS menu bar. Alternatively an aged balance list can be produced from the AGED icon on CUSTOMERS.

Tom's Aged Debtors Analysis (Summary) Report as at 28 February 2013 is shown below:

Pronto Supplies Limited
Aged Debtors Analysis (Summary)

		Report Date:	28/02/2013					Customer From:			
		Include future transactions:	No					Customer To:	ZZZZZZZZ		
		Exclude later payments:	No								

** NOTE: All report values are shown in Base Currency, unless otherwise indicated **

A/C	Name		Credit Limit	Turnover	Balance	Future	Current	Period 1	Period 2	Period 3	Older
CH001	Charisma Design	£	5,000.00	2,600.00	240.00	0.00	240.00	0.00	0.00	0.00	0.00
CR001	Crowmatic Ltd	£	5,000.00	3,664.00	3,750.00	0.00	516.00	3,234.00	0.00	0.00	0.00
DB001	David Boossey	£	5,000.00	3,550.00	720.00	0.00	720.00	0.00	0.00	0.00	0.00
JB001	John Butler & Associates	£	15,000.00	6,008.00	609.60	0.00	609.60	0.00	0.00	0.00	0.00
KD001	Kay Denz	£	10,000.00	7,070.00	144.00	0.00	144.00	0.00	0.00	0.00	0.00
LG001	L Garr & Co	£	15,000.00	8,622.00	146.40	0.00	146.40	0.00	0.00	0.00	0.00
	Totals:			31,514.00	5,610.00	0.00	2,376.00	3,234.00	0.00	0.00	0.00

The columns show (from left to right)

■ the customer account number and name

■ the credit limit (the maximum amount of credit Tom will allow on the account)

■ the turnover (total net sales for each customer in the current financial year)

■ the balance (the total balance on the customer's account)

■ any transactions due in future months

■ 'current' invoices are February invoices, period 1 is January, and so on

Note that the Report can be dated at any date required. Here it is dated 28 February.

The Report shows the following:

■ All the accounts are trading within their credit limits (ie the figure in the 'Balance' column is less than the 'Credit Limit' column) – this is a good sign.

■ The total of the Balance column shows that Pronto Supplies Limited is owed a total of £5,610.00 on 28 February. As a further check this figure could be agreed with the balance of Debtors Control Account on the Trial Balance (see page 176).

Crowmatic Ltd's account is overdue for payment. Tom can send a letter chasing payment. A range of options is available via the LETTERS icon in CUSTOMERS. The example shown on the next page is "Itemised Chase Letter 1 (Reminder)".

Pronto Supplies Limited
Unit 17 Severnvale Estate
Broadwater Road
Mereford
Wyvern
MR1 6TF

John Crow
Crowmatic Ltd
Unit 12 Severnside Estate

Mereford

MR3 6FD

04 May 2012

Dear Sir / Madam,

Your account with us is overdue, details as noted below. Please can we have your full payment by return post.

NOTE: All values are shown in Pound Sterling

Inv Ref	Date	Details		Value
10015	09/01/2013	Goods/Services	£	3234.00
Total Amount Overdue :			**£**	**3234.00**

Yours faithfully

for

Pronto Supplies Limited

aged creditors analysis

Tom also needs to check on the amounts that Pronto Supplies Limited owes its Suppliers (creditors) for goods purchased, and to make sure that there are no amounts outstanding for longer than they should be. The Aged Creditors Analysis enables him to do this. It can be printed from REPORTS on the SUPPLIERS menu bar. The layout of the columns works on the same principles as the Aged Debtors Analysis (see previous page). Alternatively the AGED icon on SUPPLIERS can also be used to produce a list of amounts due to suppliers.

Pronto Supplies Limited

Aged Creditors Analysis (Summary)

			Report Date:	28/02/2013					Supplier From:			
			Include future transactions:	No					Supplier To:	ZZZZZZZZ		
			Exclude Later Payments:	No								

** NOTE: All report values are shown in Base Currency, unless otherwise indicated **

A/C	Name		Credit Limit	Turnover	Balance	Future	Current	Period 1	Period 2	Period 3	Older
DE001	Delco PLC	£	10,000.00	9,630.00	5,228.20	0.00	5,228.20	0.00	0.00	0.00	0.00
EL001	Electron Supplies	£	15,000.00	10,500.00	2,400.00	0.00	2,400.00	0.00	0.00	0.00	0.00
MA001	MacCity	£	10,000.00	8,142.00	4,416.00	0.00	4,416.00	0.00	0.00	0.00	0.00
		Totals:		28,272.00	12,044.20	0.00	12,044.20	0.00	0.00	0.00	0.00

This report shows that:

■ Pronto Supplies Limited is up-to-date with payments to suppliers – all amounts due are 'Current', ie there is nothing outstanding for more than 30 days.

■ The total owed by Pronto Supplies Limited is £12,044.20 on 28 February. As a further check this figure should be agreed with the balance of Creditors Control Account on the Trial Balance (see page 176).

customer activity reports

Tom receives a call from John Crow of Crowmatic Limited. John asks for clarification of what is outstanding on his account. Tom needs to bring up this account on-screen; he can do this by clicking on the ACTIVITY icon on the CUSTOMERS menu bar with the appropriate account selected. The screen can be printed if required.

Alternatively Tom could select the account on the CUSTOMERS screen and click on the REPORTS icon to select the Customer Activity (Summary) Report. This report shows that invoices 10015 (£3234.00) and 10025 (£540.00) are outstanding but that a credit note 554 (£24.00) can be deducted.

Pronto Supplies Limited

Customer Activity (Summary)

			Date From:	01/01/1980						
			Date To:	28/02/2013						
			Inc b/fwd transaction:	No				Transaction From:	1	
			Exc later payment:	No				Transaction To:	99,999,999	

** NOTE: All report values are shown in Base Currency, unless otherwise indicated **

| A/C: | CR001 | | Name: | Crowmatic Ltd | | Contact: | John Crow | | Tel: | 01908 674237 |

No	Items	Type	Date	Ref	Details	Value	O/S	Debit	Credit
2	1	SI	09/01/2013	10015	Opening Balance	3,234.00 *	3,234.00	3,234.00	
50	1	SI	06/02/2013	10025	1 x Macroworx software	540.00 *	540.00	540.00	
60	1	SC	13/02/2013	554	1 x Zap USB flash memory	24.00 *	-24.00		24.00
						3,750.00	3,750.00	3,774.00	24.00

Amount Outstanding	3,750.00
Amount Paid this period	0.00
Credit Limit £	5,000.00

other useful reports

Tom has also printed a Customer List from his computer; this is an alphabetically sorted account list of customers, together with their contact numbers. A similar report – Customer Address List – produces customer addresses. These reports can be accessed from REPORTS in CUSTOMERS.

Pronto Supplies Limited
Customer List

Customer From:
Customer To: ZZZZZZZZ

A/C	Name	Contact Name	Telephone	Fax
CH001	Charisma Design	Lindsay Foster	01908 345287	01908 345983
CR001	Crowmatic Ltd	John Crow	01908 674237	01908 674345
DB001	David Boossey	David Boossey	01908 333981	01908 333761
JB001	John Butler & Associates	John Butler	01908 824342	01908 824295
KD001	Kay Denz	Kay Denz	01908 624945	01908 624945
LG001	L Garr & Co	Win Norberry	01621 333691	01621 333982

The same exercise can be carried out from the Suppliers menu bar to produce a list of Suppliers with contact numbers.

The computer will also enable Tom to print out name and address labels for Customers and Suppliers. This could be very useful when marketing products to Customers – sending out a catalogue, for example. The labels can be printed by clicking on the LABELS icon on the CUSTOMERS or SUPPLIERS menu bar and selecting an appropriate label format. The labels shown below are extracted from Tom's Customer details printed as Laser Sales Labels (A4).

Lindsay Foster	John Crow	David Boossey
Charisma Design	Crowmatic Ltd	David Boossey
36 Dingle Road	Unit 12 Severnside Estate	17 Harebell Road
Mereford	Mereford	Mereford Green
MR2 8GF	MR3 6FD	MR6 4NB

customer statements

At the end of each month Tom will print out statements and send them to his Customers. This can be done in Sage from the STATEMENT icon on the CUSTOMER menu bar. A suitable format can then be chosen from the list shown on the screen. At this point Tom could choose to email statements to his customers using the Email option in the Preview screen. The statements set out the transactions on the Customer account and state the amount owing. Statements are important documents because many customers will pay from the monthly statement rather than the invoice.

An extract from the statement for Crowmatic Limited is shown on the next page.

Pronto Supplies Limited
Unit 17 Severnvale Estate
Broadwater Road
Mereford
Wyvern
MR1 6TF

CR001

Crowmatic Ltd
Unit 12 Severnside Estate
Mereford
MR3 6FD

28/02/2013

1

NOTE: All values are shown in Pound Sterling

09/01/13	10015	Goods/Services	3,234.00 *	
06/02/13	10025	Goods/Services	540.00 *	
13/02/13	554	Credit	*	24.00

Pronto Supplies Limited
Unit 17 Severnvale Estate
Broadwater Road
Mereford
Wyvern
MR1 6TF

CR001

Crowmatic Ltd
Unit 12 Severnside Estate
Mereford
MR3 6FD

28/02/2013

1

NOTE: All values are shown in **Pound Sterling**

09/01/13	Goods/Services	3,234.00	
06/02/13	Goods/Services	540.00	
13/02/13	Credit		24.00

BANK RECONCILIATION ON THE COMPUTER

the reasons for bank reconciliation

A further routine carried out on a regular basis, with the help of the computer accounting system, is the task of tallying up the entries in the Sage bank account for a set period of time, eg a month, and the entries on the actual bank statement for the same period. This process is known as bank reconciliation. It reconciles:

■ the bank statement – what the bank states the balance actually is

with . . .

■ the bank account of a business – the balance representing what the accounting records of the business states it has in the bank

It is quite common that **differences** will arise and that the two amounts will not be the same.

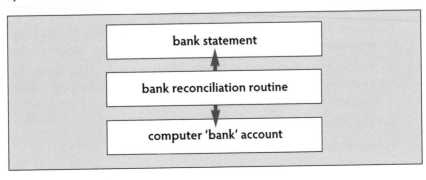

timing differences

These variations can arise from **timing differences**.

For example, a cheque that is issued by the business and sent off to a supplier will be input into the computer accounting records of the business when it is issued, but will not yet have been paid in at the bank by the supplier. Consequently the bank balance on the computer of the business writing the cheque will differ by this amount from the bank balance of the business shown on the bank statement – until, of course, the cheque is paid in and eventually deducted from the bank account. This is a 'timing difference'.

Another timing difference will occur when cheques received from customers of a business have been entered into the bank account on the computer but are still waiting to be paid into the bank on a paying-in slip. The accounting records of the business will show that the money has gone into the bank account, but the actual bank statement will only show the increase after the cheques have been paid into the bank, possibly a day or two later.

Also, there may be items on the bank statement which the business will not immediately know about and will need to enter into the accounting records after it has received the bank statement. Examples are bank charges, bank interest paid and bank interest received.

bank reconciliation in Sage

As seen on the previous page, bank reconciliation forms a link between the balances shown in the bank statement and in the accounting records of the business. All the reconciliation is doing in effect is explaining what items make up the difference between the bank statement and the bank account in the accounting records of the business.

The Bank Reconciliation screen, accessed through RECONCILE in BANK, is illustrated in the Case Study which follows. The procedure is as follows:

1. In the statement summary screen enter a statement reference (optional), the closing balance on the bank statement and the bank statement date. Any interest earned or bank charges can be added at this point. Click OK to move to the main bank reconciliation screen.

2. Check that the Matched Balance box at the bottom agrees with the opening balance on the bank statement.

3. Compare the items in the upper window on the screen with the bank statement. Click to select any items that appear on both, then click the Match button to transfer the matched item/s to the lower window. Alternatively, double-click the matched items individually to transfer them.

4. Update the computer with any items appearing on the bank statement but not in Sage by inputting them using the Adjust button.

5. When you have transferred all the matched items to the lower screen and made any adjustments, check that the Statement Balance equals the bank statement closing balance and the Difference box shows zero.

6. Click Reconcile.

Now read the Case Study which follows.

CASE STUDY

PRONTO SUPPLIES LIMITED:
BANK RECONCILIATION ROUTINE

It is 28 February 2013. Tom Cox has just printed out an online bank statement for Pronto Supplies Limited. He has access to this facility from the Albion Bank website.

The bank statement is shown below.

Tom wants to carry out a reconciliation routine and so clicks RECONCILE in BANK. This is shown on the opposite page.

ALBION BANK PLC

Online statement of account as at: 28 02 2013 15.54

Account 90 47 17 11719881 Pronto Supplies Limited

		Paid out	Paid in	Balance
31/01/2013	Opening Balance			14656.00
01/02/2013	Cheque 122991	100.00		14556.00
08/02/2013	Credit 10736		15000.00	29556.00
08/02/2013	Credit 10737		5616.00	35172.00
14/02/2013	Cheque 122992	18600.00		16572.00
15/02/2013	Credit 10738		19008.00	35580.00
15/02/2013	Credit 10738		4416.00	39996.00
15/02/2013	F Morton		547.20	40543.20
16/02/2013	DD Broadwater Properties	5400.00		35143.20
19/02/2013	Cheque 122993	12240.00		22903.20
19/02/2013	Cheque 122994	6000.00		16903.20
19/02/2013	SO Wyvern DC	350.00		16553.20
20/02/2013	BACS K Denz		523.80	17077.00
22/02/2013	Credit 10740		21360.00	38437.00
22/02/2013	Credit 10741		5760.00	44197.00
27/02/2013	Cheque 122995	189.60		44007.40
28/02/2013	BACS Kay Denz		6500.00	50507.40
28/02/2013	BACS L Garr		8500.00	59007.40
28/02/2013	BACS (multiple beneficiary)	18128.40		40879.00
28/02/2013	DD Xerax	23.76		40855.24
28/02/2013	DD Albion Bank	850.00		40005.24
28/02/2013	DD Albion Bank	150.00		39855.24
28/02/2013	Bank charges	50.00		39805.24

Note that the BACS supplier payments to Delco PLC, Electron Supplies and MacCity (see page 141) on 28 February are shown as one total (£18,128.40).

Tom compares the bank statement with the computer screen.

■ He completes the Statement Summary screen with a statement reference (he uses the date), the bank statement end balance (£39,805.24) and the statement date (28 February 2013). He clicks OK to move to the main reconciliation screen.

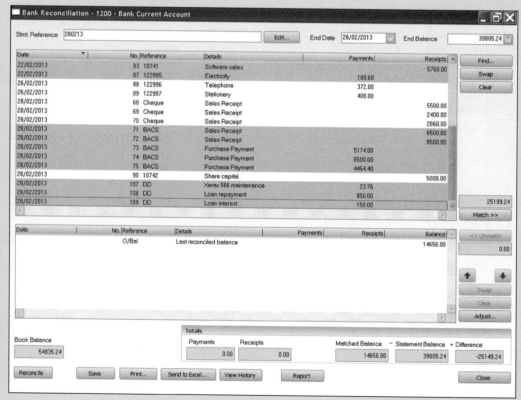

■ He checks that the opening balance on the bank statement is the same as the Matched Balance on the screen (it is £14,656.00).

■ He selects the items in the upper window that are also on the bank statement. He can use the scroll bar to move up and down or he can change the size of the upper and lower windows by dragging on the horizontal bar between them.

■ Now he clicks the Match button to transfer the matched transactions to the lower window.

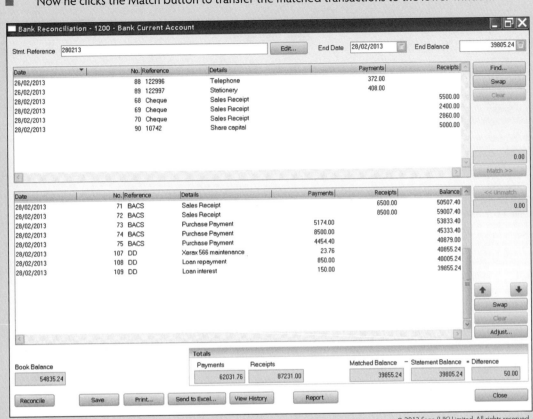

■ There is a figure of £50 in the Difference box. This is the Bank charges which have not yet been entered. Tom clicks on the Adjust button to enter this payment and chooses Bank Payment. He then enters a Bank Payment for the charges in the normal way. The nominal code is 7901 and the VAT code is T2.

■ Finally Tom is returned to the Bank Reconciliation screen where he checks that the difference box is now showing zero. At this point he prints a Bank Reconciliation report by clicking Report (see illustration, page 189). This lists the transactions that make up the difference between the actual bank statement and the balance in Sage. Now he can click Reconcile to complete the task.

All the unselected (ie 'unreconciled') items on the screen will appear next time the routine is carried out – normally when the next bank statement is received.

By carrying out this routine Tom can make sure that he has entered all his bank transactions correctly, and equally importantly, that the bank has not made any errors.

Bank Statement

1200
Bank Current Account
Currency: Pound Sterling

Book Balance: 54785.24

Pronto Supplies Limited
Unit 17 Severnvale Estate
Broadwater Road
Mereford
Wyvern
MR1 6TF

Date From: 01/01/1980
Date To: 28/02/2013

No	Date	Ref	Details	Payments £	Receipts £	Balance £
			B/Fwd Balance			14,656.00
71	28/02/2013	BACS	Sales Receipt		6,500.00	21,156.00
72	28/02/2013	BACS	Sales Receipt		8,500.00	29,656.00
73	28/02/2013	BACS	Purchase Payment	5,174.00		24,482.00
74	28/02/2013	BACS	Purchase Payment	8,500.00		15,982.00
75	28/02/2013	BACS	Purchase Payment	4,454.40		11,527.60
76	20/02/2013	BACS	Sales Receipt		523.80	12,051.40
78	08/02/2013	10736	Hardware sales		15,000.00	27,051.40
79	08/02/2013	10737	Software sales		5,616.00	32,667.40
80	15/02/2013	10738	Hardware sales		19,008.00	51,675.40
81	15/02/2013	10739	Software sales		4,416.00	56,091.40
82	22/02/2013	10740	Hardware sales		21,360.00	77,451.40
83	22/02/2013	10741	Software sales		5,760.00	83,211.40
84	12/02/2013	122992	Cash purchases	18,600.00		64,611.40
85	14/02/2013	122993	Advertising	12,240.00		52,371.40
86	15/02/2013	122994	Furniture	6,000.00		46,371.40
87	22/02/2013	122995	Electricity	189.60		46,181.80
91	01/02/2013	122991	From bank to petty cash	100.00		46,081.80
104	15/02/2013	STO	Rent 10A High St		547.20	46,629.00
105	16/02/2013	DD	Broadwater Properties rent paid	5,400.00		41,229.00
106	19/02/2013	DD	Wyvern DC	350.00		40,879.00
107	28/02/2013	DD	Xerax 566 maintenance	23.76		40,855.24
108	28/02/2013	DD	Loan repayment	850.00		40,005.24
109	28/02/2013	DD	Loan interest	150.00		39,855.24
110	28/02/2013	BANK	Bank charges	50.00		39,805.24

Tom could print a BANK STATEMENT report which replicates the bank statement and shows all the matched items (see illustration, above).

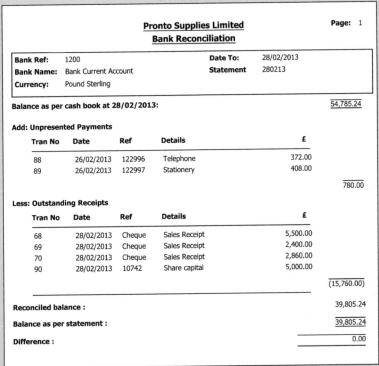

Pronto Supplies Limited
Bank Reconciliation

Page: 1

Bank Ref:	1200		Date To:	28/02/2013
Bank Name:	Bank Current Account		Statement	280213
Currency:	Pound Sterling			

Balance as per cash book at 28/02/2013: 54,785.24

Add: Unpresented Payments

Tran No	Date	Ref	Details	£
88	26/02/2013	122996	Telephone	372.00
89	26/02/2013	122997	Stationery	408.00
				780.00

Less: Outstanding Receipts

Tran No	Date	Ref	Details	£
68	28/02/2013	Cheque	Sales Receipt	5,500.00
69	28/02/2013	Cheque	Sales Receipt	2,400.00
70	28/02/2013	Cheque	Sales Receipt	2,860.00
90	28/02/2013	10742	Share capital	5,000.00
				(15,760.00)

Reconciled balance :	39,805.24
Balance as per statement :	39,805.24
Difference :	0.00

Bank Reconciliation - 1200 - Bank Current Account

Stmt. Reference 280213   Edit...   End Date 28/02/2013   End Balance 39805.24

Date		No.	Reference	Details	Payments	Receipts	
26/02/2013		88	122996	Telephone	372.00		Find...
26/02/2013		89	122997	Stationery	408.00		Swap
28/02/2013		68	Cheque	Sales Receipt		5500.00	Clear
28/02/2013		69	Cheque	Sales Receipt		2400.00	
28/02/2013		70	Cheque	Sales Receipt		2860.00	
28/02/2013		90	10742	Share capital		5000.00	

0.00

Match >>

Date		No.	Reference	Details	Payments	Receipts	Balance	
			O/Bal	Last reconciled balance			14656.00	<< Unmatch
01/02/2013		91	122991	From bank to petty cash	100.00		14556.00	0.00
08/02/2013		78	10736	Hardware sales		15000.00	29556.00	
08/02/2013		79	10737	Software sales		5616.00	35172.00	
12/02/2013		84	122992	Cash purchases	18600.00		16572.00	
15/02/2013		80	10738	Hardware sales		19008.00	35580.00	
15/02/2013		81	10739	Software sales		4416.00	39996.00	
15/02/2013		104	STO	Rent 10A High St		547.20	40543.20	
16/02/2013		105	DD	Broadwater Properties rent paid	5400.00		35143.20	
14/02/2013		85	122993	Advertising	12240.00		22903.20	
15/02/2013		86	122994	Furniture	6000.00		16903.20	
19/02/2013		106	DD	Wyvern DC	350.00		16553.20	
20/02/2013		76	BACS	Sales Receipt		523.80	17077.00	
22/02/2013		82	10740	Hardware sales		21360.00	38437.00	

Swap
Clear
Adjust...

Totals

Book Balance		Payments	Receipts		Matched Balance	− Statement Balance	= Difference
54835.24		62081.76	87231.00		39805.24	39805.24	0.00

Reconcile   Save   Print...   Send to Excel...   View History   Report   Close

OTHER MONTH-END ROUTINES

It is important for a business with a computer accounting system to establish an end-of-month routine which will include the production of the reports illustrated in the Case Studies in this chapter. Examples of other month-end routines involving the computer accounting system are explained below.

checking that all transactions have been input

The business must check that all the necessary transactions – sales and purchases transactions, payments made and received – have been input into the computer before extracting the reports.

recurring entries

Recurring entries – standing orders and direct debits – may be processed monthly, and it should become part of the month-end routine to ensure that this is done. Sage helps by displaying a warning message on the screen when you open the program up, letting you know if there are outstanding recurring entries. Recurring entries are dealt with in detail on pages 166-169.

VAT Return

A VAT-registered business may choose to print a VAT Return monthly or quarterly. This document shows how much is owed to HMRC at any time. It is accessed via COMPANY, Manage VAT (in the Task pane) and %VAT Return, or via Modules/Financials/%VAT Return. The period being reported on is entered in the top right-hand corner and the calculate button clicked. All VAT-coded transactions are automatically included in the return and options to enter adjustments, reconcile transactions, and print the return are then available.

budget reports

If budget target figures were entered in Sage in the nominal records against relevant accounts, the actual results of trading can be compared by running a budget report. A range of these is found in NOMINAL/Reports/Nominal Budget reports.

advanced month-end entries

Sage also allows you to process other monthly entries. The month-end procedure is reached from TOOLS on the main menu bar. These include:

- **clear turnover** – this resets the month-to-date turnover (eg sales and purchases) figures to zero in the customer and supplier records
- **post prepayments** – payments made in advance of the time period to which they relate; for example, an annual insurance premium can be spread out over twelve months

■ **post accruals** – payments made after the time period to which they relate; for example, a telephone bill for call charges paid at the end of a quarter can be estimated and spread over the previous three months

■ **post depreciation** – regular reductions in the value of assets which can be entered in the accounts each month

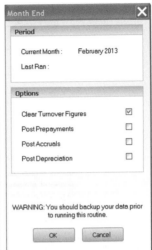

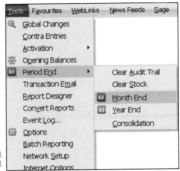

CASE STUDY

PRONTO SUPPLIES LIMITED:

VAT RETURN AND ENTERING BUDGETS

Tom wants to know his VAT liability for the month of February. He clicks on COMPANY and Manage VAT (Tasks pane) and then on the %VAT Return icon in the VAT module. He enters a date range of 01/02/13 to 28/02/13 and clicks Calculate. The program tells Tom the number of transactions found for the return. Tom clicks OK. The VAT Return boxes are automatically completed.

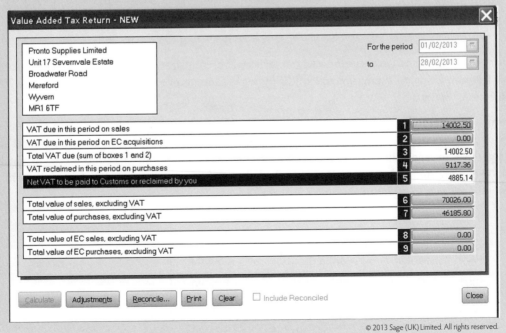

Tom clicks Print and selects the VAT Return only to run and Print.

Pronto Supplies Limited
VAT Return

Date From:	01/02/2013	Inc Current Reconciled:	No
Date To:	28/02/2013	Inc Earlier Unreconciled:	No

Transaction Number Analysis

Number of reconciled transactions included	0
Number of unreconciled transactions included (within date range)	49
Number of unreconciled transactions included (prior to date range)	0
Total number of transactions included	49

VAT due in this period on sales	1	14,002.50
VAT due in this period on EC acquisitions	2	0.00
Total VAT due (sum of boxes 1 and 2)	3	14,002.50
VAT reclaimed in this period on purchases	4	9,117.36
Net VAT to be paid to Customs or reclaimed by you	5	4,885.14
Total value of sales, excluding VAT	6	70,026.00
Total value of purchases, excluding VAT	7	46,185.80
Total value of EC sales, excluding VAT	8	0.00
Total value of EC purchases, excluding VAT	9	0.00

Tom does not want to Reconcile the VAT transactions at present; he will do this when he runs a quarterly VAT Return for online submission to HMRC. He clicks Close to exit the screen and chooses the "Don't Reconcile" option.

Tom also wants to be able to monitor his targeted sales against actual results. He could have entered budget figures when he set up his Nominal accounts (see Chapter 5). Now he wants to transfer some target sales to Sage so he highlights each of his sales accounts in the Nominal Ledger screen (ie numbers 4000 to 4002) and clicks Record. He enters the following Budget targets in the Budgets column for the months of January and February:

	January	February
4000	75000	50000
4001	15000	15000
4002	1000	1000

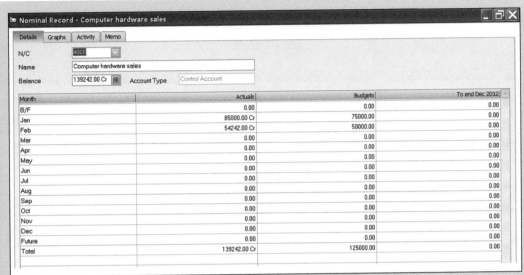

After each entry he clicks Save and Next. Now he can run a report showing the budgets he has entered. He keeps the three accounts highlighted and clicks Reports/Nominal Budget Reports/Nominal Ledger Budgets (months 1-6)

Pronto Supplies Limited   Page: 1

Nominal Ledger Budgets (months 1-6)

Nominal Code From
Nominal Code To   99999999

N/C	Name	Month 1	Month 2	Month 3	Month 4	Month 5	Month 6
4000	Computer hardware sales	75,000.00	50,000.00	0.00	0.00	0.00	0.00
4001	Computer software sales	15,000.00	15,000.00	0.00	0.00	0.00	0.00
4002	Computer consultancy	1,000.00	1,000.00	0.00	0.00	0.00	0.00
		91,000.00	66,000.00	0.00	0.00	0.00	0.00

Tom checks his actual sales figures against budgeted figures by going to the Financials module and clicking on Variance. He enters a date range of January 2013 to February 2013 to display the Budget Report for the period. He is pleased to see that his total product sales for the period exceed budget by a variance (difference) of £14,956.50.

(See illustration on next page.)

Pronto Supplies Limited

Budget Report

Page: 1

From: Month 1, January 2013
To: Month 2, February 2013

Chart of Accounts: Default Layout of Accounts

	Period				Year to Date			
	Actual	Ratio(%)	Budget	Variance	Actual	Ratio(%)	Budget	Variance
Sales								
Product Sales	171,956.50	99.74	157,000.00	14,956.50	171,956.50	99.74	157,000.00	14,956.50
Other Sales	456.00	0.26	0.00	456.00	456.00	0.26	0.00	456.00
	172,412.50	100.00	157,000.00	15,412.50	172,412.50	100.00	157,000.00	15,412.50
Purchases								
Purchases	93,366.00	54.15	0.00	93,366.00	93,366.00	54.15	0.00	93,366.00
	93,366.00	54.15	0.00	93,366.00	93,366.00	54.15	0.00	93,366.00
Direct Expenses								
Sales Promotion	22,600.00	13.11	0.00	22,600.00	22,600.00	13.11	0.00	22,600.00
	22,600.00	13.11	0.00	22,600.00	22,600.00	13.11	0.00	22,600.00
Gross Profit/(Loss):	56,446.50	32.74	157,000.00	(100,553.50)	56,446.50	32.74	157,000.00	(100,553.50)
Overheads								
Gross Wages	16,230.00	9.41	0.00	16,230.00	16,230.00	9.41	0.00	16,230.00
Rent and Rates	9,800.00	5.68	0.00	9,800.00	9,800.00	5.68	0.00	9,800.00
Heat, Light and Power	308.00	0.18	0.00	308.00	308.00	0.18	0.00	308.00
Printing and Stationery	597.00	0.35	0.00	597.00	597.00	0.35	0.00	597.00
Telephone and Computer charges	585.00	0.34	0.00	585.00	585.00	0.34	0.00	585.00
Equipment Hire and Rental	19.80	0.01	0.00	19.80	19.80	0.01	0.00	19.80
Bank Charges and Interest	200.00	0.12	0.00	200.00	200.00	0.12	0.00	200.00
	27,739.80	16.09	0.00	27,739.80	27,739.80	16.09	0.00	27,739.80
Net Profit/(Loss):	28,706.70	16.65	157,000.00	(128,293.30)	28,706.70	16.65	157,000.00	(128,293.30)

EXPORTING REPORT DATA FOR REPORTING PURPOSES

exporting data to Excel

As this chapter has shown, the reporting facilities within Sage are very comprehensive. There may be situations, however, where a business may want to export data for management reporting and 'what if' situations which require the data manipulation facilities of a spreadsheet. Sage allows the user to export data from the Reports Preview window and from certain windows, lists and grids within the program direct to Microsoft Excel. This will then allow the user to edit and format the data to create reports as required.

To export data in the form of a report, preview the report required and then click the Export button. The report can then be saved in a variety of types including Excel files. In the example on the next page an Aged Debtors Analysis has been exported to Excel.

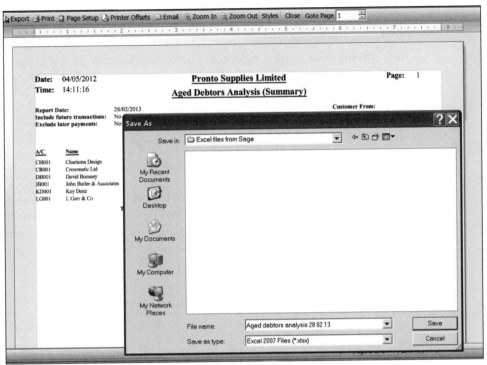

To export data from a screen to Excel, eg customer list, click on the File menu, then Office Integration and Contents to Microsoft Excel (as shown below). Excel will open automatically and show the data transferred. It can then be saved within the Excel program.

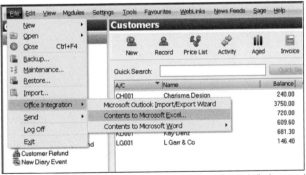

exporting reports for email

A report can be emailed directly from a Preview screen using the Email button. The report can be sent as a 'pdf' file and automatically attached to an email.

Tom in the Pronto Supplies Case Study, for example, could send customer statements by email, or he could send information to his accountant in the form of a Trial Balance or Audit Trail.

screenshots

An image of the screen can be 'exported' to another program using the 'Print Scr' button on the keyboard. The image is held in the computer's memory until it is pasted into another program, eg Word or Paint. It can then be saved and given a suitable filename.

Such images are useful for demonstration purposes (they have been used extensively in this publication) and in a training environment where the student needs to show, or print a copy of, something that appeared on-screen.

retention of records

Business records are normally stored for at least **six years plus the present year** (and a minimum of three years for payroll data). There are a number of legal reasons why financial data should be kept for this period of time. One reason is that accounting records should be kept so that they can be inspected by HM Revenue & Customs if required in the case of a tax inspection.

CHAPTER SUMMARY

- A computer accounting system has the advantage that it can provide a wide range of useful printed reports quickly and accurately. These are useful both for the management of the business and also for accounts assistants.

- Reports can be produced to help with checking the accuracy of the records. These are often produced at the end of each month and include:
  - the trial balance – a full list of the Nominal account balances
  - the audit trail – a numbered list of transactions set out in order of input on the computer

- Reports can be produced to help with day-to-day dealings with customers and suppliers. Month-end reports include:
  - 'aged' analyses – separate lists of customers and suppliers which show when payments are due and if any payments are overdue
  - activity reports – lists of transactions on individual accounts which need to be looked into
  - customer statements of account

  Other day-to-day useful printouts include customer and supplier account lists and label lists – useful for mailing purposes.

- Another regular routine is the bank reconciliation, which agrees the entries on the actual bank statement with those in the bank account records of the organisation.

- The end-of-month is the time to process recurring entries and other regular account transfers.

- A VAT Return shows how much is owed to HMRC.

- A budget report shows how actual results compare with targets.

- Data can be exported to other computer programs and sent by email to other users.

- Financial records of a business must be kept for a minimum of 6 years.

KEY TERMS

trial balance	a list of Nominal account balances set out in debit and credit columns, the totals of which should be the same
audit trail	a numbered list of transactions on the computer produced in order of input
aged debtor analysis	a list of Customer (debtor) balances which are split up according to the length of time they have been outstanding
aged creditor analysis	a list of Supplier (creditor) balances which are split up according to the length of time they have been outstanding
activity report	a list of transactions on individual Nominal, Customer and Supplier accounts
bank reconciliation	the process of checking the bank statement entries against the accounting records of an organisation and identifying the differences that exist between the two documents
VAT Return	a document showing how much is owed to HMRC and how it has been calculated
budget report	provides a comparison of target figures against actual figures

EXERCISES

PRONTO SUPPLIES INPUTTING TASKS

Set the program date to 28 February 2013.

Task 1

Print a Chase letter to Crowmatic requesting payment of their overdue account. Check it against the copy on page 180.

Task 2

Following the instructions on pages 185-189, carry out a bank reconciliation from RECONCILE in BANK.

Check that the opening balance is the same on both the bank statement and the 'reconcile' screen.

Remember to click on the screen only the items which appear in the bank statement.

Carry out any 'adjustments' that need to be done (ie inputting any items on the bank statement which have not yet been input into the computer accounting system).

Check that the Matched Balance is the same as the Statement Balance, ie that the difference is zero, before proceeding to Reconcile. Print a Bank Reconciliation Report and BANK STATEMENT and check them against the ones on pages 188-189.

Task 3

Follow the procedure in the Case Study on pages 191-192 to produce a VAT Return for the month of February.

Reminder! Have you made a back-up?

13 CORRECTIONS, ADJUSTMENTS AND JOURNALS

Chapter introduction

- When you are operating a computer accounting program it is inevitable that errors will be made. These might be your own input errors or they might be errors on the part of a customer or a supplier. Whatever the source of the error might be, it will have to be put right.

- The Corrections function contained in Sage will enable you to change most details on invoices, credit notes and payments. It is most commonly used for internal corrections – before any documents are sent out of the business.

- If a significant mistake – for example a wrong amount – is discovered after an invoice has been sent out, the invoice will normally be cancelled by a credit note and a new invoice issued in its place. An invoice or credit note can also be cancelled if it has been input on the computer but has not yet been sent out.

- The computer will warn the user, by means of an on-screen message, if an obvious inputting error is being made – for example, a date in the wrong financial year.

- Sage provides a Check Data function that should be run regularly. This will highlight and report on some types of errors.

- If data on the computer has become corrupted or is in such a mess that it needs to be input again, Sage provides a rebuild function which will set up all or part of the accounts again ready for the re-input of data. This is a very drastic measure.

- The computer also allows you to make adjustments to the records, if for example:

  - you need to 'write off' a customer account because you consider you will never get the money – the customer may have become bankrupt, for example

  - you need to refund a customer because he or she has paid too much

  - you need to cancel a cheque you have written or you have received a cheque which has been returned unpaid for some reason by the customer's bank

- The JOURNAL function in Sage is used for transferring amounts from one nominal account to another and for entering non-regular transactions and payroll values. Knowledge of how to use debits and credits is needed in order to process journals.

THE CORRECTIONS FUNCTION

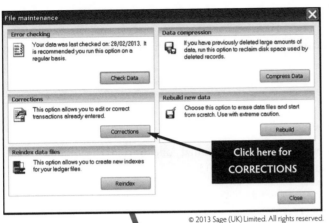

You will be able to correct most input errors within Sage using the CORRECTIONS function which is part of MAINTENANCE reached through FILE on the main menu bar.

This leads to a screen which lists all the transactions which have passed through the computer accounting system and are available for correction. You highlight the transaction which needs correcting (see screen below) and click on Edit Item to bring up the screen shown at the bottom of the page. The correction has already been made on this screen.

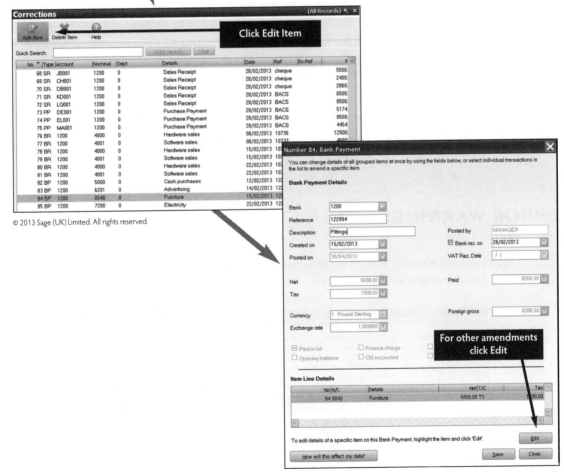

The last screen on the previous page allows correction of:

■ the account to which the invoice is posted

■ the product description

■ the reference and date

Further amendments can be made to an individual item highlighted in the bottom box by clicking Edit. These include:

■ the nominal code

■ the amounts charged

■ the VAT rate and VAT amount

In the example shown (on the previous page) the nominal code for transaction number 66, a purchase invoice, has been changed from 5000 to 0030.

CORRECTION BY DOCUMENT

Documents such as invoices have to be checked carefully before they are despatched because once they have been sent out by the business they cannot be changed. They must instead be replaced. For example, an invoice sent to a customer with a wrong price used, or a mistake in calculation, a wrong discount, or a wrong VAT code, will need to be refunded in full by the issue of a credit note. A second and correct invoice will then have to be sent to the customer.

The net effect of all this on the accounting system and the input into a computer accounting system is that the final amount owing by the customer will be correct.

If, on the other hand, a problem is discovered with an invoice or credit note before it has been sent out, it can be deleted in CORRECTIONS and a replacement document issued and input.

ERROR WARNINGS

Sage will warn the user by an on-screen message if an obvious inputting error is suspected. Some examples are shown below.

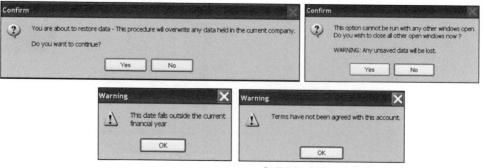

CHECK DATA

The File Maintenance option offers a Check Data routine which should be run on a regular basis. An on-screen report will advise any problems or findings. These include data corruption, missing data and date errors.

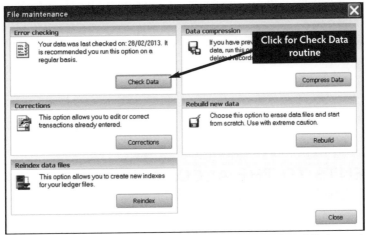

REBUILD

The REBUILD function is exactly what it says it is. Sage provides the facility to reconstruct selections of data files. This could happen for one of two reasons:

- the data is corrupted – something has gone wrong with the computer and the data cannot be used because the program will not work properly

- the data is dummy data – for example in a training situation where new 'companies' are set up each time a new set of exercises is started and the old data has to be deleted

Rebuild can be reached from MAINTENANCE through the FILE menu:

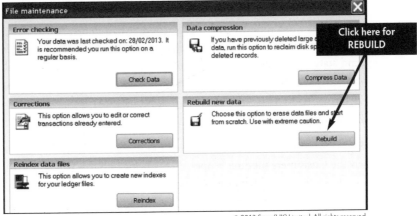

The screen looks like this . . .

You will need to deselect, ie remove the ticks from the data files that you want to reconstruct.

Rebuilding the nominal accounts will also involve reconstructing the Chart of Accounts (see page 57). You will be asked which business type you want – including the default layout.

As you can see, REBUILD is a drastic remedy to be used only when all else fails.

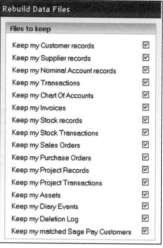

ADJUSTMENTS TO THE ACCOUNTS

A business may from time-to-time need to make adjustments to the data which has already been input into the computer accounting system. Situations where this happens include:

- A credit customer is going or has gone 'bust' (bankrupt) and cannot pay invoices – the account will need to be 'written off' as a bad debt

- A credit customer has paid too much and a refund payment has to be made (by cheque or BACS)

- a cheque paid to the business by a credit customer has 'bounced' – it has been returned by the bank after it has been paid in and the money is taken off the account of the business by the bank

- a cheque issued by the business needs to be cancelled – it may have been lost in the post or it may have been stopped

We will look at each of the procedures in turn.

write offs

All businesses from time-to-time will encounter bad debts. A **bad debt** is a credit customer who does not pay. It may be that the customer has gone 'bust' or that the cost of continuing to send statements, reminders and demands is too high in relation to the amount owing. A business will decide in these circumstances to **write off** the debt in the accounts. This involves:

- debiting 'Bad Debts Account' set up in NOMINAL

- crediting the customer with the amount due – wiping it off the account

In Sage this transfer is carried out through the Write Off/Refund option on the vertical toolbar when the Customers module is open. This brings up the WRITE OFF, REFUNDS AND RETURNS Wizard which gives a choice of accounting adjustments and customer accounts.

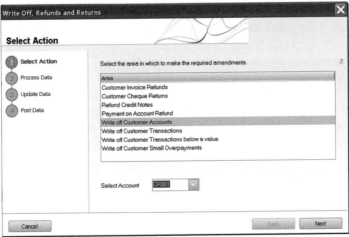

Screens then follow which allow the business to select the outstanding invoices to write off (all of them if the whole account is being written off) and then to date and confirm the details.

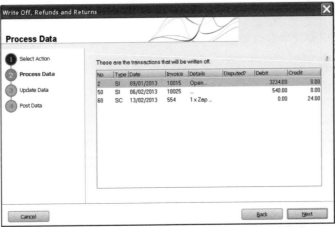

After this procedure the customer account will show as a nil balance and a corresponding Bad Debts Account in NOMINAL will show the write off amount as an expense to the business. The Debtors Control Account value will also be decreased by the amount of the write off. Eventually a write off – like any expense – will reduce the business profits.

customer refunds

A business may sometimes be asked by a credit customer to send a refund cheque. This could happen when a customer, who has been sold goods on credit and has paid for them, has then decided (with the agreement of the business) to return them. The business will have to refund this amount.

The computer accounting entries in Sage will again be made through the WRITE OFF, REFUNDS AND RETURNS Wizard. If payment has already been made, as in the above example, the 'Refund Credit Notes' option will be chosen as the refund amount will appear with this description on the account. The accounting entries here are:

- adjusting the customer's account with the refunded amount (a debit)
- deducting the refund amount from the relevant Bank account (a credit)

adjusting for returned cheques

A **returned cheque** is a cheque which has been received by a business and paid in but returned by the cheque issuer's bank for a variety of reasons: there may be a lack of funds, or the cheque may have been stopped, or it may be technically incorrect (eg unsigned by the customer).

The appropriate computer accounting entries in Sage will be made through the WRITE OFF, REFUNDS AND RETURNS Wizard under 'Customer Cheque Returns'. The cheque screen is shown below.

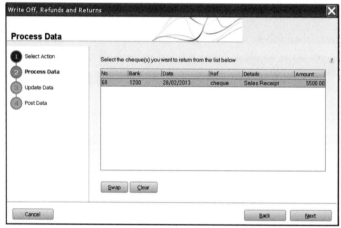

Here a cheque for £5,500 received from John Butler & Associates has been returned from their bank, marked 'Refer to Drawer'. This means that there is not sufficient money in their account and so the money will be deducted from Pronto Supplies Limited's bank account.

cancelling a cheque

A business may wish to delete from the accounting records a cheque that it has issued. For example, the cheque may have been lost in the post or it may be cancelled before it leaves the business. In these circumstances a new cheque will be issued and input into the computer accounting system.

The appropriate computer accounting entries in Sage will be made using the WRITE OFF, REFUNDS AND RETURNS Wizard (Suppliers) under 'Supplier Cheque Returns'. The screens appear as follows:

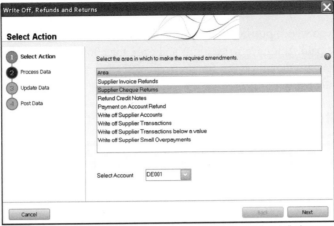

Subsequent screens allow selection or entry of the cheque details, date and details.

The accounting entries created by this process for this are:

■ adding the amount back to the Bank Current Account because the cheque is cancelled (a debit)

■ increasing the balance of the supplier's account and the Creditors Control Account with the amount of the cheque (a credit)

JOURNAL ENTRIES

Journal entries enable you to make transfers from one nominal account to another. They are used, for example, after completing a VAT Return to transfer VAT due to HMRC from the Sales VAT and Purchase VAT control accounts to the VAT Liability account. They are also another way of putting things right when you have input the wrong nominal account.

Journals are also used to enter opening balances, advanced accounting adjustments (such as depreciation of fixed assets), and a variety of non-regular transactions.

journals and double-entry

You need to be confident about **double-entry** bookkeeping and using debits and credits when doing journal entries. You will have to decide which accounts have debit entries and which accounts have credit entries. The rule is that for every transaction there are balancing debit and credit entries:

debits = money paid into the bank
purchases and expenses
an increase in an asset

credits = payments out of the bank
sales and income
an increase in a liability

If you are still in any doubt about debits and credits, use CORRECTIONS wherever possible to adjust account entries.

example

Suppose you were inputting a batch of Bank Payments which included a number of bills that had to be paid. You have written out a cheque for £96 to RPower for a gas bill, but when inputting it you thought it was for electricity and so posted it to electricity (nominal account 7200) instead of gas (7201).

the solution

You could use CORRECTIONS, but as you are a double-entry expert you choose to correct your mistake using a journal entry. You bring up the screen by clicking on the JOURNALS icon on the NOMINAL menu bar:

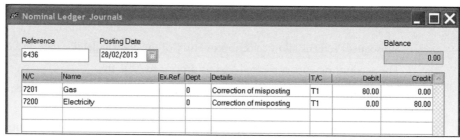

The procedure is:

■ enter your reference (this could be the transaction number you can find by opening up the FINANCIALS module and locating the transaction)

■ enter the nominal code of the account to which you are going to post the debit; here it is Gas Account because you are recording an expense

■ enter the reason for the transaction – here you are adjusting a misposting

■ enter the VAT tax code input on the original (wrong) entry

■ enter the net amount in the debit column (ie the amount before VAT has been added on) – here the net amount is £80 and VAT (assumed here at standard rate) is £16 and the total is £96; note that neither the VAT nor the total appear on the screen because you are not adjusting the VAT; *only the net amount* has gone to the wrong account

then on the next line . . .

■ enter the nominal code of the account to which you are going to post the credit; here it is Electricity Account because you are effectively refunding the amount to the account – it is an income item and so a credit

■ enter the remaining data as you did for the debit, but enter the net amount in the right-hand credit column

■ make sure the Balance box reads zero – meaning that the debit equals the credit – and SAVE

journals for non-regular transactions

Certain types of transactions are traditionally entered as journals in accounting. These include entry of opening balances, purchase of fixed assets and payroll journals.

Some unusual transactions can only be entered as journals, such as owner drawings in goods, assets introduced and cash sale bad debts.

Journals should include a "narrative", ie a brief description of the transaction. This is entered in the Details column in Sage.

opening balances

When a business is started there are always some accounting entries to make. For example, the owner will have introduced some capital (money invested) into the business bank account. The two journals below are typical examples of start-up journals. They could be entered in Sage once the appropriate nominal accounts have been identified.

Date	Details	Debit	Credit
2013		£	£
1 Jan	Bank	10,000	
	Capital/Shares		10,000
	Opening capital introduced		

Date	Details	Debit	Credit
2013		£	£
1 Feb	Cash	100	
	Bank	5,000	
	Inventory (stock)	1,000	
	Machinery	2,500	
	Creditors Control		850
	Capital/Shares		7,750
		8,600	8,600
	Assets and liabilities at the start of business		

Now look back at page 60 in Chapter 5 where a Trial Balance was used to enter opening balances via the Nominal Ledger in Sage. This could have been entered as a journal as shown on the next page. Note the inclusion of a Suspense account balance to compensate for the Debtors and Creditors Control account balances already entered (see page 45).

N/C	Name	Ex.Ref	Dept	Details	T/C	Debit	Credit
	Reference: Opening balances			Posting Date: 31/01/2013		Balance	0.00
0020	Plant and Machinery		0	Opening balance	T9	35000.00	0.00
0030	Office Equipment		0	Opening balance	T9	15000.00	0.00
0040	Furniture and Fixtures		0	Opening balance	T9	25000.00	0.00
1200	Bank Current Account		0	Opening balance	T9	14656.00	0.00
2200	Sales Tax Control Account		0	Opening balance	T9	0.00	17920.00
2201	Purchase Tax Control Account		0	Opening balance	T9	26600.00	0.00
2300	Loans		0	Opening balance	T9	0.00	35000.00
3000	Ordinary Shares		0	Opening balance	T9	0.00	75000.00
4000	Computer hardware sales		0	Opening balance	T9	0.00	85000.00
4001	Computer software sales		0	Opening balance	T9	0.00	15000.00
4002	Computer consultancy		0	Opening balance	T9	0.00	2400.00
5000	Materials Purchased		0	Opening balance	T9	69100.00	0.00
6201	Advertising		0	Opening balance	T9	12400.00	0.00
7000	Gross Wages		0	Opening balance	T9	16230.00	0.00
7100	Rent		0	Opening balance	T9	4500.00	0.00
7103	General Rates		0	Opening balance	T9	450.00	0.00
7200	Electricity		0	Opening balance	T9	150.00	0.00
7502	Telephone		0	Opening balance	T9	275.00	0.00
7504	Office Stationery		0	Opening balance	T9	175.00	0.00
9998	Suspense Account		0	Opening balance	T9	10784.00	0.00
						230320.00	230320.00

purchase of fixed assets

It is possible to enter the purchase of a fixed asset as a credit purchase or simple bank transaction in Sage, coded appropriately in the nominal range of 0010 to 0059 (see the example on page 88 in Chapter 7). However, it is traditional in accounting to enter it using a journal. Below is an example of the journal entry for the purchase of machinery and the entry that could be made in Sage.

Date	Details	Debit	Credit
2013 15 Apr		£	£
	Plant & Machinery	1,000	
	VAT	200	
	Bank		1,200
		1,200	1,200
	Purchase of binding machine, serial number X7439288/5		

N/C	Name	Ex.Ref	Dept	Details	T/C	Debit	Credit
	Reference: J150413			Posting Date: 15/04/2013		Balance	0.00
0020	Plant and Machinery		0	Binder serial no X7439288/5	T1	1000.00	0.00
2201	Purchase Tax Control Accou...		0	VAT on new binder	T1	200.00	0.00
1200	Bank Current Account		0	BACS Binder Supplies	T9	0.00	1200.00

Sales of fixed assets may also be entered as journal.

If an asset is introduced by the owner of a business rather than being purchased by the business, a similar entry would be made but with the credit entry in the Capital account, ie the value of the asset introduced is owed back to the owner. In the example below, a vehicle valued at £8000 has been introduced into the business by the owner.

Date	Details	Debit	Credit
		£	£
2013			
17 Jul	Vehicles	8,000	
	Capital/Shares		8,000
	Introduction of vehicle registration WV60 TVL		
	to business by owner		

	Nominal Ledger Journals								_ □ X

Reference	Posting Date							Balance	
J170713	17/07/2013							0.00	

N/C	Name	Ex.Ref	Dept	Details	T/C	Debit	Credit
0050	Motor Vehicles		0	Vehicle reg WV60 TVL from owner	T9	8000.00	0.00
3000	Ordinary Shares		0	Vehicle reg WV60 TVL from owner	T9	0.00	8000.00

owner drawings in goods

The owners of businesses that operate as sole traders or partnerships (as opposed to limited companies) may pay themselves in the form of Drawings. Normally this is in the form of money, but it can be in the form of goods taken from the business. For example the owner of a retail clothing business may take items of clothing from time-to-time. The values involved in these transactions are recorded as journals. Below is an example:

Date	Details	Debit	Credit
		£	£
2013			
1 Oct	Drawings	600	
	Sales		500
	VAT		100
		600	600
	Clothing taken by owner		

The Drawings Account in Sage is 3050 by default (Sole Trader Chart of Accounts) where it effectively reduces owner capital (nominal code 3000) invested in the business.

If the business is VAT registered then VAT must be accounted for on owner drawings in goods as sales VAT and the owner drawings value should include VAT (as in the example above).

cash sale bad debt

We have looked at bad debt write off of a customer invoice or account (see page 202), but what if a cheque received against a cash sale is returned and there is no way of contacting the purchaser to obtain an alternative method of payment? Below is an example of a journal to enter a cash sale cheque returned for £120 inclusive of VAT.

Date	Details	Debit	Credit
2013		£	£
20 Nov	Bad debt write off	100	
	VAT *	20	
	Bank		120
		120	120
	Returned cheque for cash sales written off		

*There are special rules relating to reclaiming VAT on bad debts.

Note that the sales account is not adjusted as the sale has gone through the system. It is the payment for the sale that has not been received.

VAT codes on journals in Sage

The default setting for the tax code in the journals entry screen is T9. This is because many journals do not involve VAT. Where the journal is a correction of a value involving VAT (as in the example on page 206) the original VAT code for the transaction should be used. Sage does not however calculate any VAT here and any value adjustment to the VAT accounts (Sales Tax Control or Purchase Tax Control) should be entered as a separate line as in the example of the asset purchase above.

payroll journals

The use of the journal as a means of entering payroll values ensures that the complex elements of payroll are correctly posted and tracked through the accounting system. These values will be generated either manually or by computerised payroll software (eg Sage Payroll) and include:

- Gross wages
- Net wages
- Statutory deductions (income tax and employee National Insurance contributions)
- Employer National Insurance contributions
- Non-statutory deductions, eg pension contributions, charity donations, internal club payments, savings scheme contributions (eg SAYE)
- Amounts due to HMRC (income tax, national insurance, student loan deductions)

Once the above values have been calculated, the relevant entries can be made in the appropriate nominal accounts to record:

(a) the total expense of the payroll to the business (made up of gross pay plus other costs such as employer National Insurance and employer pension contributions)

(b) any resultant liability to outside bodies, eg HMRC, Pension Fund provider

(c) net amounts due to employees when pay day arrives

Below is an example of total payroll values and the relevant Sage journal entries:

Pay element	Value (£)	Nominal code
Gross pay	22,352	7000
Tax	2,510	2210
National Insurance (employee)	965	2211
National Insurance (employer)	1,105	2211
National Insurance (employer)	1,105	7006
Pension (employee contribution)	1,032	2230
Pension (employer contribution)	1,032	2230
Pension (employer contribution)	1,032	7007
Net pay	17,845	2220

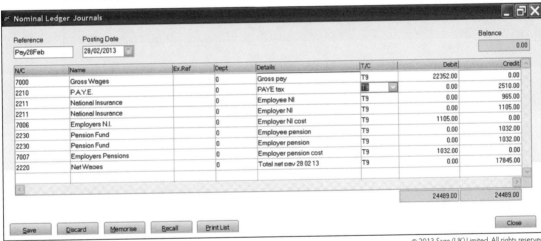

Note that, as always in journals, the total debit value must equal the total credit value.

Payments will be made from the bank account (perhaps by BACS) to pay individual employees on pay day, and to discharge any liabilities (eg to HMRC and pension provider) by the due dates. These will be entered as bank payments in Sage using the appropriate nominal code. In the example above, a bank payment of £17,845 would be entered in Sage on pay day, coded 2220.

A split bank payment of £4,580 would be made to HMRC by 22nd of the following month – £2,510 coded 2210 (PAYE) and £2,070 coded 2211 (National Insurance). A bank payment of £2,064 would be made to the pension provider by the due date, coded 2230 (Pension Fund).

CASE STUDY

PRONTO SUPPLIES LIMITED:
CORRECTIONS AND ADJUSTMENTS

It is 28 February 2013. Tom is still finalising his accounts. He encounters a number of situations which require him to carry out corrections and adjustments straightaway.

Incorrect cash payment description

Tom realises that the cash purchase made on 15 February using cheque number 122994 was for Fittings, not Furniture.

Tom identifies the transaction from the audit trail he has printed out. It is transaction 86. Tom goes into CORRECTIONS from FILE MAINTENANCE and selects transaction 86. He clicks 'Edit item' on the Corrections toolbar and changes 'Furniture' to 'Fittings' in the Description field.

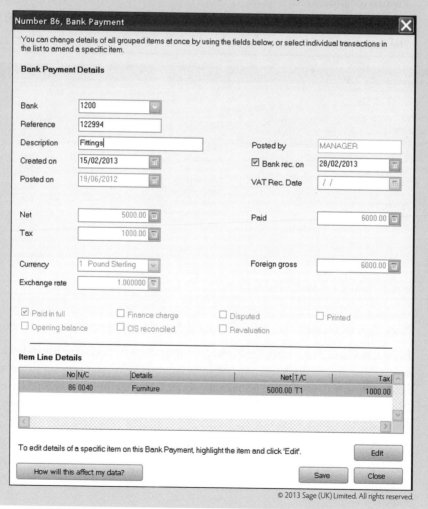

Clicking on the EDIT button then brings up another screen (see below). Tom has to make the same amendment and then CLOSE and SAVE.

Number 86, Bank Payment ✕

Bank Payment Details

N/C	0040
Details	Fittings
Date	15/02/2013
Department	0
Ex.Ref	
Project Ref	
Cost Code	

journal entries

On checking the paperwork relating to the accounts for the month Tom spots that a bill from RPower has been paid but the expense has been posted by mistake to Electricity Account instead of Gas account.

The bill was for £158 plus VAT.

Tom decides to carry out journal entries to switch the expense from one account to the other. In double-entry bookkeeping terms this means:

debit   Gas Account (code 7201) £158 – recording an expense

credit   Electricity Account (code 7200) £158 – recording a refund

Tom accesses the Journal through the Journals icon on the Nominal menu bar. The journal screen after input appears as follows:

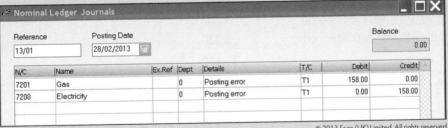

Nominal Ledger Journals

Reference	Posting Date						Balance
13/01	28/02/2013						0.00

N/C	Name	Ex.Ref	Dept	Details	T/C	Debit	Credit
7201	Gas		0	Posting error	T1	158.00	0.00
7200	Electricity		0	Posting error	T1	0.00	158.00

Note that:

■   no VAT is involved here because it is only the net amount (amount before VAT is added on) that has gone to the wrong account

■   the reference used is taken from Tom's journal numbering system

■   the Balance box shows as zero because the debit entry equals the credit entry – as you would expect (the Balance is the difference between the entries)

Tom can keep a printed record of his journals by going to Reports in the Nominal module and printing Day Books: Nominal Ledger.

Pronto Supplies Limited

Day Books: Nominal Ledger

Date From:	28/02/2013								N/C From:		
Date To:	28/02/2013								N/C To:	99999999	
Transaction From:	1								Dept From:	0	
Transaction To:	99,999,999								Dept To:	999	

No	Type	N/C	Date	Ref	Ex.Ref	Details	Dept	T/C	Debit	Credit	V	B
111	JD	7201	28/02/2013	13/01		Posting error	0	T9	158.00		-	-
112	JC	7200	28/02/2013	13/01		Posting error	0	T9		158.00	-	-
								Totals:	158.00	158.00		

cancelling a customer payment

John Butler has phoned to ask Tom to cancel the cheque for £5,500.00 which he recently sent because he has a query on the goods charged.

Tom cancels the payment on his computer through WRITE OFF/REFUND on the vertical toolbar of the Customers module. He chooses Customer Cheque Returns in the WRITE OFF, REFUNDS AND RETURNS Wizard, selects John Butler's account and completes the wizard to delete the payment.

payroll journals

Tom needs to enter a journal for his February payroll. The values have been generated as follows:

Pay element	£
Gross pay	16,780
Tax	2,200
National Insurance (employee)	1,250
National Insurance (employer)	1,320
Net pay	13,330

He enters these amounts into Sage via JOURNALS using a reference of 13/02 and date of 28 February 2013.

Nominal Ledger Journals

Reference	Posting Date		Balance	
13/02	28/02/2013		0.00	

N/C	Name	Ex.Ref	Dept	Details	T/C	Debit	Credit
7000	Gross Wages		0	Gross pay	T9	16780.00	0.00
2210	P.A.Y.E.		0	PAYE tax	T9	0.00	2200.00
2211	National Insurance		0	Employee NI	T9	0.00	1250.00
2211	National Insurance		0	Employer NI	T9	0.00	1320.00
7006	Employers N.I. (Non-Directo...		0	Employer NI cost	T9	1320.00	0.00
2220	Net Wages		0	Net pay 28 02 13	T9	0.00	13330.00

checking corrections and adjustments

Sage does not automatically generate a report as a result of corrections to transaction data, so to confirm that the adjustments have been made, the audit trail should be checked.

The way in which a correction is reported depends on how important the change is in accounting terms. Some changes result in a simple substitution, such as a change to Details or Reference (eg the 'furniture' to 'fittings' change in the Case Study). Some result in the original transaction being amended and an additional entry being inserted on the audit trail showing what has been deleted, eg where a major alteration like a change to the nominal code has been made.

Changes to amounts of Journals transactions require a different treatment as they cannot be changed in CORRECTIONS. The way to do this is to choose the Reversals option from the Nominal toolbar. This will enable you to reverse (cancel out) the original transaction and to then enter the correct journal debit and credit entries.

CHAPTER SUMMARY

- Errors inevitably occur when processing accounts on the computer. Errors can involve incorrect descriptions, incorrect prices, wrong VAT codes and wrong accounts used.

- Most errors within Sage can be corrected using the CORRECTIONS routine within MAINTENANCE. This will enable corrections to be made to invoices, credit notes and payments.

- After financial documents such as invoices and credit notes have been sent out they can normally only be corrected by document – for example an invoice overcharge adjusted by a credit note.

- On-screen warnings may appear in the case of some inputting errors.

- Certain data errors can be detected by running the Check Data option.

- If computer files become corrupted beyond repair the Sage REBUILD function can be used to reconstruct the ledgers. This may result in data being lost in the process. REBUILD is also used in a training context.

- The computer accounting records may also be adjusted for situations such as account write-offs, refunds to customers, returned customer cheques and cheques to suppliers that need to be cancelled.

- Adjustments to Nominal accounts can be carried out by transfers through the JOURNALS function within Sage. This process requires a knowledge of double-entry bookkeeping.

- Journals are used for non-regular transactions and the entry of payroll values.

KEY TERMS

write off	the removal of a Customer (or Supplier) account balance from the accounting records
bad debt	a debt that is never likely to be paid and so will need to be written off
returned cheque	a cheque that has been paid into a bank account but has been returned unpaid by the bank either because of lack of funds, or because of some technical irregularity on the cheque
journal	the part of the accounting system which enables you to make transfers from one nominal account to another, and to enter new balances directly into nominal accounts
double-entry	the system of bookkeeping which involves each transaction having two entries made – a debit and a credit; computer accounting programs (which are largely single-entry systems) deal with the double-entry automatically

EXERCISES

PRONTO SUPPLIES INPUTTING TASKS

Ensure the program date is set at 28 February 2013.

Task 1

Correct cheque 122994 (transaction 86) in the Case Study on page 214 using CORRECTIONS.

Task 2

Carry out the Journal entries for the misposting in the Case Study on page 215. Use Ref 13/01.

Task 3

Cancel the cheque for £5,500.00 from John Butler & Associates using the WRITE OFF, REFUNDS AND RETURNS Wizard.

Task 4

Enter the payroll journal on page 216 using reference 13/02.

Task 5

When you have completed your corrections, print out a Trial Balance. Check the figures on the Trial Balance with the figures on page 289.

Reminder! Have you made a back-up?

14 DOUBLE-ENTRY BOOKKEEPING AND MANUAL SYSTEMS

Chapter introduction

■ Earlier chapters in this book have shown how computer accounting involves the use of 'accounts' and 'ledgers' maintained on computer files. It is easy to accept these terms at face value when you are sitting in front of a computer – but they make much more sense once you know how they work in a manual accounting system.

■ The basis of many manual accounting systems is a set of double-entry accounts grouped into separate ledgers – eg sales ledger, purchases ledger. Each time a transaction is recorded, it is entered twice in the accounts, once as a debit and once as a credit.

■ The basis of computer accounting is the input of a financial transaction as a single entry on the screen. The computer then processes that entry to two separate accounts (or three accounts if VAT is involved). In other words, the computer does the double-entry for you.

■ The problem with manual double-entry bookkeeping is knowing which entry is the debit and which is the credit. This is best understood when it is seen as part of the 'dual aspect' of double-entry bookkeeping, which sets down the principles of which entry is which. These principles are sometimes needed in computer accounting, for example when you are processing a journal entry or a nominal opening balance. You then have to decide whether an amount should be entered as a debit or as a credit. If you understand the principles of manual double-entry bookkeeping you are at a great advantage.

■ Remember that double-entry bookkeeping is only one part of the accounting process, whether a manual or a computer accounting system is used. The first step is the financial transaction and the document it generates, the second is the listing and summarising of financial transactions and the third is the entry of this data in the accounts. The final stage is the summary of the accounts in the Trial Balance and the production of reports such as the Profit & Loss Statement and the Balance Sheet from the double-entry records. We will start off in this chapter by looking at this overall accounting system.

THE ACCOUNTING SYSTEM

The overall accounting system as it relates to both manual and computer accounting is a simple series of stages which starts off with financial transactions such as sales and purchases and concludes with information used by management such as aged debtor summaries and profit and loss statements. The stages can be summarised as follows:

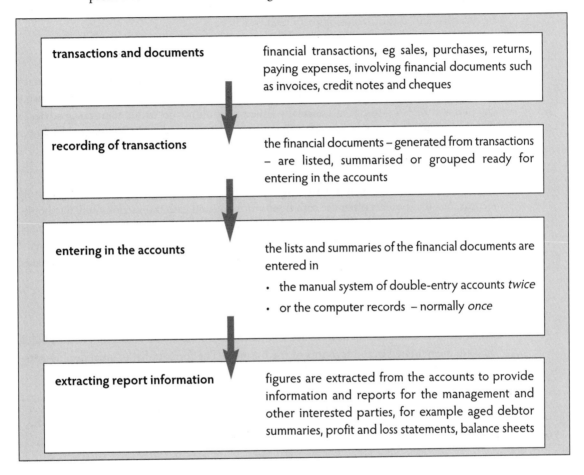

transactions and documents — financial transactions, eg sales, purchases, returns, paying expenses, involving financial documents such as invoices, credit notes and cheques

recording of transactions — the financial documents – generated from transactions – are listed, summarised or grouped ready for entering in the accounts

entering in the accounts — the lists and summaries of the financial documents are entered in
- the manual system of double-entry accounts *twice*
- or the computer records – normally *once*

extracting report information — figures are extracted from the accounts to provide information and reports for the management and other interested parties, for example aged debtor summaries, profit and loss statements, balance sheets

stage 1 – transactions and documents

Financial transactions involve financial documents. You will already be familiar with many of these.

sale and purchase of goods and services – the invoice

When a business buys or sells goods or a service the seller prepares an invoice which sets out the amount owing, the date on which it should be paid and the details of the goods sold or the service provided.

refunds – the credit note

If the buyer returns goods which are bought on credit or has a problem with a service supplied on credit, the seller will issue a credit note which is sent to the buyer, reducing the amount of money owed.

small cash payments – the petty cash voucher

If the business operates a petty cash system for making small cash payments, the payments will be recorded and authorised using petty cash vouchers.

paying-in slips, cheques and remittance advices

Businesses need to pay money into the bank current account, and draw out cash and make payments. Money can be paid in on paying-in slips or electronically. Payments made using cheques and BACS transfers are normally issued in conjunction with a remittance advice, a document sent to the person receiving the money, explaining what the payment represents.

stage 2 – recording transactions

Businesses need to list and summarise these documents ready for entry into the accounting records. Manual systems often use cash books for bank and cash transactions and 'day books' for listing sales, purchases and returns. Each day book will usually be totalled on a regular basis. Computer systems often use the **batch** system which is a grouping of the items with an overall total to check against the computer input. It is common to find batches for sales, purchases, returns, cheques received, cheques issued.

stage 3 – entering transactions in the accounts

When the financial documents have been suitably listed in a day book or grouped in a batch they are then entered in the accounts of the business. The format of a manual double-entry account with a debit entry might look like this:

Debit						Computer Account			Credit	
Date	Details	Folio	£	p	Date	Details	Folio	£	p
01 02 13	Bank	CB007	450.00						
↑	↑	↑	↑	↑	↑	↑	↑	
date of the trans- action	name of the account in which the other entry is made	page or reference number of the other account	amount of the trans- action	date of the trans- action	name of the account in which the other entry is made	page or reference number of the other account	amount of the trans- action	

The double-entry system used by many manual systems involves two entries for each amount or total (or three entries if VAT is involved). This form of account and the way it works is explained in more detail on page 225.

A computer system, as you know, needs only one entry to be made for each transaction, but will require the account code of the other entry when that single entry is made.

Most accounting systems use the **ledger** system to organise the accounts. The word 'ledger' means 'book' but is used freely by both manual and computer systems to represent a section of the accounts kept on paper or on the computer. The ledgers can be summarised as follows:

■ **sales ledger** — the accounts of customers who have bought on credit (also known as debtors), referred to in computer accounting as CUSTOMERS

■ **purchases ledger** — the accounts of suppliers (creditors) who have sold to the business on credit, referred to in computer accounting as SUPPLIERS

■ **cash book ledger** — the cash and bank accounts of the business – referred to in computer accounting as BANK

■ **main 'general' ledger** — all the other accounts – expenses, income, assets (items owned) and liabilities (items owed), also referred to in computer accounting as NOMINAL

stage 4 – extracting report information

Financial data in the accounts is only useful when it can be extracted and used by the management of the business or presented to outsiders such as shareholders. The advantage of computer accounting systems is that reports can be generated automatically from a menu. You may encounter a number of different reports in your studies:

■ **trial balance** — a list of account balances in two columns, which will show whether or not the bookkeeping (in a manual system) has been accurate

■ **account activity** — a list of the transactions on a particular account which may need investigation, eg an expense account or the account of a customer

■ **aged debtors analysis** — a listing of the balances of credit customers, setting out what they owe, when they need to pay and if any payments are overdue

■ **aged creditors analysis** — a listing of the balances of suppliers, setting out when payments need to be made

■ **financial statements** — these include the **profit and loss statement**, which states what profit/loss has been made and the **balance sheet** which sets out what a business owns and owes and how it is financed

Now study the diagram on the next page which summarises the various stages in a manual and a computer accounting system. The workings of double-entry used in a manual system are explained on page 225.

the accounting system – a summary

TRANSACTIONS AND DOCUMENTS

invoices – sales and purchases

paying-in slips – money paid into the bank

remittance advices – payments received

credit notes – credit refunds made

cheques – suppliers and expenses paid

sources of accounting information

⬇

recording of accounting information

MANUAL BOOKKEEPING	*or*	COMPUTER ACCOUNTING

MANUAL BOOKKEEPING

double-entry – two entries in the accounts for each transaction

paper-based accounts in 'ledgers'
- sales ledger – customer accounts
- purchases ledger – supplier accounts
- cash book – bank and cash accounts
- main ('nominal' or 'general') ledger – all the other accounts

or

COMPUTER ACCOUNTING

single-entry – one entry on the screen for most transactions

accounts in 'ledgers' on computer file
- sales ledger – customer accounts
- purchases ledger – supplier accounts
- 'Bank' – bank and cash accounts
- nominal ledger – all the other accounts

⬇   ⬇

extracting reports from the accounts

AGED REPORTS
balances of the Customer and Supplier accounts to help with Credit Control and timing of payments

TRIAL BALANCE
a list of the balances of all the accounts to check bookkeeping accuracy

ACCOUNT ACTIVITY
transaction lists of individual accounts, eg expense accounts, Customer accounts

⬇   ⬇

FINANCIAL STATEMENTS
- profit and loss statement – showing how much profit (or loss) has been made
- balance sheet – showing what the business owns and owes

DOUBLE-ENTRY ACCOUNTS

Double-entry bookkeeping in a manual accounting system involves entries being made in accounts for each transaction – debit entries (on the left-hand side of the account) and credit entries (on the right-hand side of the account). If a transaction does not involve VAT there will be two entries: an equal debit and credit. If VAT is involved there will be three entries, but the debit(s) must always equal the credit(s).

The questions faced by anyone operating the system are:

■ deciding which two (or three) accounts should be used for each transaction, and more critically …

■ deciding which entry is the debit and which is the credit

There are simple rules which guide you here, but, as with learning to drive a car, the early stages require both thought and concentration!

We will first look at the layout of a typical double-entry account. The illustration here shows an account for computer equipment purchased.

Debit					Computer Account				Credit	
Date	Details	Folio	£	p	Date	Details	Folio	£	p	
01 02 13	Bank	CB007	450.00							
date of the trans- action	name of the account in which the other entry is made	page or reference number of the other account	amount of the trans- action							

Note the following:

■ the name of the account – Computer Account – is written at the top

■ the account is divided into two identical halves, separated by a central double vertical line: the left-hand side is called the 'debit' side ('debit' is abbreviated to 'Dr'), the right-hand side is called the 'credit' (or 'Cr') side

A note for UK drivers! – **Dr**ive on the left   **Cr**ash on the right

■ the date, details and amount of the transaction are entered in the columns:

– in the 'details' column is entered the name of the other account involved in the bookkeeping transaction – here it is the Bank Account

– the 'folio' column is used as a cross-referencing system to the other entry of the double-entry bookkeeping transaction – here CB007 stands for page 7 in the Cash Book where the Bank Account entry is made

In a manual bookkeeping system each account would occupy a whole page or more, but in textbooks to save space it is usual to simplify the format and put several accounts on a page.

The Computer Account set out in this way is shown at the bottom of this page.

You will see that the Folio column has gone and the column divisions have also disappeared. It is all much simpler, with just a single vertical line dividing the debit and credit sides.

The problem remains: if you are given a transaction to enter, how do you decide which is the debit entry and which is the credit entry?

dual aspect theory of double-entry

The principle of double-entry bookkeeping is that every business transaction has a dual aspect: one account gains value (the debit), the other gives value (the credit). The Computer Account shows a gain in value for the business (the debit), ie the new computer, while the Bank Account will give value as the purchase price is paid (the credit).

practical aspects of double-entry

If this sounds too theoretical, look at the practical aspects of the system. For each double-entry transaction (ignoring any VAT for the sake of simplicity):

- one account is debited (entry on the left of the account)
- another account is credited (entry on the right of the account)

The practical rules for debits and credits are:

debit entry	credit entry
■ money paid into the bank	■ money paid out of the bank
■ purchases made, expenses paid	■ an income item
■ an asset (item owned) is acquired or increased	■ a liability (item owed) is incurred or increased

Look at the example below and read the text in the grey boxes:

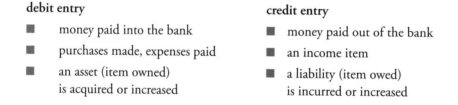

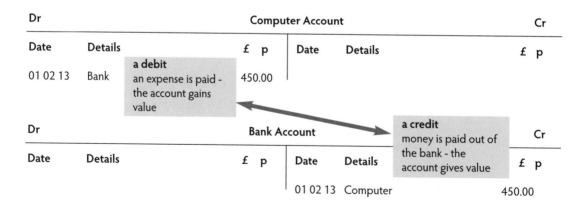

CASE STUDY

HARRY PORTER LIMITED:
DOUBLE-ENTRY TRANSACTIONS

Harry Porter runs a magic and jokes shop. During the first week of July 2013 he has five transactions to enter in his double-entry accounts:

2 Jul 2013   Sale of goods for £12,000 cheque received.

3 Jul 2013   Payment of wages of £1,200 by cheque.

4 Jul 2013   Purchase of goods for £3,000, paid for by cheque.

5 Jul 2013   Received loan of £5,000 from D B Dore, and paid cheque into bank.

6 Jul 2013   Purchase of computer costing £4,000, paid for by cheque.

For the sake of simplicity VAT and wages journals have been ignored.

If you look at these five transactions for Harry Porter Limited, you will see that they all involve the bank account. One invariable rule for the bank account is that money received is recorded on the left-hand (debit) side, and money paid out is recorded on the right-hand (credit) side. By applying this rule, you can say that for a bank account:

Money in is a debit (on the left); money out is a credit (on the right)

Using this rule, the bank account for Harry Porter Limited, after entering the five transactions, appears as follows:

Dr			Bank Account			Cr
Date	Details	£ p	Date	Details		£ p
2013		money in	2013		money out	
02 Jul	Sales	12,000.00	03 Jul	Wages		1,200.00
05 Jul	D B Dore Loan	5,000.00	04 Jul	Purchases		3,000.00
			06 Jul	Computer		4,000.00

It is now a simple step to work out onto which side, debit or credit, the entries are recorded in the other accounts involved. If you bear in mind that money received is a debit (left-hand side) and money paid out is a credit (right-hand side), by looking at any double-entry transaction which involves the bank account you should:

■ identify on which side of the bank account, debit (money in) or credit (money out), the item is recorded

■ record the other double-entry item on the other side of the appropriate account

We are now in a position to set out the other accounts involved in the five transactions entered in the bank account. Note that in each case the description in the account is 'Bank'.

transaction

2 July 2013: sale of goods for £12,000, cheque received

double-entry

Debit Bank Account (money in); Credit Sales Account (an income item)

Dr			Sales Account			Cr
Date	**Details**	**£ p**	**Date**	**Details**		**£ p**
2013			2013			
			02 Jul	Bank		12,000.00

transaction

3 July 2013: payment of wages £1,200 by cheque

double-entry

Debit Wages Account (an expense); Credit Bank Account (money paid out)

Dr			Wages Account			Cr
Date	**Details**	**£ p**	**Date**	**Details**		**£ p**
2013			2013			
03 Jul	Bank	1,200.00				

transaction

4 July 2013: purchase of goods for £3,000, paid for by cheque

double-entry

Debit Purchases Account (an expense); Credit Bank Account (money paid out)

Dr			Purchases Account			Cr
Date	**Details**	**£ p**	**Date**	**Details**		**£ p**
2013			2013			
04 Jul	Bank	3,000.00				

transaction

5 July 2013: received loan from D B Dore, £5,000, and paid cheque into bank

double-entry

Debit Bank Account (money in); Credit D B Dore Loan Account (a liability)

Dr				D B Dore Loan Account		Cr
Date	Details	£ p	Date	Details		£ p
2013			2013			
			05 Jul	Bank		5,000.00

transaction

6 July 2013: purchase of computer costing £4,000, paid for by cheque

double-entry

Debit Computer Account (asset acquired); Credit Bank Account (money paid out)

Dr				Computer Account		Cr
Date	Details	£ p	Date	Details		£ p
2013			2013			
06 Jul	Bank	4,000.00				

Note that the acquisition of a computer is the purchase of an item which will be retained in the business. It is therefore a fixed asset and will be recorded in a separate account, and not in Purchases Account, which is used solely for recording the purchase of goods which the business is going to sell – ie magic and joke products.

DOUBLE-ENTRY FOR CREDIT SALES AND CREDIT PURCHASES

So far in this chapter we have examined the treatment of double-entry transactions involving the bank account, and have used the bank account as a guide to working out which entry is a debit and which is a credit. In business many entries will involve the bank account, because cash, cheques and BACS are common methods of payment.

There will, however, be some transactions which do not involve the bank account. Purchases and sales on credit (ie where payment is made later) are the most common, and the double-entry rules for these follow the same logic: the bookkeeper, on entering a credit purchase or credit sale, records the item in the sales account or purchases account as normal, but then records the second entry in the relevant account in the name of either the customer or the supplier, instead of in the bank account, because no money has yet changed hands. The entries (again ignoring any VAT) are therefore:

■ credit sale	Debit	Customer's Account	
	Credit	Sales Account	
■ credit purchase	Credit	Supplier's Account	
	Debit	Purchases Account	

Let us now take an example of a credit sale made by Harry Porter Limited, and payment received after thirty days. On 10 July 2013 Harry Porter Limited sells goods invoiced at £5,000 on credit to Owl Promotions. The ledger entries are: debit Owl Promotions' Account; credit Sales Account.

Dr			Sales Account			Cr
Date	**Details**	**£ p**	**Date**	**Details**	**£ p**	
2013			2013			
			10 Jul	Owl Promotions	5,000.00	

Dr			Owl Promotions			Cr
Date	**Details**	**£ p**	**Date**	**Details**	**£ p**	
2013			2013			
10 Jul	Sales	5,000.00				

On 10 August, thirty days after this sale has been made, Harry Porter Limited receives a cheque for £5,000 from Owl Promotions in settlement of the amount due; the cheque is paid into the bank. Harry Porter Limited's bookkeeper will:

■ debit Bank Account £5,000 (money received)

■ credit the account of Owl Promotions £5,000

The accounts will appear as set out below. Note the existing entry from 10 July on the account of Owl Promotions.

Dr			Bank Account			Cr
Date	**Details**	**£ p**	**Date**	**Details**	**£ p**	
2013			2013			
10 Aug	Owl Promotions	5,000.00				

Dr			Owl Promotions			Cr
Date	**Details**	**£ p**	**Date**	**Details**	**£ p**	
2013			2013			
10 Jul	Sales	5,000.00	10 Aug	Bank	5,000.00	

Credit purchases made by a business are recorded in a similar way. If Harry Porter Limited purchases £2,500 of goods from H A Gridd Supplies on 12 July, and is given 30 days in which to pay, the entries in the books will be:

- debit Purchases Account £2,500
- credit H A Gridd Supplies' Account £2,500

Dr			Purchases Account			Cr
Date	**Details**	**£ p**	**Date**	**Details**		**£ p**
2013			2013			
12 Jul	H A Gridd Supplies	2,500.00				

Dr			H A Gridd Supplies			Cr
Date	**Details**	**£ p**	**Date**	**Details**		**£ p**
2013			2013			
			12 Jul	Purchases		2,500.00

Settlement of the invoice by Harry Porter Limited in thirty days' time will be recorded by the bookkeeper with the following entries:

- debit H A Gridd Supplies Account £2,500
- credit Bank Account £2,500 (money paid out)

Dr			H A Gridd Supplies			Cr
Date	**Details**	**£ p**	**Date**	**Details**		**£ p**
2013			2013			
12 Aug	Bank	2,500.00	12 Jul	Purchases		2,500.00

Dr			Bank Account			Cr
Date	**Details**	**£ p**	**Date**	**Details**		**£ p**
2013			2013			
			12 Aug	H A Gridd Supplies		2,500.00

balancing off accounts

You will probably have noticed that in the above examples, the accounts of the customer (Owl Promotions) and the supplier (H A Gridd Supplies) have finished up with the same amounts on each side. In these cases, nothing is owing to Harry Porter Limited, or is owed by Harry Porter Limited.

In practice, as the business trades, there will be many entries on both sides of customer and supplier accounts. It is a useful exercise to balance off each account periodically, to see how much in total each customer owes, and how much is owed to each supplier of the business. This balancing off procedure is also applied to other accounts in the books of the business. A computer accounting system will, of course, do this balancing automatically.

CHAPTER SUMMARY

■   The accounting system of a business involves a number of stages:

- •   financial transactions and the documents they generate

- •   recording and listing of transactions ready for entering in the accounts

- •   entering the data into the accounts of the business – either manual accounts or a computer accounting system

- •   extracting report information from the accounts

■   Double-entry bookkeeping transactions involve two entries, a credit and a debit. Debits are recorded on the left-hand side of an account, credits on the right-hand side.

■   The dual aspect theory of double-entry accounting states that one account gains value (the debit entry) while the other gives value (the credit entry).

■   In practical terms, debit entries include:

- •   money paid into the bank

- •   an expense incurred or a purchase made

- •   an acquisition of an asset or an increase in that asset

- •   money owing by customers (debtors)

■   In practical terms, credit entries include:

- •   money paid out of the bank

- •   income item

- •   a liability incurred or increased

- •   money owed to suppliers (creditors)

KEY TERMS

batch	a group of items totalled together for input into an accounting system
ledger	a section of the accounts of a business
trial balance	a list of the balances of accounts compiled to check the accuracy of the bookkeeping
account activity	a list of the transactions on a particular account
aged debtors analysis	a list of credit customers showing what they owe and if payment is overdue
aged creditors analysis	a list of suppliers showing what they are owed and when payment is due
profit and loss statement	a financial statement showing the amount of profit or loss made by a business
balance sheet	a financial statement showing what a business owns and owes and how it is financed

EXERCISES

You are a trainee accountant in the firm of Arthur Andrews & Co. Your job is to assist with the accounts of start-up businesses, a number of which have no double-entry records. You are to carry out the following tasks. VAT can be ignored here. The answers are on page 236 (immediately after this chapter).

14.1   Will Abbott has kept his bank account up-to-date, but has not got around to the other double-entry items. Rule out the other accounts for him, and make the appropriate entries.

Dr			Bank Account			Cr
2013		£	2013			£
1 Feb	Sales	5,000	1 Feb	Purchases		3,500
2 Feb	Sales	7,500	2 Feb	Wages		2,510
3 Feb	Bank Loan	12,500	3 Feb	Van purchase		12,500
5 Feb	Sales	9,300	3 Feb	Purchases		5,000
			4 Feb	Rent paid		780

14.2   Sarah Banks has opened up a health food shop 'Just Nuts', but has not yet started to write up the books. As she is inexperienced she asks you to set up an accounting system for her.

She provides you with the following list of transactions for the first week's trading, starting on Monday 8 June 2013. You are to enter the double-entry accounts for her.

Monday
Paid £5,000 cheque as capital into the bank; purchases of £4,000, paid by cheque.
Paid £750 sales into the bank; paid week's rent £75 by cheque.

Tuesday
Paid £500 sales into the bank; made purchases of £425 by cheque.

Wednesday
Paid £420 sales into the bank; bought computer £890 by cheque.

Thursday
Paid £550 sales into the bank; made purchases £510 by cheque.

Friday
Paid £925 sales into the bank; paid assistant's wages £75 by cheque.

14.3   Anu Sharma has made a mess of recording entries in the bank account. You are to set out the bank account as it should appear, rule up the other double-entry accounts and make the appropriate entries.

Dr			Bank Account			Cr
2013		£	2013			£
1 Jan	Purchases	1,000	2 Jan	Sales		5,000
5 Jan	Wages	2,700	3 Jan	Sales		7,000
5 Jan	Rent paid	150	4 Jan	Bank Loan		5,500
8 Jan	Rates paid	6,210	9 Jan	Machine purchased		4,000
9 Jan	Sales	5,205	10 Jan	Sales		9,520
10 Jan	Purchases	6,750	12 Jan	Wages		2,850
11 Jan	Car purchase	5,500	12 Jan	Rent paid		150

14.4   Sam McRae is a lazy individual and has not entered up his double-entry accounts. He has listed all his transactions, and mentions that all cheques are paid into the bank account on the day of receipt. You are to draw up the accounts for Sam McRae and make the necessary entries.

2013

1 March   Received £5,000 cheque as loan from brother

2 March   Bought goods £200; paid by cheque

3 March   Bought goods £1,200 on credit from H Lomax

4 March   Sold goods £800; cheque received

5 March   Sold goods £1,200 on credit to V Firth

6 March   Paid rent £955 by cheque

9 March   Bought cash register £1,200 on credit from Broadheath Business Supplies

10 March   Paid wages £780 by cheque

11 March   Bought goods on credit £5,920 from W Gould

12 March   V Firth pays for goods £1,200 by cheque

15 March   Bought goods £1,650 on credit from H Lomax

16 March   Made payment £750 by cheque to H Lomax

ANSWERS TO CHAPTER 14 EXERCISES

Task 14.1

Dr			Sales			Cr
Date	**Details**	**£**	**Date**	**Details**		**£**
			1 Feb	Bank		5,000
			2 Feb	Bank		7,500
			5 Feb	Bank		9,300

Dr			Purchases			Cr
Date	**Details**	**£**	**Date**	**Details**		**£**
1 Feb	Bank	3,500				
3 Feb	Bank	5,000				

Dr			Wages			Cr
Date	**Details**	**£**	**Date**	**Details**		**£**
2 Feb	Bank	2,510				

Dr			Motor vehicles			Cr
Date	**Details**	**£**	**Date**	**Details**		**£**
3 Feb	Bank	12,500				

Dr			Rent paid			Cr
Date	**Details**	**£**	**Date**	**Details**		**£**
4 Feb	Bank	780				

Dr			Bank loan			Cr
Date	**Details**	**£**	**Date**	**Details**		**£**
			3 Feb	Bank		12,500

Task 14.2

Dr					Bank		Cr
Date	Details	£		Date	Details		£
8 Jun	Capital	5,000		8 Jun	Purchases		4,000
8 Jun	Sales	750		8 Jun	Rent		75
9 Jun	Sales	500		9 Jun	Purchases		425
10 Jun	Sales	420		10 Jun	Computer		890
11 Jun	Sales	550		11 Jun	Purchases		510
12 Jun	Sales	925		12 Jun	Wages		75

Dr			Capital			Cr
Date	Details	£	Date	Details		£
			8 Jun	Bank		5,000

Dr			Purchases			Cr
Date	Details	£	Date	Details		£
8 Jun	Bank	4,000				
9 Jun	Bank	425				
11 Jun	Bank	510				

Dr			Sales			Cr
Date	Details	£	Date	Details		£
			8 Jun	Bank		750
			9 Jun	Bank		500
			10 Jun	Bank		420
			11 Jun	Bank		550
			12 Jun	Bank		925

Dr			Computer			Cr
Date	Details	£	Date	Details		£
10 Jun	Bank	890				

Dr		Rent				Cr
Date	Details	£	Date	Details		£
8 Jun	Bank	75				

Dr		Wages				Cr
Date	Details	£	Date	Details		£
12 Jun	Bank	75				

Task 14.3

Dr		Bank			Cr
Date	Details	£	Date	Details	£
2 Jan	Sales	5,000	1 Jan	Purchases	1,000
3 Jan	Sales	7,000	5 Jan	Wages	2,700
4 Jan	Bank loan	5,500	5 Jan	Rent Paid	150
9 Jan	Sales	5,205	8 Jan	Rates paid	6,210
10 Jan	Sales	9,520	9 Jan	Machinery	4,000
			10 Jan	Purchases	6,750
			11 Jan	Motor Veh's	5,500
			12 Jan	Wages	2,850
			12 Jan	Rent paid	150

Dr		Purchases			Cr
Date	Details	£	Date	Details	£
1 Jan	Bank	1,000			
10 Jan	Bank	6,750			

Dr		Sales			Cr
Date	Details	£	Date	Details	£
			2 Jan	Bank	5,000
			3 Jan	Bank	7,000
			9 Jan	Bank	5,205
			10 Jan	Bank	9,520

Dr			Bank loan			Cr
Date	Details	£	Date	Details		£
			4 Jan	Bank		5,500

Dr			Wages			Cr
Date	Details	£	Date	Details		£
5 Jan	Bank	2,700				
12 Jan	Bank	2,850				

Dr			Rent paid			Cr
Date	Details	£	Date	Details		£
5 Jan	Bank	150				
12 Jan	Bank	150				

Dr			Rates paid			Cr
Date	Details	£	Date	Details		£
8 Jan	Bank	6,210				

Dr			Machinery			Cr
Date	Details	£	Date	Details		£
9 Jan	Bank	4,000				

Dr			Motor vehicles			Cr
Date	Details	£	Date	Details		£
11 Jan	Bank	5,500				

Task 14.4

Dr			Bank			Cr
Date	**Details**	**£**	**Date**	**Details**		**£**
1 Mar	Loan	5,000	2 Mar	Purchases		200
4 Mar	Sales	800	6 Mar	Rent		955
12 Mar	V Firth	1,200	10 Mar	Wages		780
			16 Mar	H Lomax		750

Dr			Loan			Cr
Date	**Details**	**£**	**Date**	**Details**		**£**
			1 Mar	Bank		5,000

Dr			Purchases			Cr
Date	**Details**	**£**	**Date**	**Details**		**£**
2 Mar	Bank	200				
3 Mar	H Lomax	1,200				
11 Mar	W Gould	5,920				
15 Mar	H Lomax	1,650				

Dr			H Lomax			Cr
Date	**Details**	**£**	**Date**	**Details**		**£**
16 Mar	Bank	750	3 Mar	Purchases		1,200
			15 Mar	Purchases		1,650

Dr			Sales			Cr
Date	**Details**	**£**	**Date**	**Details**		**£**
			4 Mar	Bank		800
			5 Mar	V Firth		1,200

Dr			V Firth			Cr
Date	**Details**	**£**	**Date**	**Details**		**£**
5 Mar	Sales	1200	12 Mar	Bank		1200

Dr				Rent paid		Cr
Date	Details	£	Date	Details		£
6 Mar	Bank	955				

Dr				Cash register		Cr
Date	Details	£	Date	Details		£
9 Mar	Broadheath	1,200				

Dr				Broadheath Business Supplies		Cr
Date	Details	£	Date	Details		£
			9 Mar	Cash register		1,200

Dr				Wages		Cr
Date	Details	£	Date	Details		£
10 Mar	Bank	780				

Dr				W Gould		Cr
Date	Details	£	Date	Details		£
			11 Mar	Purchases		5,920

EXTENDED EXERCISE –
INTERLINGO TRANSLATION SERVICES

Introduction

This is a 'standalone' extended exercise which puts into practice all the computer accounting skills you will have developed while working through this book. As with the main text, the use of Products, Sales Order Processing, Invoicing and Purchase Order Processing are optional. Activities 4 and 5 use the batch entry system. Activity 6 uses Products, Sales Order Processing, Invoicing and Purchase Order Processing to process the same data. Thus if you wish to use these modules, you can skip Activities 4 and 5.

It features a small company run by Jo Lane who has set up a translation bureau 'Interlingo' which sells language books and CDs as a sideline. Jo has been operating for a month using a manual bookkeeping system and has then decided to set up the accounting records in a Sage system in the second month.

The activities to be covered are:

1   Setting up the business in Sage.

2   Setting up customer and supplier records and inputting opening balances.

3   Setting up the Nominal Ledger in Sage and inputting opening balances from the Trial Balance produced at the end of the first month of trading.

4   Setting up product records, selling from stock and purchasing new stock (optional).

5   Processing and printing stock and service sales invoices and credit notes (optional).

6   Processing purchase invoices and credit notes.

7   Processing payments received – including payments from credit customers, contra entry and cash payments from small translation jobs, and books and CDs over the counter.

8   Processing payments made to suppliers and for running expenses.

9   Setting up a Petty Cash Account and processing Petty Cash Payments.

10   Setting up recurring payments through the bank current account.

11   Printing month-end reports and extracting information from the computer accounting records for use in the business.

ACTIVITY **1** – SETTING UP THE BUSINESS IN SAGE

introduction

Interlingo Translation Services is a small business run by Jo Lane, a linguist who has worked as a translator with the European Commission in Brussels and has now settled back in her home town of Mereford. Jo rents a small office in the town and employs three members of staff.

Interlingo Translation Services provides translation services and also sells books and CDs.

translation services

Larger clients, for example importers and exporters who need documents translated into English and sales literature translated into foreign languages are supplied by Jo on credit terms (ie they are invoiced and pay later).

Small local 'private' translating jobs which come about from local adverts are normally paid for on a cash basis (ie cash or cheque) and are not invoiced.

language books and CDs

Jo has found that selling language books and CDs is a useful sideline. They are all sold on cash and credit terms, but are bought on credit from the publishers.

the accounting system

Interlingo Translation Services was set up on 2 July 2013. The business is registered for VAT and after a month of using a manual accounting system Jo has decided to transfer her accounts to Sage 50 software and sign up for a year's telephone technical support. Her main problem, common to so many small businesses, is that of time – finding time to process her accounts and to see how she is getting on in financial terms.

Jo has chosen Sage 50 because it will enable her to:

- process the invoices issued to customers who are supplied on credit
- record the cash sales of books and CDs and small translation jobs
- pay the publishers of the books and CDs on the due date
- keep a record of money received and paid out
- control the stock of books and CDs
- print out reports which will tell her who has not paid on time
- print out reports which will tell her what she is spending

In short Jo hopes that Sage will help her save time (and money) in running her accounting system.

back-ups

Remember to back-up your data after each inputting Task, just as Jo would.

task 1

Ensure that the computer is set up correctly. A Sage Rebuild may be necessary.

The financial year should be set to start in July 2013. This can be done in SETTINGS or as part of the Rebuild process.

As part of this process you should adopt the 'General Business: Standard Accounts' as the chart of accounts to be used.

task 2

Set up the details of the business in Sage. Company Preferences in SETTINGS can be used if you are not using the ActiveSetup Wizard.

- Enter the address details:

    Interlingo Translation Services

    14 Privet Road

    Mereford

    MR5 1HP

    Tel: 01908 335876

    Fax: 01908 335899

    Email: mail@interlingo.co.uk

    www.interlingo.co.uk

    VAT Reg: 416 1385 51

- Ensure that T1 (standard-rated VAT) is set at 20% (Settings/Configuration/Tax Codes) and that the VAT scheme is set to Standard VAT in (Settings/Company Preferences).

- Set the program date to 31 July 2013 (SETTINGS).

ACTIVITY 2 – SETTING UP THE CUSTOMER AND SUPPLIER RECORDS

introduction

Interlingo Translation sells on credit to five businesses that use its translation services on a regular basis. Jo will have to set up the details of these customers on the computer.

The business also buys its books and CDs from two wholesale suppliers. These will also have to be input onto the computer.

task 1

The defaults for the customers, reached through SETTINGS, should be set up as follows:

Configuration Editor (Terms):

Payment due days	30 days
Terms	Payment 30 days of invoice

Customer Defaults:

VAT rate	20% standard rate (code T1)
Default nominal code	4000

task 2

Input the details and opening balance for each of the five customers through RECORD in CUSTOMERS. The opening balance in each case is the total of the invoice already issued and is a gross amount. You do not need to deal with VAT at this stage. Do not post these invoices as a separate batch.

The credit limits and 'Terms Agreed' will also need to be entered (in the Credit Control tab).

Account name	**RS Export Agency**
Account reference	RS001
Address	46 Chancery Street Mereford MR1 9FD
Contact name	Raspal Singh

Telephone 01908 564187, Fax 01908 564911

Email rsingh@zipnet.co.uk

Credit limit £1,000

Invoice reference 10010 for £850.00 issued on 06 07 13.

Account name	**Playgames PLC**
Account reference	PL001
Address	Consul House
	Viney Street
	Mereford
	MR2 6PL
Contact name	Jacquie Mills

Telephone 01908 749724, Fax 01908 749355
Email mail@playgames.com
www.playgames.com
Credit limit £1,000
Invoice reference 10011 for £795.00 issued on 12 07 13

Account name	**Rotherway Limited**
Account reference	RT001
Address	78 Sparkhouse Street
	Millway
	MY5 8HG
Contact name	Darsha Patel

Telephone 01987 875241, Fax 01987 875267
Email mail@rotherway.co.uk
www.rotherway.co.uk
Credit limit £2,000
Special terms: 2.5% settlement discount for payment within 7 days of invoice date.
No opening balance.

Account name	**Hill & Dale & Co, Solicitors**
Account reference	HD001
Address	17 Berkeley Chambers
	Penrose Street
	Mereford
	MR2 6GF
Contact name	Helen Lexington

Telephone 01908 875432, Fax 01908 875444
Email hlex@hilldale.co.uk
Credit limit £1,000
Invoice reference 10013 for £345.00 issued on 19 07 13.

Account name	**Schafeld Ltd**
Account reference	SC001
Address	86 Tanners Lane
	Millway
	MY7 5VB
Contact name	Hans Rautmann

Telephone 01987 619086, Fax 01987 619097
Email hrautmann@schafeld.com
www.schafeld.com
Credit limit £1,000
Invoice reference 10014 for £800.00 issued on 20 07 13.

task 3

Print out a Day Books: Customer Invoices (Detailed) Report and check your printout against the printout on page 290. The batch total should be £2,790.

task 4

The SUPPLIER defaults (reached through SETTINGS) should be set up as follows:

VAT rate 20% standard rate (code T1)

Default nominal code   5000

task 5

Input the details and opening balance for the two suppliers of books and CDs through RECORD in SUPPLIERS. The credit limits and payment terms agreed will also need to be entered on the Credit Control screen. The 'Terms Agreed' box will also need to be ticked.

Account name	**TDI Wholesalers**
Account reference	TD001
Address	Markway Estate
	Nottingham
	NG1 7GH
Contact name	Ron Beasley

Telephone 0115 295992, Fax 0115 295976, Email sales@tdi.co.uk
www.tdi.co.uk
Credit limit granted £5,000, payment terms 30 days of invoice date
Invoice reference 2347 for £780.00 issued on 05 07 13.
TDI Wholesalers supply Jo with language CDs, which are standard-rated for VAT.

Account name	Bardners Books
Account reference	BB001
Address	Purbeck House
	College Street
	Cambridge
	CB3 8HP
Contact name	Sarah Rooney

Telephone 01223 400652, Fax 01223 400648
Email sales@bardners.co.uk
www.bardners.co.uk
Credit limit granted £2,000, payment terms 30 days of invoice date
Invoice reference 9422 for £420.00 issued on 06 07 13.
Bardners Books supply Jo with language books, which are zero-rated for VAT. This supplier account may therefore be set up with a default tax code of T0.

task 6

Print out a Day Books: Supplier Invoices (Detailed) Report and check your printout against the printout on page 290. The batch total should be £1,200.

task 7

Print out a Trial Balance Report for July from FINANCIALS to check the total of the Debtors Control Account (the total of the Customer invoices) and the Creditors Control Account (the total of the Supplier invoices). The report should appear as follows:

Interlingo Translation Services
Period Trial Balance

Page: 1

To Period: Month 1, July 2013

N/C	Name	Debit	Credit
1100	Debtors Control Account	2,790.00	
2100	Creditors Control Account		1,200.00
9998	Suspense Account		1,590.00
	Totals:	2,790.00	2,790.00

Reminder! Have you made a back-up?

ACTIVITY 3 – SETTING UP THE NOMINAL LEDGER

introduction

Interlingo Translation Services has been set up in Sage with a default Chart of Accounts (nominal accounts list) which can be used as a structure for the nominal account balances which were outstanding at the end of July.

Jo has already set up a Trial Balance on a spreadsheet. The figures are shown below. The right-hand column shows the Nominal Account number which Jo has allocated to each account from the list of Nominal Accounts. The grey backgrounds show where the default account name needs changing.

	Dr	Cr	Account
	£	£	
Office computers	5,000		0020
Office equipment	2,500		0030
Furniture and fixtures	3,000		0040
Debtors control account	2,790		1100
Bank current account	8,295		1200
Creditors control account		1,200	2100
Sales tax control account		814	2200
Purchase tax control account	623		2201
P.A.Y.E.		700	2210
National Insurance		900	2211
Loans		5,000	2300
Ordinary Shares		15,000	3000
Translation services income		3,660	4000
Sales of language books		456	4100
Sales of language CDs		950	4101
Purchases of books	300		5000
Purchases of CDs	750		5001
Advertising	550		6201
Gross wages	3,600		7000
Rent	250		7100
General rates	129		7103
Electricity	61		7200
Postage & Carriage	86		7501
Office Stationery	471		7502
Telephone and Fax	275		7550
	28,680	28,680	

task 1

Ensure the program date is set at 31 July 2013.

Select the accounts that you wish to enter in the records from the NOMINAL opening screen. Use the account numbers in the right-hand column. Do not worry if the account names are different - they will be amended in Task 3. But do not select the Debtors Control Account or the Creditors Control Account as they should already show their balances.

Select RECORD from NOMINAL and enter the balance of each account from the Trial Balance, using the 31 July date. You may need to click on the Balance field or the O/B button to bring up the balance entry screen. Ensure that the amount is recorded in the correct debit or credit box.

task 2

Print out a Trial Balance for July 2013 from FINANCIALS. Check it against the one on page 291.

task 3

Now change the account names that need changing (see the accounts with grey backgrounds on page 249) in RECORD in NOMINAL. Print out a further Trial Balance to check your corrections. The print out should appear as shown below. Check your input against this Report.

Interlingo Translation Services
Period Trial Balance

To Period: Month 1, July 2013

N/C	Name	Debit	Credit
0020	Office Computers	5,000.00	
0030	Office Equipment	2,500.00	
0040	Furniture and Fixtures	3,000.00	
1100	Debtors Control Account	2,790.00	
1200	Bank Current Account	8,295.00	
2100	Creditors Control Account		1,200.00
2200	Sales Tax Control Account		814.00
2201	Purchase Tax Control Account	623.00	
2210	P.A.Y.E.		700.00
2211	National Insurance		900.00
2300	Loans		5,000.00
3000	Ordinary Shares		15,000.00
4000	Translation services income		3,660.00
4100	Sales of language books		456.00
4101	Sales of language CDs		950.00
5000	Purchases of books	300.00	
5001	Purchases of CDs	750.00	
6201	Advertising	550.00	
7000	Gross Wages	3,600.00	
7100	Rent	250.00	
7103	General Rates	129.00	
7200	Electricity	61.00	
7501	Postage and Carriage	86.00	
7502	Office Stationery	471.00	
7550	Telephone and Fax	275.00	
	Totals:	28,680.00	28,680.00

Reminder! Have you made a back-up?
This back-up is very important as you may need to restore it at the beginning of Activity 6 on page 254

ACTIVITY 4 – ISSUING INVOICES AND CREDIT NOTES

introduction

It is 31 August and Jo has to process customer invoices and a credit note for work done during the month. She uses batch entry to enter the details into Sage 50.

task 1

Set the program date to 31 August 2013. Input the following invoices using the batch entry system. Be careful to code books as zero-rated for VAT (T0).

invoice	account	date	net	VAT	description
10015	HD001	10 08 2013	520.00	104.00	Translation of sales contracts
10016	PL001	16 08 2013	120.00	24.00	Translation of sales literature
10017	RS001	20 08 2013	100.00	20.00	Translation of shipping docs
10018	SC001	20 08 2013	160.00	32.00	Translation of sales contracts
10019	RT001	22 08 2013	320.00	62.40*	16 Beginners French CDs
10020	RT001	31 08 2013	180.00	0.00	10 German First Course books
10020	RT001	31 08 2013	220.00	0.00	10 French Second Course books
10020	RT001	31 08 2013	480.00	93.60*	20 Advanced Italian CDs

Note: the VAT value is reduced because of the settlement discount offered. You may need to amend the VAT figure in Sage.

task 2

Hill & Dale & Co, who have passed substantial work to Interlingo, have written formally to ask for a 10% discount backdated to the beginning of the month.

Amend the customer record and enter the following credit note to Hill & Dale & Co:

ref	account	date	net	VAT	description
501	HD001	31 08 2013	52.00	10.40	Refund of 10% discount, invoice 10015

task 3

Print out detailed Day Books reports for the customer invoices and credit note entered. Check them against those on page 292.

Reminder! Have you made a back-up?

ACTIVITY 5 – PROCESSING PURCHASE INVOICES AND CREDIT NOTES

introduction

Jo's purchases on credit are her supplies of language CDs and books. During August she received two invoices in total. They are shown below and on the next page.

task 1

Set the program date to 31 August 2013.

Input the two invoices below and on the next page as a batch into Invoices in SUPPLIERS.

Note that the Nominal code for CDs is 5001 and for books is 5000.

task 2

Interlingo's customer RS Export Agency supplies delivery services for Interlingo and is therefore both a customer and a supplier. A supplier account should be set up (see page 245 for address details) using an appropriate account number and then the following supplier invoice details entered. The nominal code is 5100 (Carriage).

invoice	date	net	VAT	description
72/554	15 08 2013	100.00	20.00	Same day delivery to London

task 3

Print out a Day Books: Supplier Invoices (Detailed) and check your printout against the printout on page 293. The transaction dates are 15 August to 20 August. The total should be £3,069.75.

INVOICE

TDI Wholesalers
Markway Estate, Nottingham, NG1 7GH
Tel 0115 295992 Fax 0115 295976 www.TDI.co.uk

invoice to

Interlingo Translation Services	
14 Privet Road	
Mereford	
MR5 1HP	

invoice no	2561
account	3023
your reference	13
date/tax point	15 08 13

product code	description	quantity	price	unit	net	VAT	total
2421	Beginners French CDs	100	10.00	set	1000.00	200.00	1200.00
2634	Advanced Italian CDs	50	12.00	set	600.00	120.00	720.00
					goods total		1600.00
					VAT		320.00
					TOTAL		1920.00

INVOICE

BARDNERS BOOKS

Purbeck House, College Street, Cambridge CB3 8HP
Tel 01223 400652 Fax 01223 400648 www.Bardners.co.uk

invoice to

Interlingo Translation Services	
14 Privet Road	
Mereford	
MR5 1HP	

invoice no	11231
account	IL9987
your reference	14
date/tax point	20 08 13

product code	description	quantity	price	unit	total	VAT zero-rate	total
G778	German First Course	60	8.95	each	537.00	00.00	537.00
2634	French Second Course	45	10.95	each	492.75	00.00	492.75
					goods total		1029.75
					VAT		00.00
					TOTAL		1029.75

task 4

Jo discovers that ten of the sets of Beginners French CDs are faulty. She sends them back and asks for a credit note. This arrives on 31 August. Input the document (see below) into Credit in SUPPLIERS (Nominal Code 5001) and print out a Day Books: Suppliers Credits (Detailed) Report. Check your printout against the printout on page 293.

credit note from TDI Wholesalers (extract)

Interlingo Translation Services	
14 Privet Road	
Mereford	
MR5 1HP	

credit note no	1919
account	3023
your reference	13
date/tax point	28 08 13

product code	description	quantity	price	unit	net	VAT	total
2421	Beginners French CDs	10	10.00	set	100.00	20.00	120.00
					goods total		100.00
					VAT		20.00
					TOTAL		120.00

REASON FOR CREDIT
Faulty CDs returned

Reminder! Have you made a back-up?

ACTIVITY 6 – PRODUCTS, ORDER PROCESSING AND INVOICING

The data in Activity 6 is the same as in Activities 4 and 5 but is processed using the Products, Sales Order Processing, Invoicing and Purchase Order Processing modules rather than by 'batch entry'. If you have already worked through Activities 4 and 5 and you wish to use these modules, you will need to restore the back-up taken at the end of Activity 3 on page 250 (see page 15 for how to restore). If not, skip to Activity 7.

introduction

During August Jo has the following tasks to perform:

■ Enter her stock of products into the computer system.

■ Re-order stock and process supplier invoices and credit notes

■ Process customer orders and raise customer invoices and credit notes

task 1

It is 1 August. Set up product records for the following items as at 1 August. Decide on your own product codes. Ensure the correct sales and purchase nominal codes are entered and that the default VAT code for books is zero-rated (T0).

Print out or preview a Product Details report and compare it with the one on page 294. Your codes may be different.

supplier	description	category	nominal code (sales)	opening balance	cost price (£)	sales price (£)
TDI Wholesalers	Beginners French CD	CDs	4101	33	10.00	20.00 each
TDI Wholesalers	Advanced Italian CD	CDs	4101	29	12.00	24.00 each
Bardners Books	German First Course	Books	4100	19	8.95	18.00 each
Bardners Books	French Second Course	Books	4100	11	10.95	22.00 each

task 2

Place the following orders with suppliers for the above stock items, using PURCHASE ORDER PROCESSING. Set the auto-numbering for purchase orders to start at 13. The purchase code for CDs is 5001 and for Books 5000. Print or preview a Purchase Order List and compare it with the one on page 295.

Order no 13

Date 07 08 13

TDI Wholesalers

100 Beginners French CDs @ £10.00 each

50 Advanced Italian CDs @ £12.00 each

Order no 14

Date 07 08 13

Bardners Books

60 German First Course Books @ £8.95 each

45 French Second Course Books @ £10.95 each

task 3

Enter the delivery of orders placed with suppliers (see Task 2) as follows:

Order no 13   TDI Wholesalers

10 08 13   All goods delivered

Order no 14   Bardners Books

15 08 13   30 German First Course Books (30 to follow)

45 French Second course Books

Order no 15   Bardners Books

20 08 13   30 German First Course Books (balance of order)

task 4

Enter supplier invoices as shown on pages 252-253 using the PURCHASE ORDER PROCESSING Update option. Print or preview a Day Books: Supplier Invoices (Detailed) report and check it against the one on page 295.

task 5

On 20 August Jo discovered that 10 of the Beginners French CDs were faulty and returned them to the supplier. She used the Products "Out" option to reduce the stock figure. Process the credit note shown on page 253. NB This cannot be done through PURCHASE ORDER PROCESSING. It must be entered as a batch credit note.

task 6

Process the following service sales invoices using INVOICING. Note: this can be done either by using the Service option in the invoicing form and typing in the text, or by setting up "non-stock" or "service" product records for these items in the PRODUCTS module. You will need to set the auto-numbering function for invoicing to start at 10015. Do not update the ledgers yet.

invoice no	account	date	net	VAT	description
10015	HD001	10 08 13	520.00	104.00	Translation of sales contracts
10016	PL001	16 08 13	120.00	24.00	Translation of sales literature
10017	RS001	20 08 13	100.00	20.00	Translation of shipping documents
10018	SC001	20 08 13	160.00	32.00	Translation of sales contracts

task 7

Process the following sales orders from stock and produce relevant sales invoices. For simplicity, the dates for sales order, product delivery and sales invoice can be on the same day. Do not update the ledgers yet.

account	cust order ref	order date	net	VAT	description
RT001	13/79	22 08 13	320.00	62.40	16 Beginners French CDs @ £20.00 each
RT001	13/80	31 08 13	880.00	93.60	20 Advanced Italian CDs @ £24.00 each
					10 German First Course @ £18.00 each
					10 French Second Course @ £22.00 each

task 8

Jo has agreed that her customer Hill & Dale & Co should receive 10% discount in return for substantial translation work given to Interlingo. This is to be backdated to the beginning of the month. First amend the auto-numbering for credit notes to start at 501 and then raise a service credit note in INVOICING as follows:

account	credit note no.	date	net	VAT	description
HD001	501	31 08 13	52.00	10.40	Refund of 10% discount, invoice 10015

Finally amend the customer record to include the new discount arrangement.

Now update the sales ledger with invoices and credit notes raised in tasks 6, 7 and 8. Print the Update Ledgers report and check it against the one on page 296.

task 9

Interlingo's customer RS Export Agency supplies delivery services for Interlingo and is therefore both a customer and a supplier. A supplier account should be set up (see page 245 for address details) using an appropriate account number and then the following supplier invoice details entered. The nominal code is 5100 (Carriage).

invoice	date	net	VAT	description
72/554	15 08 2013	100.00	20.00	Same day delivery to London

Reminder! Have you made a back-up?

ACTIVITY 7 – PROCESSING PAYMENTS RECEIVED

introduction

Jo has received payments from a number of different sources during August:

- payments from customers who have bought on credit during July
- cash payments for small translation jobs
- cash payments for books and CDs

They all have to be input into the computer accounting system.

task 1

Ensure the program date is set at 31 August 2013.

Input in BANK (Customer) the following payments received during August and paid into the bank current account on the dates indicated. The reference number is the paying-in slip number.

account	date	customer	amount (£)	reference
HD001	09 08 13	Hill & Dale & Co	345.00	100110
PL001	16 08 13	Playgames PLC	795.00	100112
RS001	23 08 13	RS Export Agency	850.00	100114
RT001	26 08 13	Rotherway Limited	*374.40	100116
SC001	31 08 13	Schafeld Ltd	800.00	100118
		Total	3,164.40	

This pays invoice 10019 less settlement discount of £8.00.

task 2

Print out a Day Books: Customer Receipts (Summary) report for the month from BANK and check your printout against the printout on page 296.

task 3

Jo has also paid the takings from cash sales (ie from small translation jobs, books and CDs) into the bank current account each week. She has totalled up each week's takings from these three sources and paid them in on one paying-in slip each Friday (the reference is shown in the right-hand column). The manual records she has kept show the cash receipts as follows:

date paid in	description	net	VAT	gross	reference
9 08 2013	Translations	96.00	19.20	115.20	100111
	CDs	240.00	48.00	288.00	
	Books	160.00	T0 code	160.00	
	Paying-in slip total			563.20	
16 08 2013	Translations	116.00	23.20	139.20	100113
	CDs	180.00	36.00	216.00	
	Books	107.00	T0 code	107.00	
	Paying-in slip total			462.20	
23 08 2013	Translations	104.00	20.80	124.80	100115
	CDs	220.00	44.00	264.00	
	Books	84.00	T0 code	84.00	
	Paying-in slip total			472.80	
30 08 2013	Translations	82.00	16.40	98.40	100117
	CDs	190.00	38.00	228.00	
	Books	113.00	T0 code	113.00	
	Paying-in slip total			439.40	

Input each of these cash receipts in BANK as BANK RECEIPTS. Remember to use the correct Nominal Codes for each type of sale: 4000 for translations, 4100 for books, 4101 for CDs. The reference in the right-hand column is the paying-in slip reference and should be used for each line of input.

You could use the Memorise/Recall option here if you wish. After entering the first bank receipt on 9 August, but before saving, click Memorise and give the file a name (eg Cash Sales). Now Save but when you are ready to enter the next receipt for 16 August, click Recall and choose the file saved. You will simply need to amend some of the details before saving. You can recall the file as many times as you like.

task 4

Print out a Day Books: Bank Receipts (Detailed) Report for the month from BANK and check your printout against the printout on page 297.

task 5

Process a set off (contra entry) for the amount owed by RS Export Agency against the amount owed to RS Export Agency. Use the Contra Entries option in the Tools menu.

task 6

Some cash customers pay Interlingo by debit or credit card. Jo enters these into the Card Receipts account (1250) in BANK and transfers the totals when they appear on her bank statement.

Input the receipts detailed below. The amounts are inclusive of VAT where the item is VATable so you will need to calculate the goods value and VAT. Preview or print a Day Books: Credit Card Receipts (Detailed) Report and check it against the one on page 297.

date	ref	details	total value
30 08 13	Cards	Card sales CDs	120.00
30 08 13	Cards	Card sales books	72.00

Reminder! Have you made a back-up?

ACTIVITY **8** – PAYING SUPPLIERS AND EXPENSES

introduction

During August Jo has had to pay her suppliers (of books and CDs) who have invoiced her in July on 30 days terms. She has also had to pay a number of expenses.

task 1

Ensure the program date is set at 31 August 2013.

Input in BANK (Supplier) these two outstanding items which were paid on 2 August:

TDI Wholesalers	Invoice 2347	£780.00	Due 05 08 2013	Cheque 120006
Bardners Books	Invoice 9422	£420.00	Due 06 08 2013	Cheque 120007

If possible, print out remittance advices from the computer to accompany the cheques.

task 2

Print out a Day Books: Supplier Payments (Summary) report for 2 August from BANK and check your printout against the printout on page 298.

task 3

Input the following expense payments through Payment in BANK.

In most cases you will need to work out the nominal codes from the Trial Balance on page 250.

The cheque number should be used as the reference.

The tax code is T1 unless indicated otherwise.

date	cheque	details	net	VAT
07 08 2013	120009	Office furniture	140.00	28.00
08 08 2013	120010	Advertising	600.00	120.00
15 08 2013	120011	Rent	250.00	50.00
17 08 2013	120012	Stationery	126.00	25.20
20 08 2013	120013	Rates	129.00	T2
22 08 2013	BACS	HMRC	1,600.00*	T9
22 08 2013	120014	Telephone	186.00	37.20
24 08 2013	120015	Electricity	84.00	16.80
30 08 2013	120016	Postages	45.60	T2
		Totals	3,160.60	277.20
				3,437.80

*This pays PAYE £700 and NI £900 due for July. You will need to enter this payment on two lines: £700 coded 2210 and £900 coded 2211

task 4

Print out a Day Books: Bank Payments (Detailed) report for 7-31 August from BANK and check your printout against the printout on page 298.

task 5

Jo has a company credit card for telephone and online cash purchases. She enters this expenditure on the Company Credit Card account (1240) in BANK. She will transfer the total amount due to the card merchant from the Bank Account to the Card Account when it is taken by direct debit from the Bank Account at the end of next month.

Input the following card payment made on 19 August. Choose the appropriate nominal code for advertising. Use a reference of "C/Card".

£84 inclusive of VAT paid to Mereford Publications for advertising in specialist language magazine

Print or preview a Day Books: Credit Card Payments (Detailed) report and check it against the one on page 299.

Reminder! Have you made a back-up?

ACTIVITY 9 – SETTING UP A PETTY CASH SYSTEM

introduction

Jo finds that her office assistant, Ella, often needs to make small payments in cash for items such as postage stamps and stationery for the office. She therefore decides to set up a petty cash system and cashes a cheque for £80 on 6 August to provide the funds.

task 1

Set the program date to 31 August 2013.

Process a Transfer in BANK for the £80 cheque (No. 120008) cashed on 6 August 2013. The accounts involved are Bank Current Account 1200 and Petty Cash Account 1230.

task 2

Input into BANK (Payments) Petty Cash Account the transactions represented by the four petty cash vouchers shown below and on the next page.

Note that on one of them you will have to calculate the VAT on screen.

Postage stamps are VAT exempt (Tax code T2).

task 3

Print out a Day Books: Cash Payments (Detailed) report from BANK and check your printout against the printout on page 299. Remember to select Petty Cash Account on the Bank opening screen first.

The net total should be £72.00 and the VAT total £7.20.

petty cash voucher		Number *0001*	
	date	*7 Aug 2013*	
description			amount
		£	p
Copy paper		*16*	*00*
		16	*00*
	VAT	*3*	*20*
VAT receipt obtained		*19*	*20*
signature	*Ella Smith*		
authorised	*Jo Lane*		

petty cash voucher   Number *0002*

                                          date   *7 Aug 2013*

description   amount

                                          | £ | p |
Postage stamps | 24 | 00 |

                              VAT | | |
                                          | 24 | 00 |

signature   *Ella Smith*
authorised   *Jo Lane*

---

petty cash voucher   Number *0003*

                                          date   *15 Aug 2013*

description   amount

                                          | £ | p |
Box files | 24 | 00 |

                              VAT | | |
Receipt obtained (VAT not shown) | 24 | 00 |

signature   *Ella Smith*
authorised   *Jo Lane*

> note that the receipt in this case does not show the VAT that has been charged – it will have to be worked out on input

---

petty cash voucher   Number *0004*

                                          date   *22 Aug 2013*

description   amount

                                          | £ | p |
Postage stamps | 12 | 00 |

                              VAT | | |
                                          | 12 | 00 |

signature   *Ella Smith*
authorised   *Jo Lane*

Reminder! Have you made a back-up?

ACTIVITY **10** – SETTING UP RECURRING PAYMENTS IN BANK

introduction

Jo has set up monthly standing order and direct debit payments through the bank current account. She can process these in Sage by setting up Recurring Payments in RECURRING in BANK. Click on the ADD button at the bottom of the screen to bring up the necessary window.

task 1

Set up a Recurring Payment for the following:

Bank Account	1200
Payment type	Direct Debit (Transaction ref: DD)
Payee	Suresafe Insurance (premises insurance)
Nominal code	7104
Tax code	T2
Amount	£98.50 per month
Frequency	12 monthly payments, starting 10 August 2013

task 2

Set up a Recurring Payment for the following:

Bank Account	1200
Payment type	Standing order (Transaction ref: STO)
Payee	Albion Bank (standing charge)
Nominal code	7901
Tax code	T2
Amount	£15.00 per month
Frequency	Monthly, until further notice, starting 25 August 2013

task 3

Set the program date to 31 August 2013 and process the Recurring Payments for August in BANK.

task 4

Print out a Trial Balance of the business as at 31 August 2013. It should agree with the Trial Balance shown on the next page.

Interlingo Translation Services
Period Trial Balance

To Period: Month 2, August 2013

N/C	Name	Debit	Credit
0020	Office Computers	5,000.00	
0030	Office Equipment	2,500.00	
0040	Furniture and Fixtures	3,140.00	
1100	Debtors Control Account	1,871.20	
1200	Bank Current Account	8,565.70	
1230	Petty Cash	0.80	
1240	Company Credit Card		84.00
1250	Credit Card Receipts	192.00	
2100	Creditors Control Account		2,829.75
2200	Sales Tax Control Account		1,405.20
2201	Purchase Tax Control Account	1,241.40	
2300	Loans		5,000.00
3000	Ordinary Shares		15,000.00
4000	Translation services income		4,906.00
4009	Discounts Allowed	8.00	
4100	Sales of language books		1,392.00
4101	Sales of language CDs		2,680.00
5000	Purchases of books	1,329.75	
5001	Purchases of CDs	2,250.00	
5100	Carriage	100.00	
6201	Advertising	1,220.00	
7000	Gross Wages	3,600.00	
7100	Rent	500.00	
7103	General Rates	258.00	
7104	Premises Insurance	98.50	
7200	Electricity	145.00	
7501	Postage and Carriage	167.60	
7502	Office Stationery	633.00	
7550	Telephone and Fax	461.00	
7901	Bank Charges	15.00	
	Totals:	**33,296.95**	**33,296.95**

Trial Balance of Interlingo Translation Services as at 31 August 2013

Reminder! Have you made a back-up?

ACTIVITY 11 – JOURNALS

task 1

Jo made a payment of £600.00 plus VAT on 8 08 13 (cheque no 120010) coded as Advertising. £200.00 of this was for the printing of marketing brochures.

Process a journal, reference 13/11 dated 26 August, to transfer £200.00 from Advertising (6201) to P.R. Literature and Brochures (6203). There is no need to amend VAT.

task 2

Also on 26 August Jo prepares wages for her small team of employees, payable on the last day of the month. The values she has calculated are as follows:

Pay element	£
Gross pay	4,210
Tax	718
National Insurance (employee)	433
National Insurance (employer)	500
Net pay	3,059

Process a journal reference 13/12 to enter these values into the accounts in preparation for pay day.

task 3

Print out a Day Books: Nominal Ledger Report for 26 August and compare it to that on page 300.

Reminder! Have you made a back-up?

ACTIVITY **12** – END-OF-MONTH PROCEDURES

introduction

At the end of August Jo is ready to print out her end-of-month reports.

task 1

Jo has printed a bank statement online, shown below. Carry out a bank reconciliation as at 31 August 2013. You will also need to match the Contra Receipt and Contra Payment on screen to reconcile them.

ALBION BANK PLC				
Online statement of account as at: 31 08 2013				
Account 90 47 17 11894422 Interlingo Translation Services Ltd				
		Paid out	Paid in	Balance
31/07/2013	Balance b/f			8295.00
05/08/2013	120006	780.00		7515.00
05/08/2013	120007	420.00		7095.00
06/08/2013	120008	80.00		7015.00
09/08/2013	Credit 100111		563.20	7578.20
09/08/2013	120009	168.00		7410.20
09/08/2013	Credit 100110		345.00	7755.20
10/08/2013	DD Suresafe	98.50		7656.70
10/08/2013	120010	720.00		6936.70
16/08/2013	Credit 100112		795.00	7731.70
16/08/2013	Credit 100113		462.20	8193.90
19/08/2013	120011	300.00		7893.90
19/08/2013	120012	151.20		7742.70
22/08/2013	BACS HMRC	1600.00		6142.70
22/08/2013	120013	129.00		6013.70
23/08/2013	Credit 100114		850.00	6863.70
23/08/2013	Credit 100115		472.80	7336.50
25/08/2013	Albion Bank	15.00		7321.50
26/08/2013	Credit 100116		374.40	7695.90
30/08/2013	Credit 100117		439.40	8135.30
30/08/2013	Credit 100118		800.00	8935.30

Print a Bank Reconciliation Report and check it against the one on page 301.

task 2

Preview or print the following reports and check them where shown:

- an Aged Debtors Analysis (Summary) from Reports in CUSTOMERS (see page 301)

- a Summary Audit Trail from Reports in FINANCIALS (see pages 302-303)

task 3

Jo offers a settlement discount to her account customer Rotherway Limited. Obtain a Customer Activity (Detailed) Report (see page 304).

task 4

Print out a Supplier Activity (Detailed) Report for TDI Wholesalers (see page 304).

task 5

Jim Draxman, a friend of Jo, who is helping her with her marketing, asks her for a list of the names and addresses of her customers as soon as possible.

Produce a suitable list, either from Labels or from a Customer Address List Report (both accessible in CUSTOMERS) ready for sending electronically by email (see page 305).

Reminder! Have you made a back-up?

SAGE PRINTOUT CHECKLIST

The Sage printouts that follow are provided so that students and individuals carrying out the processing exercises and extended activities can periodically check their progress.

The page numbers for the relevant printouts can be found by referring to the index below.

Chapter 4

Task 3

Pronto Supplies Limited

Day Books: Customer Invoices (Summary)

Date From:	01/01/2013					Customer From:		
Date To:	31/01/2013					Customer To:	ZZZZZZZ	

Transaction From:	1
Transaction To:	99,999,999

Tran No.	Items	Tp	Date	A/C Ref	Inv Ref	Details	Net Amount	Tax Amount	Gross Amount
1	1	SI	05/01/2013	JB001	10013	Opening Balance	5,500.00	0.00	5,500.00
2	1	SI	05/01/2013	CH001	10014	Opening Balance	2,400.00	0.00	2,400.00
3	1	SI	09/01/2013	CR001	10015	Opening Balance	3,234.00	0.00	3,234.00
4	1	SI	10/01/2013	DB001	10016	Opening Balance	3,400.00	0.00	3,400.00
5	1	SI	10/01/2013	KD001	10017	Opening Balance	6,500.00	0.00	6,500.00
6	1	SI	17/01/2013	LG001	10019	Opening Balance	8,500.00	0.00	8,500.00
						Totals:	29,534.00	0.00	29,534.00

Task 4

Pronto Supplies Limited

Day Books: Supplier Invoices (Summary)

Date From:	01/01/2013					Supplier From:		
Date To:	31/01/2013					Supplier To:	ZZZZZZZ	

Transaction From:	1
Transaction To:	99,999,999

Tran No.	Item	Type	Date	A/C Ref	Inv Ref	Details	Net Amount	Tax Amount	Gross Amount
7	1	PI	04/01/2013	DE001	4563	Opening Balance	5,750.00	0.00	5,750.00
8	1	PI	05/01/2013	EL001	8122	Opening Balance	8,500.00	0.00	8,500.00
9	1	PI	09/01/2013	MA001	9252	Opening Balance	4,500.00	0.00	4,500.00
						Totals	18,750.00	0.00	18,750.00

Task 5

Pronto Supplies Limited

Period Trial Balance

To Period: Month 1, January 2013

N/C	Name	Debit	Credit
1100	Debtors Control Account	29,534.00	
2100	Creditors Control Account		18,750.00
9998	Suspense Account		10,784.00
	Totals:	29,534.00	29,534.00

Chapter 6

Task 4

Pronto Supplies Limited

Day Books: Customer Invoices (Detailed)

Date From:	11/02/2013							Customer From:			
Date To:	15/02/2013							Customer To:	ZZZZZZZZ		
Transaction From:	1							N/C From:			
Transaction To:	99,999,999							N/C To:	99999999		
Dept From:	0										
Dept To:	999										

Tran No.	Type	Date	A/C Ref	N/C	Inv Ref	Dept.	Details	Net Amount	Tax Amount	T/C	Gross Amount	V	B
54	SI	11/02/2013	DB001	4000	10027	0	1 x Printer EF102 Multi	600.00	120.00	T1	720.00	N	-
55	SI	12/02/2013	LG001	4000	10028	0	2 x Zap external drive	162.00	32.40	T1	194.40	N	-
56	SI	13/02/2013	KD001	4001	10029	0	1 x Macroworx software V9	450.00	87.30	T1	537.30	N	-
57	SI	15/02/2013	CH001	4000	10030	0	2 x Monitor 17 inch	200.00	40.00	T1	240.00	N	-
58	SI	15/02/2013	JB001	4002	10031	0	2 hours consultancy	108.00	21.60	T1	129.60	N	-
							Totals:	1,520.00	301.30		1,821.30		

Task 5

Pronto Supplies Limited

Day Books: Customer Credits (Detailed)

Date From:	12/02/2013							Customer From:			
Date To:	13/02/2013							Customer To:	ZZZZZZZZ		
Transaction From:	1							N/C From:			
Transaction To:	99,999,999							N/C To:	99999999		
Dept From:	0										
Dept To:	999										

Tran No.	Type	Date	A/C Ref	N/C	Inv Ref	Dept.	Details	Net Amount	Tax Amount	T/C	Gross Amount	V	B
59	SC	12/02/2013	CH001	4000	553	0	1 x Power lead 3 mtr	16.00	3.20	T1	19.20	N	-
60	SC	13/02/2013	CR001	4000	554	0	1 x Zap USB flash memory drive	20.00	4.00	T1	24.00	N	-
							Totals:	36.00	7.20		43.20		

Task 5

Pronto Supplies Limited

Period Trial Balance

To Period: Month 2, February 2013

N/C	Name	Debit	Credit
0020	Plant and Machinery	35,000.00	
0030	Office Equipment	15,000.00	
0040	Furniture and Fixtures	25,000.00	
1100	Debtors Control Account	31,907.30	
1200	Bank Current Account	14,656.00	
2100	Creditors Control Account		18,750.00
2200	Sales Tax Control Account		18,313.30
2201	Purchase Tax Control Account	26,600.00	
2300	Loans		35,000.00
3000	Ordinary Shares		75,000.00
4000	Computer hardware sales		86,302.00
4001	Computer software sales		15,450.00
4002	Computer consultancy		2,628.00
5000	Materials Purchased	69,100.00	
6201	Advertising	12,400.00	
7000	Gross Wages	16,230.00	
7100	Rent	4,500.00	
7103	General Rates	450.00	
7200	Electricity	150.00	
7502	Office Stationery	175.00	
7550	Telephone and Fax	275.00	
	Totals:	251,443.30	251,443.30

Chapter 7

Task 3

Pronto Supplies Limited

Day Books: Supplier Invoices (Detailed)

Date From:		25/02/2013						**Supplier From:**			DE001	
Date To:		25/02/2013						**Supplier To:**			DE001	
Transaction From:		1						**N/C From:**				
Transaction To:		99,999,999						**N/C To:**			99999999	
Dept From:		0										
Dept To:		999										

Tran No.	Type	Date	A/C Ref	N/C	Inv Ref	Dept	Details	Net Amount	Tax Amount	T/C	Gross Amount	V	B
66	PI	25/02/2013	DE001	0030	11377	0	Laptop X70	400.00	78.00	T1	478.00	N	-
67	PI	25/02/2013	DE001	0030	11377	0	Laser Multi-Printer P28	360.00	70.20	T1	430.20	N	-
							Totals	760.00	148.20		908.20		

Pronto Supplies Limited
Period Trial Balance

To Period: Month 2, February 2013

N/C	Name	Debit	Credit
0020	Plant and Machinery	35,000.00	
0030	Office Equipment	15,760.00	
0040	Furniture and Fixtures	25,000.00	
1100	Debtors Control Account	31,907.30	
1200	Bank Current Account	14,656.00	
2100	Creditors Control Account		30,172.60
2200	Sales Tax Control Account		18,313.30
2201	Purchase Tax Control Account	28,500.60	
2300	Loans		35,000.00
3000	Ordinary Shares		75,000.00
4000	Computer hardware sales		86,302.00
4001	Computer software sales		15,450.00
4002	Computer consultancy		2,628.00
5000	Materials Purchased	77,862.00	
6201	Advertising	12,400.00	
7000	Gross Wages	16,230.00	
7100	Rent	4,500.00	
7103	General Rates	450.00	
7200	Electricity	150.00	
7502	Office Stationery	175.00	
7550	Telephone and Fax	275.00	
	Totals:	262,865.90	262,865.90

Chapter 8

Task 2

Pronto Supplies Limited
Product Details

Page: 1

| Product From: | | Category From: | 1 |
| Product To: | ZZZZZZZZZZZZ | Category To: | 999 |

| **Product Code:** | AP300 | **Product Description:** | Power lead 3 mtr |

Category:	3	In Stock:	6.00	Units of Sale:	each
Category Desc:	Accessories and peripherals	On Order:	0.00	Supplier part refn:	
Department Code:	0	Allocated:	0.00	Supplier A/C:	
Tax Code:	T1	Location:		Purchase Price:	9.50
Nominal Code:	4000	Selling Price:	16.00	Reorder Level:	0.00
Date Last Pur:		Last Purchase Qty:	0.00	Date Last Sale:	

| **Product Code:** | AP301 | **Product Description:** | Zap external drive |

Category:	3	In Stock:	5.00	Units of Sale:	each
Category Desc:	Accessories and peripherals	On Order:	0.00	Supplier part refn:	
Department Code:	0	Allocated:	0.00	Supplier A/C:	
Tax Code:	T1	Location:		Purchase Price:	52.00
Nominal Code:	4000	Selling Price:	90.00	Reorder Level:	0.00
Date Last Pur:		Last Purchase Qty:	0.00	Date Last Sale:	

| **Product Code:** | AP302 | **Product Description:** | Zap USB flash memory drive |

Category:	3	In Stock:	9.00	Units of Sale:	pack 5
Category Desc:	Accessories and peripherals	On Order:	0.00	Supplier part refn:	
Department Code:	0	Allocated:	0.00	Supplier A/C:	
Tax Code:	T1	Location:		Purchase Price:	11.00
Nominal Code:	4000	Selling Price:	20.00	Reorder Level:	0.00
Date Last Pur:		Last Purchase Qty:	0.00	Date Last Sale:	

| **Product Code:** | H200 | **Product Description:** | Desktop computer 3000i |

Category:	1	In Stock:	2.00	Units of Sale:	each
Category Desc:	Hardware	On Order:	0.00	Supplier part refn:	
Department Code:	0	Allocated:	0.00	Supplier A/C:	
Tax Code:	T1	Location:		Purchase Price:	360.00
Nominal Code:	4000	Selling Price:	600.00	Reorder Level:	0.00
Date Last Pur:		Last Purchase Qty:	0.00	Date Last Sale:	

| **Product Code:** | H201 | **Product Description:** | Monitor 17 inch |

Category:	1	In Stock:	7.00	Units of Sale:	each
Category Desc:	Hardware	On Order:	0.00	Supplier part refn:	
Department Code:	0	Allocated:	0.00	Supplier A/C:	
Tax Code:	T1	Location:		Purchase Price:	65.00
Nominal Code:	4000	Selling Price:	100.00	Reorder Level:	0.00
Date Last Pur:		Last Purchase Qty:	0.00	Date Last Sale:	

| **Product Code:** | H202 | **Product Description:** | Processor G240 |

Category:	1	In Stock:	2.00	Units of Sale:	each
Category Desc:	Hardware	On Order:	0.00	Supplier part refn:	
Department Code:	0	Allocated:	0.00	Supplier A/C:	
Tax Code:	T1	Location:		Purchase Price:	500.00
Nominal Code:	4000	Selling Price:	799.00	Reorder Level:	0.00
Date Last Pur:		Last Purchase Qty:	0.00	Date Last Sale:	

| **Product Code:** | H203 | **Product Description:** | Printer EF102 Multi |

Category:	1	In Stock:	3.00	Units of Sale:	each
Category Desc:	Hardware	On Order:	0.00	Supplier part refn:	
Department Code:	0	Allocated:	0.00	Supplier A/C:	
Tax Code:	T1	Location:		Purchase Price:	420.00
Nominal Code:	4000	Selling Price:	600.00	Reorder Level:	0.00
Date Last Pur:		Last Purchase Qty:	0.00	Date Last Sale:	

continued

Pronto Supplies Limited
Product Details

Page: 2

Product Code:	S100	Product Description:	Macroworx software Version 9		
Category:	2	In Stock:	5.00	Units of Sale:	each
Category Desc:	Software	On Order:	0.00	Supplier part refn:	
Department Code:	0	Allocated:	0.00	Supplier A/C:	
Tax Code:	T1	Location:		Purchase Price:	230.00
Nominal Code:	4001	Selling Price:	450.00	Reorder Level:	0.00
Date Last Pur:		Last Purchase Qty:	0.00	Date Last Sale:	

Task 4

Pronto Supplies Limited
Sales Order List

Page: 1

Order No From:	1	Customer From:		Order Date From:	01/01/1980
Order No To:	9,999,999	Customer To:	ZZZZZZZ	Order Date To:	31/12/2019

Order	Date	A/C	Name	Stock Description	Quantity Ordered	Units	Disc Amt.	Net
1000	04/02/2013	JB001	John Butler & Associates	Monitor 17 inch	4.00		0.00	400.00
				Less Net Value Discount				0.00
				Net Amount				400.00
1001	04/02/2013	CH001	Charisma Design	Power lead 3 mtr	1.00	each	0.00	16.00
				Less Net Value Discount				0.00
				Net Amount				16.00
1002	04/02/2013	CR001	Crowmatic Ltd	Macroworx software Version 9	1.00		0.00	450.00
				Less Net Value Discount				0.00
				Net Amount				450.00

Task 6

Pronto Supplies Limited
Update Ledgers

Page: 1

Inv	Type	Tran	Date	A/C	N/C	Stock Code	Details	Quantity	Net	Tax	Gross
551	SC	48	06/02/2013	DB001	4001	S100	Macroworx software Version 9	1.00	-450.00	-90.00	-540.00
							Total for Invoice 551		-450.00	-90.00	-540.00
552	SC	49	06/02/2013	LG001	4000	AP302	Zap USB flash memory drive	2.00	-40.00	-8.00	-48.00
							Total for Invoice 552		-40.00	-8.00	-48.00
10023	SI	50	05/02/2013	JB001	4000	H201	Monitor 17 inch	4.00	400.00	80.00	480.00
							Total for Invoice 10023		400.00	80.00	480.00
10024	SI	51	06/02/2013	CH001	4000	AP300	Power lead 3 mtr	1.00	16.00	3.20	19.20
							Total for Invoice 10024		16.00	3.20	19.20
10025	SI	52	06/02/2013	CR001	4001	S100	Macroworx software Version 9	1.00	450.00	90.00	540.00
							Total for Invoice 10025		450.00	90.00	540.00
10026	SI	53	08/02/2013	KD001	4002		2 hours consultancy		120.00	24.00	144.00
							Total for Invoice 10026		120.00	24.00	144.00
							Grand Total for All:		496.00	99.20	595.20

Pronto Supplies Limited
Day Books: Customer Invoices (Detailed)

Page: 1

Date From:		05/02/2013						Customer From:				
Date To:		08/02/2013						Customer To:		ZZZZZZZ		
Transaction From:		1						N/C From:				
Transaction To:		99,999,999						N/C To:		99999999		
Dept From:		0										
Dept To:		999										

Tran No.	Type	Date	A/C Ref	N/C	Inv Ref	Dept.	Details	Net Amount	Tax Amount	T/C	Gross Amount	V	B
50	SI	05/02/2013	JB001	4000	10023	0	Monitor 17 inch	400.00	80.00	T1	480.00	N	-
51	SI	06/02/2013	CH001	4000	10024	0	Power lead 3 mtr	16.00	3.20	T1	19.20	N	-
52	SI	06/02/2013	CR001	4001	10025	0	Macroworx software Version 9	450.00	90.00	T1	540.00	N	-
53	SI	08/02/2013	KD001	4002	10026	0	2 hours consultancy	120.00	24.00	T1	144.00	N	-
							Totals:	986.00	197.20		1,183.20		

Pronto Supplies Limited
Day Books: Customer Credits (Detailed)

Page: 1

Date From:		06/02/2013						Customer From:				
Date To:		06/02/2013						Customer To:		ZZZZZZZ		
Transaction From:		1						N/C From:				
Transaction To:		99,999,999						N/C To:		99999999		
Dept From:		0										
Dept To:		999										

Tran No.	Type	Date	A/C Ref	N/C	Inv Ref	Dept.	Details	Net Amount	Tax Amount	T/C	Gross Amount	V	B
48	SC	06/02/2013	DB001	4001	551	0	Macroworx software Version 9	450.00	90.00	T1	540.00	N	-
49	SC	06/02/2013	LG001	4000	552	0	Zap USB flash memory drive	40.00	8.00	T1	48.00	N	-
							Totals:	490.00	98.00		588.00		

Task 8

Pronto Supplies Limited
Product Re-Order Levels

Page: 1

Product From:			Category From:	1
Product To:	ZZZZZZZZZZZ		Category To:	999

Code & Supplier	Product Description	Quantity In Stock	Quantity Allocated	Quantity On Order	Reorder Level	Last Purchase Quantity	Purchase Price
H200 DE001	Desktop computer 3000i	2.00	0.00	0.00	2.00	0.00	360.00
H202 EL001	Processor G240	2.00	0.00	0.00	3.00	0.00	500.00
S100 MA001	Macroworx software Version 9	5.00	0.00	0.00	5.00	0.00	230.00

Task 9

Pronto Supplies Limited Page: 1
Purchase Order List

| Order Number From | 1 | Order Date From | 01/01/1980 | Supplier From | | Stock Code From | |
| Order Number To | 9,999,999 | Order Date To | 31/12/2019 | Supplier To | ZZZZZZZ | Stock Code To | ZZZZZZZZZZZZZZZZZZZZZ |

Order Number 2000   **Order Date** 11/02/2013   **Account Ref** DE001   **Name** Delco PLC

Stock Code	Description	Unit Of Sale	Quantity Order	Discount	Net Amount	Tax Amount	Gross Amount
H200	Desktop computer 3000i	each	10.00	0.00	3,600.00	720.00	4,320.00
			10.00	0.00	3,600.00	720.00	4,320.00

Order Number 2001   **Order Date** 11/02/2013   **Account Ref** EL001   **Name** Electron Supplies

Stock Code	Description	Unit Of Sale	Quantity Order	Discount	Net Amount	Tax Amount	Gross Amount
H202	Processor G240	each	4.00	0.00	2,000.00	400.00	2,400.00
			4.00	0.00	2,000.00	400.00	2,400.00

Order Number 2002   **Order Date** 11/02/2013   **Account Ref** MA001   **Name** MacCity

Stock Code	Description	Unit Of Sale	Quantity Order	Discount	Net Amount	Tax Amount	Gross Amount
S100	Macroworx software Version 9	each	16.00	0.00	3,680.00	736.00	4,416.00
			16.00	0.00	3,680.00	736.00	4,416.00
			30.00	0.00	9,280.00	1,856.00	11,136.00

Pronto Supplies Limited Page: 1
Day Books: Supplier Invoices (Detailed)

Date From:	20/02/2013			Supplier From:	
Date To:	25/02/2013			Supplier To:	ZZZZZZZZ
Transaction From:	1			N/C From:	
Transaction To:	99,999,999			N/C To:	99999999
Dept From:	0				
Dept To:	999				

Tran No.	Type	Date	A/C Ref	N/C	Inv Ref	Dept	Details	Net Amount	Tax Amount	T/C	Gross Amount	V	B
54	PI	20/02/2013	DE001	5000	11365	0	Desktop computer 3000i	3,600.00	720.00	T1	4,320.00	N	-
55	PI	25/02/2013	EL001	5000	8576	0	Processor G240	2,000.00	400.00	T1	2,400.00	N	-
56	PI	25/02/2013	MA001	5000	2947	0	Macroworx software Version	3,680.00	736.00	T1	4,416.00	N	-
							Totals	9,280.00	1,856.00		11,136.00		

Task 13

Pronto Supplies Limited Page: 1
Product Movement (In / Out)

| Date From: | 01/01/1980 | Stock Code From: | |
| Date To: | 31/12/2019 | Stock Code To: | ZZZZZZZZZZZZZZZZZZZZZZZZZZZ |

Code	Description	In	Out	Balance
AP300	Power lead 3 mtr	7.00	1.00	6.00
AP301	Zap external drive	5.00	2.00	3.00
AP302	Zap USB flash memory drive	12.00	0.00	12.00
H200	Desktop computer 3000i	12.00	0.00	12.00
H201	Monitor 17 inch	7.00	6.00	1.00
H202	Processor G240	6.00	0.00	6.00
H203	Printer EF102 Multi	3.00	1.00	2.00
S100	Macroworx software Version 9	22.00	2.00	20.00
		74.00	12.00	62.00

Pronto Supplies Limited
Product Activity

Page: 1

Product From:	
Product To:	ZZZZZZZZZZZZZ
Date From:	01/01/1980
Date To:	31/12/2019

Category From:	1
Category To:	999

Product Code: AP300   **Product Description:** Power lead 3 mtr

Type	Date	Ref	Details	Quantity	Quantity Used	Cost Price	Sales Price
AI	01/02/2013	O/BAL	Bfwd Product	6.00	1.00	9.50	0.00
GO	04/02/2013	1001	Goods Out	1.00	0.00	9.50	16.00
GR	12/02/2013	553	Goods Returned	1.00	0.00	9.50	16.00

Quantity In Stock   6.00

Product Code: AP301   **Product Description:** Zap external drive

Type	Date	Ref	Details	Quantity	Quantity Used	Cost Price	Sales Price
AI	01/02/2013	O/BAL	Bfwd Product	5.00	2.00	52.00	0.00
GO	12/02/2013	10028	Goods Out	2.00	0.00	52.00	81.00

Quantity In Stock   3.00

Product Code: AP302   **Product Description:** Zap USB flash memory drive

Type	Date	Ref	Details	Quantity	Quantity Used	Cost Price	Sales Price
AI	01/02/2013	O/BAL	Bfwd Product	9.00	0.00	11.00	0.00
GR	06/02/2013	552	Goods Returned	2.00	0.00	11.00	20.00
GR	13/02/2013	554	Goods Returned	1.00	0.00	11.00	20.00

Quantity In Stock   12.00

Product Code: H200   **Product Description:** Desktop computer 3000i

Type	Date	Ref	Details	Quantity	Quantity Used	Cost Price	Sales Price
AI	01/02/2013	O/BAL	Bfwd Product	2.00	0.00	360.00	0.00
GI	20/02/2013	2000	Goods In	10.00	0.00	360.00	0.00

Quantity In Stock   12.00

Product Code: H201   **Product Description:** Monitor 17 inch

Type	Date	Ref	Details	Quantity	Quantity Used	Cost Price	Sales Price
AI	01/02/2013	O/BAL	Bfwd Product	7.00	6.00	65.00	0.00
GO	04/02/2013	1000	Goods Out	4.00	0.00	65.00	100.00
GO	15/02/2013	10030	Goods Out	2.00	0.00	65.00	100.00

Quantity In Stock   1.00

Product Code: H202   **Product Description:** Processor G240

Type	Date	Ref	Details	Quantity	Quantity Used	Cost Price	Sales Price
AI	01/02/2013	O/BAL	Bfwd Product	2.00	0.00	500.00	0.00
GI	21/02/2013	2001	Goods In	2.00	0.00	500.00	0.00
GI	25/02/2013	2001	Goods In	2.00	0.00	500.00	0.00

Quantity In Stock   6.00

Product Code: H203   **Product Description:** Printer EF102 Multi

Type	Date	Ref	Details	Quantity	Quantity Used	Cost Price	Sales Price
AI	01/02/2013	O/BAL	Bfwd Product	3.00	1.00	420.00	0.00
GO	11/02/2013	10027	Goods Out	1.00	0.00	420.00	600.00

Quantity In Stock   2.00

Product Code: S100   **Product Description:** Macroworx software Version 9

Type	Date	Ref	Details	Quantity	Quantity Used	Cost Price	Sales Price
AI	01/02/2013	O/BAL	Bfwd Product	5.00	2.00	230.00	0.00
GO	04/02/2013	1002	Goods Out	1.00	0.00	230.00	450.00
GR	06/02/2013	551	Goods Returned	1.00	0.00	230.00	450.00
GI	22/02/2013	2002	Goods In	16.00	0.00	230.00	0.00
GO	13/02/2013	10029	Goods Out	1.00	0.00	230.00	450.00

Quantity In Stock   20.00

Pronto Supplies Limited   Page: 1

Product Audit Trail

Stock Code From		**Date From** 01/01/1980	**Supp From**		**Nom Code From**	
Stock Code To ZZZZZZZZZZZZZZZZZZZZ		**Date To** 31/12/2019	**Supp To**		**Nom Code To** 99999999	
Cat From 1					**Dept From** 0	
Cat To 999					**Dept To** 999	

Type	Stock Code	Description	Date	Ref	Details	Quantity	Cost Price	Sales Price	Quantity Used
AI	AP300	Power lead 3 mtr	01/02/2013	O/BAL	Bfwd Product	6.00	9.50	0.00	1.00
AI	H203	Printer EF102 Multi	01/02/2013	O/BAL	Bfwd Product	3.00	420.00	0.00	1.00
AI	S100	Macroworx software Version 9	01/02/2013	O/BAL	Bfwd Product	5.00	230.00	0.00	2.00
AI	AP301	Zap external drive	01/02/2013	O/BAL	Bfwd Product	5.00	52.00	0.00	2.00
AI	AP302	Zap USB flash memory drive	01/02/2013	O/BAL	Bfwd Product	9.00	11.00	0.00	0.00
AI	H202	Processor G240	01/02/2013	O/BAL	Bfwd Product	2.00	500.00	0.00	0.00
AI	H201	Monitor 17 inch	01/02/2013	O/BAL	Bfwd Product	7.00	65.00	0.00	6.00
AI	H200	Desktop computer 3000i	01/02/2013	O/BAL	Bfwd Product	2.00	360.00	0.00	0.00
GO	AP300	Power lead 3 mtr	04/02/2013	1001	Goods Out	-1.00	9.50	16.00	0.00
GO	H201	Monitor 17 inch	04/02/2013	1000	Goods Out	-4.00	65.00	100.00	0.00
GO	S100	Macroworx software Version 9	04/02/2013	1002	Goods Out	-1.00	230.00	450.00	0.00
GR	S100	Macroworx software Version 9	06/02/2013	551	Goods Returned	1.00	230.00	450.00	0.00
GR	AP302	Zap USB flash memory drive	06/02/2013	552	Goods Returned	2.00	11.00	20.00	0.00
GO	H203	Printer EF102 Multi	11/02/2013	10027	Goods Out	-1.00	420.00	600.00	0.00
GO	AP301	Zap external drive	12/02/2013	10028	Goods Out	-2.00	52.00	81.00	0.00
GR	AP300	Power lead 3 mtr	12/02/2013	553	Goods Returned	1.00	9.50	16.00	0.00
GO	S100	Macroworx software Version 9	13/02/2013	10029	Goods Out	-1.00	230.00	450.00	0.00
GR	AP302	Zap USB flash memory drive	13/02/2013	554	Goods Returned	1.00	11.00	20.00	0.00
GO	H201	Monitor 17 inch	15/02/2013	10030	Goods Out	-2.00	65.00	100.00	0.00
GI	H200	Desktop computer 3000i	20/02/2013	2000	Goods In	10.00	360.00	0.00	0.00
GI	H202	Processor G240	21/02/2013	2001	Goods In	2.00	500.00	0.00	0.00
GI	S100	Macroworx software Version 9	22/02/2013	2002	Goods In	16.00	230.00	0.00	0.00
GI	H202	Processor G240	25/02/2013	2001	Goods In	2.00	500.00	0.00	0.00

Pronto Supplies Limited

Period Trial Balance

Page: 1

To Period: Month 2, February 2013

N/C	Name	Debit	Credit
0020	Plant and Machinery	35,000.00	
0030	Office Equipment	15,000.00	
0040	Furniture and Fixtures	25,000.00	
1100	Debtors Control Account	31,907.30	
1200	Bank Current Account	14,656.00	
2100	Creditors Control Account		30,172.60
2200	Sales Tax Control Account		18,313.30
2201	Purchase Tax Control Account	28,500.60	
2300	Loans		35,000.00
3000	Ordinary Shares		75,000.00
4000	Computer hardware sales		86,302.00
4001	Computer software sales		15,450.00
4002	Computer consultancy		2,628.00
5000	Materials Purchased	78,622.00	
6201	Advertising	12,400.00	
7000	Gross Wages	16,230.00	
7100	Rent	4,500.00	
7103	General Rates	450.00	
7200	Electricity	150.00	
7502	Office Stationery	175.00	
7550	Telephone and Fax	275.00	
	Totals:	262,865.90	262,865.90

Chapter 9

Task 1

Pronto Supplies Limited

Day Books: Customer Receipts (Summary)

Date From:	28/02/2013									Bank From:	1200
DateTo:	28/02/2013									Bank To:	1200

Transaction From:	1				Customer From :	
Transaction To:	99,999,999				Customer To:	ZZZZZZZ

Bank 1200   **Currency** Pound Sterling

No	Type	Date	Account	Ref	Details	Net £	Tax £	Gross £	B	Bank Rec. Date
68	SR	28/02/2013	JB001	cheque	Sales Receipt	5,500.00	0.00	5,500.00	N	
69	SR	28/02/2013	CH001	cheque	Sales Receipt	2,400.00	0.00	2,400.00	N	
70	SR	28/02/2013	DB001	cheque	Sales Receipt	2,860.00	0.00	2,860.00	N	
71	SR	28/02/2013	KD001	BACS	Sales Receipt	6,500.00	0.00	6,500.00	N	
72	SR	28/02/2013	LG001	BACS	Sales Receipt	8,500.00	0.00	8,500.00	N	
					Totals £	25,760.00	0.00	25,760.00		

Task 2

Pronto Supplies Limited

Day Books: Supplier Payments (Summary)

Date From:	28/02/2013									Bank From:	1200
DateTo:	28/02/2013									Bank To:	1200

Transaction From:	1				Supplier From:	
Transaction To:	99,999,999				Supplier To:	ZZZZZZZ

Bank 1200   **Currency** Pound Sterling

No	Type	Date	Supplier	Ref	Details	Net £	Tax £	Gross £	B	Bank Rec. Date
73	PP	28/02/2013	DE001	BACS	Purchase Payment	5,174.00	0.00	5,174.00	N	
74	PP	28/02/2013	EL001	BACS	Purchase Payment	8,500.00	0.00	8,500.00	N	
75	PP	28/02/2013	MA001	BACS	Purchase Payment	4,454.40	0.00	4,454.40	N	
					Totals £	18,128.40	0.00	18,128.40		

Task 4

Pronto Supplies Limited

Period Trial Balance

To Period: Month 2, February 2013

N/C	Name	Debit	Credit
0020	Plant and Machinery	35,000.00	
0030	Office Equipment	15,760.00	
0040	Furniture and Fixtures	25,000.00	
1100	Debtors Control Account	5,610.00	
1200	Bank Current Account	22,811.40	
2100	Creditors Control Account		12,044.20
2200	Sales Tax Control Account		18,313.30
2201	Purchase Tax Control Account	28,500.60	
2300	Loans		35,000.00
3000	Ordinary Shares		75,000.00
4000	Computer hardware sales		86,302.00
4001	Computer software sales		15,450.00
4002	Computer consultancy		2,628.00
4009	Discounts Allowed	13.50	
5000	Materials Purchased	77,862.00	
6201	Advertising	12,400.00	
7000	Gross Wages	16,230.00	
7100	Rent	4,500.00	
7103	General Rates	450.00	
7200	Electricity	150.00	
7502	Office Stationery	175.00	
7550	Telephone and Fax	275.00	
	Totals:	244,737.50	244,737.50

Chapter 10

Task 1

Pronto Supplies Limited   Page: 1

Day Books: Bank Receipts (Detailed)

Date From:	01/01/1980		Bank From:	1200
DateTo:	31/12/2019		Bank To:	1200

Transaction From:	1	N/C From:	
Transaction To:	99,999,999	N/C To:	99999999

Dept From:	0
Dept To:	999

Bank: 1200   **Currency:** Pound Sterling

No	Type	N/C	Date	Ref	Details	Dept	Net £	Tax £	T/C	Gross £	V	B	Bank Rec. Date
78	BR	4000	08/02/2013	10736	Hardware sales	0	12,500.00	2,500.00	T1	15,000.00	N	N	
79	BR	4001	08/02/2013	10737	Software sales	0	4,680.00	936.00	T1	5,616.00	N	N	
80	BR	4000	15/02/2013	10738	Hardware sales	0	15,840.00	3,168.00	T1	19,008.00	N	N	
81	BR	4001	15/02/2013	10739	Software sales	0	3,680.00	736.00	T1	4,416.00	N	N	
82	BR	4000	22/02/2013	10740	Hardware sales	0	17,800.00	3,560.00	T1	21,360.00	N	N	
83	BR	4001	22/02/2013	10741	Software sales	0	4,800.00	960.00	T1	5,760.00	N	N	
						Totals £	59,300.00	11,860.00		71,160.00			

Task 2

Pronto Supplies Limited

Day Books: Bank Payments (Detailed)

Date From:	01/01/1980		Bank From:	1200
DateTo:	31/12/2019		Bank To:	1200

Transaction From:	1		N/C From:	
Transaction To:	99,999,999		N/C To:	99999999

Dept From:	0
Dept To:	999

Bank: 1200   **Currency:** Pound Sterling

No	Type	N/C	Date	Ref	Details	Dept	Net £	Tax £ T/C	Gross £	V	B	Bank Rec. Date
84	BP	5000	12/02/2013	122992	Cash purchases	0	15,500.00	3,100.00 T1	18,600.00	N	N	
85	BP	6201	14/02/2013	122993	Advertising	0	10,200.00	2,040.00 T1	12,240.00	N	N	
86	BP	0040	15/02/2013	122994	Furniture	0	5,000.00	1,000.00 T1	6,000.00	N	N	
87	BP	7200	22/02/2013	122995	Electricity	0	158.00	31.60 T1	189.60	N	N	
88	BP	7550	26/02/2013	122996	Telephone	0	310.00	62.00 T1	372.00	N	N	
89	BP	7502	26/02/2013	122997	Stationery	0	340.00	68.00 T1	408.00	N	N	
						Totals £	**31,508.00**	**6,301.60**	**37,809.60**			

Task 4

Pronto Supplies Limited

Period Trial Balance

Page: 1

To Period: Month 2, February 2013

N/C	Name	Debit	Credit
0020	Plant and Machinery	35,000.00	
0030	Office Equipment	15,760.00	
0040	Furniture and Fixtures	30,000.00	
1100	Debtors Control Account	5,610.00	
1200	Bank Current Account	61,161.80	
2100	Creditors Control Account		12,044.20
2200	Sales Tax Control Account		30,173.30
2201	Purchase Tax Control Account	34,802.20	
2300	Loans		35,000.00
3000	Ordinary Shares		80,000.00
4000	Computer hardware sales		132,442.00
4001	Computer software sales		28,610.00
4002	Computer consultancy		2,628.00
4009	Discounts Allowed	13.50	
5000	Materials Purchased	93,362.00	
6201	Advertising	22,600.00	
7000	Gross Wages	16,230.00	
7100	Rent	4,500.00	
7103	General Rates	450.00	
7200	Electricity	308.00	
7502	Office Stationery	515.00	
7550	Telephone and Fax	585.00	
	Totals:	**320,897.50**	**320,897.50**

Chapter 11

Task 2

Pronto Supplies Limited

Day Books: Cash Payments (Detailed)

Date From:	01/02/2013	Bank From:	1230
DateTo:	28/02/2013	Bank To:	1230
Transaction From:	1	N/C From:	
Transaction To:	99,999,999	N/C To:	99999999
Dept From:	0		
Dept To:	999		

Bank: 1230   Currency: Pound Sterling

No	Type	N/C	Date	Ref	Details	Dept	Net £	Tax £ T/C	Gross £ V B	Bank Rec. Date
93	CP	7502	07/02/2013	PC101	Copy paper	0	36.00	7.20 T1	43.20 N	-
94	CP	7501	14/02/2013	PC102	Postage stamps	0	25.00	0.00 T2	25.00 N	-
95	CP	7502	20/02/2013	PC103	Envelopes	0	16.00	3.20 T1	19.20 N	-
96	CP	7501	28/02/2013	PC104	Postage stamps	0	5.00	0.00 T2	5.00 N	-
97	CP	5003	28/02/2013	PC105	Packing tape	0	4.00	0.80 T1	4.80 N	-
						Totals £	86.00	11.20	97.20	

Task 3

Pronto Supplies Limited

Day Books: Cash Receipts (Detailed)

Date From:	26/02/2013	Bank From:	1235
DateTo:	28/02/2013	Bank To:	1235
Transaction From:	1	N/C From:	
Transaction To:	99,999,999	N/C To:	99999999
Dept From:	0		
Dept To:	999		

Bank: 1235   Currency: Pound Sterling

No	Type	N/C	Date	Ref	Details	Dept	Net £	Tax £ T/C	Gross £ V B	Bank Rec. Date
96	CR	4000	26/02/2013	10743	Hardware sales	0	5,000.00	1,000.00 T1	6,000.00 N	-
97	CR	4001	26/02/2013	10743	Software sales	0	480.00	96.00 T1	576.00 N	-
98	CR	4000	27/02/2013	10744	Hardware sales	0	1,200.00	240.00 T1	1,440.00 N	-
99	CR	4001	27/02/2013	10745	Software sales	0	890.00	178.00 T1	1,068.00 N	-
100	CR	4000	28/02/2013	10746	Hardware sales	0	600.00	120.00 T1	720.00 N	-
101	CR	4001	28/02/2013	10746	Software sales	0	120.00	24.00 T1	144.00 N	-
						Totals £	8,290.00	1,658.00	9,948.00	

Task 5 (a)

Pronto Supplies Limited

Audit Trail (Summary)

Date From:	01/01/1980				Customer From:	
Date To:	31/12/2019				Customer To:	ZZZZZZZ
Transaction From:	1				Supplier From:	
Transaction To:	99,999,999				Supplier To:	ZZZZZZZ
Dept From:	0				N/C From:	
Dept To:	999				N/C To:	99999999
Exclude Deleted Tran:	No					

No	Type	Date	A/C	N/C	Dept	Ref	Details	Net	Tax	T/C	Pd	Paid	V	B
1	SI	05/01/2013	JB001	9998	0	10013	Opening Balance	5,500.00	0.00	T9	Y	5,500.00	-	-
2	SI	05/01/2013	CH001	9998	0	10014	Opening Balance	2,400.00	0.00	T9	Y	2,400.00	-	-
3	SI	09/01/2013	CR001	9998	0	10015	Opening Balance	3,234.00	0.00	T9	N	0.00	-	-
4	SI	10/01/2013	DB001	9998	0	10016	Opening Balance	3,400.00	0.00	T9	Y	3,400.00	-	-
5	SI	10/01/2013	KD001	9998	0	10017	Opening Balance	6,500.00	0.00	T9	Y	6,500.00	-	-
6	SI	17/01/2013	LG001	9998	0	10019	Opening Balance	8,500.00	0.00	T9	Y	8,500.00	-	-
7	PI	04/01/2013	DE001	9998	0	4563	Opening Balance	5,750.00	0.00	T9	Y	5,750.00	-	-
8	PI	05/01/2013	EL001	9998	0	8122	Opening Balance	8,500.00	0.00	T9	Y	8,500.00	-	-
9	PI	09/01/2013	MA001	9998	0	9252	Opening Balance	4,500.00	0.00	T9	Y	4,500.00	-	-
10	JD	31/01/2013	0020	0020	0	O/Bal	Opening Balance	35,000.00	0.00	T9	Y	35,000.00	-	-
11	JC	31/01/2013	9998	9998	0	O/Bal	Opening Balance	35,000.00	0.00	T9	Y	35,000.00	-	-
12	JD	31/01/2013	0030	0030	0	O/Bal	Opening Balance	15,000.00	0.00	T9	Y	15,000.00	-	-
13	JC	31/01/2013	9998	9998	0	O/Bal	Opening Balance	15,000.00	0.00	T9	Y	15,000.00	-	-
14	JD	31/01/2013	0040	0040	0	O/Bal	Opening Balance	25,000.00	0.00	T9	Y	25,000.00	-	-
15	JC	31/01/2013	9998	9998	0	O/Bal	Opening Balance	25,000.00	0.00	T9	Y	25,000.00	-	-
16	JD	31/01/2013	1200	1200	0	O/Bal	Opening Balance	14,656.00	0.00	T9	Y	14,656.00	-	-
17	JC	31/01/2013	9998	9998	0	O/Bal	Opening Balance	14,656.00	0.00	T9	Y	14,656.00	-	-
18	JC	31/01/2013	2200	2200	0	O/Bal	Opening Balance	17,920.00	0.00	T9	Y	17,920.00	-	-
19	JD	31/01/2013	9998	9998	0	O/Bal	Opening Balance	17,920.00	0.00	T9	Y	17,920.00	-	-
20	JD	31/01/2013	2201	2201	0	O/Bal	Opening Balance	26,600.00	0.00	T9	Y	26,600.00	-	-
21	JC	31/01/2013	9998	9998	0	O/Bal	Opening Balance	26,600.00	0.00	T9	Y	26,600.00	-	-
22	JC	31/01/2013	2300	2300	0	O/Bal	Opening Balance	35,000.00	0.00	T9	Y	35,000.00	-	-
23	JD	31/01/2013	9998	9998	0	O/Bal	Opening Balance	35,000.00	0.00	T9	Y	35,000.00	-	-
24	JC	31/01/2013	3000	3000	0	O/Bal	Opening Balance	75,000.00	0.00	T9	Y	75,000.00	-	-
25	JD	31/01/2013	9998	9998	0	O/Bal	Opening Balance	75,000.00	0.00	T9	Y	75,000.00	-	-
26	JC	31/01/2013	4000	4000	0	O/Bal	Opening Balance	85,000.00	0.00	T9	Y	85,000.00	-	-
27	JD	31/01/2013	9998	9998	0	O/Bal	Opening Balance	85,000.00	0.00	T9	Y	85,000.00	-	-
28	JC	31/01/2013	4001	4001	0	O/Bal	Opening Balance	15,000.00	0.00	T9	Y	15,000.00	-	-
29	JD	31/01/2013	9998	9998	0	O/Bal	Opening Balance	15,000.00	0.00	T9	Y	15,000.00	-	-
30	JC	31/01/2013	4002	4002	0	O/Bal	Opening Balance	2,400.00	0.00	T9	Y	2,400.00	-	-
31	JD	31/01/2013	9998	9998	0	O/Bal	Opening Balance	2,400.00	0.00	T9	Y	2,400.00	-	-
32	JD	31/01/2013	5000	5000	0	O/Bal	Opening Balance	69,100.00	0.00	T9	Y	69,100.00	-	-
33	JC	31/01/2013	9998	9998	0	O/Bal	Opening Balance	69,100.00	0.00	T9	Y	69,100.00	-	-
34	JD	31/01/2013	6201	6201	0	O/Bal	Opening Balance	12,400.00	0.00	T9	Y	12,400.00	-	-
35	JC	31/01/2013	9998	9998	0	O/Bal	Opening Balance	12,400.00	0.00	T9	Y	12,400.00	-	-
36	JD	31/01/2013	7000	7000	0	O/Bal	Opening Balance	16,230.00	0.00	T9	Y	16,230.00	-	-
37	JC	31/01/2013	9998	9998	0	O/Bal	Opening Balance	16,230.00	0.00	T9	Y	16,230.00	-	-
38	JD	31/01/2013	7100	7100	0	O/Bal	Opening Balance	4,500.00	0.00	T9	Y	4,500.00	-	-
39	JC	31/01/2013	9998	9998	0	O/Bal	Opening Balance	4,500.00	0.00	T9	Y	4,500.00	-	-
40	JD	31/01/2013	7103	7103	0	O/Bal	Opening Balance	450.00	0.00	T9	Y	450.00	-	-
41	JC	31/01/2013	9998	9998	0	O/Bal	Opening Balance	450.00	0.00	T9	Y	450.00	-	-
42	JD	31/01/2013	7200	7200	0	O/Bal	Opening Balance	150.00	0.00	T9	Y	150.00	-	-
43	JC	31/01/2013	9998	9998	0	O/Bal	Opening Balance	150.00	0.00	T9	Y	150.00	-	-
44	JD	31/01/2013	7502	7502	0	O/Bal	Opening Balance	175.00	0.00	T9	Y	175.00	-	-
45	JC	31/01/2013	9998	9998	0	O/Bal	Opening Balance	175.00	0.00	T9	Y	175.00	-	-
46	JD	31/01/2013	7550	7550	0	O/Bal	Opening Balance	275.00	0.00	T9	Y	275.00	-	-
47	JC	31/01/2013	9998	9998	0	O/Bal	Opening Balance	275.00	0.00	T9	Y	275.00	-	-
48	SI	05/02/2013	JB001	4000	0	10023	4 x Monitor 17 inch	400.00	80.00	T1	N	0.00	N	-
49	SI	06/02/2013	CH001	4000	0	10024	1 x Power lead 3 mtr	16.00	3.20	T1	N	0.00	N	-
50	SI	06/02/2013	CR001	4001	0	10025	1 x Macroworx software Version	450.00	90.00	T1	N	0.00	N	-
51	SI	08/02/2013	KD001	4002	0	10026	2 hours consultancy	120.00	24.00	T1	N	0.00	N	-
52	SC	06/02/2013	DB001	4001	0	551	1 x Macroworx software Version	450.00	90.00	T1	Y	540.00	N	-
53	SC	06/02/2013	LG001	4000	0	552	2 x Zap USB flash memory drive	40.00	8.00	T1	N	0.00	N	-
54	SI	11/02/2013	DB001	4000	0	10027	1 x Printer EF102 Multi	600.00	120.00	T1	N	0.00	N	-
55	SI	12/02/2013	LG001	4000	0	10028	2 x Zap external drive	162.00	32.40	T1	N	0.00	N	-
56	SI	13/02/2013	KD001	4001	0	10029	1 x Macroworx software Version	450.00	87.30	T1	Y	537.30	N	-
57	SI	15/02/2013	CH001	4000	0	10030	2 x Monitor 17 inch	200.00	40.00	T1	N	0.00	N	-
58	SI	15/02/2013	JB001	4002	0	10031	2 hours consultancy	108.00	21.60	T1	N	0.00	N	-
59	SC	12/02/2013	CH001	4000	0	553	1 x Power lead 3 mtr	16.00	3.20	T1	N	0.00	N	-
60	SC	13/02/2013	CR001	4000	0	554	1 x Zap USB flash memory drive	20.00	4.00	T1	N	0.00	N	-
61	PI	20/02/2013	DE001	5000	0	11365	10 x Desktop Computer 3000i	3,600.00	720.00	T1	N	0.00	N	-
62	PI	25/02/2013	EL001	5000	0	8576	4 x Processor G240	2,000.00	400.00	T1	N	0.00	N	-
63	PI	25/02/2013	MA001	5000	0	2947	16 x Macroworx Software	3,680.00	736.00	T1	N	0.00	N	-
64	PC	06/02/2013	DE001	5000	0	7223	1 x Pro 704 Computer	480.00	96.00	T1	Y	576.00	N	-
65	PC	08/02/2013	MA001	5000	0	552	1 x 10 Optical Mouse	38.00	7.60	T1	Y	45.60	N	-
66	PI	25/02/2013	DE001	0030	0	11377	Laptop X70	400.00	78.00	T1	N	0.00	N	-
67	PI	25/02/2013	DE001	0030	0	11377	Laser Multi-Printer P28	360.00	70.20	T1	N	0.00	N	-
68	SR	28/02/2013	JB001	1200	0	Cheque	Sales Receipt	5,500.00	0.00	T9	Y	5,500.00	-	N
69	SR	28/02/2013	CH001	1200	0	Cheque	Sales Receipt	2,400.00	0.00	T9	Y	2,400.00	-	N

Task 5 (a) continued

Pronto Supplies Limited
Audit Trail (Summary)

No	Type	Date	A/C	N/C	Dept	Ref	Details	Net	Tax	T/C	Pd	Paid	V	B
70	SR	28/02/2013	DB001	1200	0	Cheque	Sales Receipt	2,860.00	0.00	T9	Y	2,860.00	-	N
71	SR	28/02/2013	KD001	1200	0	BACS	Sales Receipt	6,500.00	0.00	T9	Y	6,500.00	-	N
72	SR	28/02/2013	LG001	1200	0	BACS	Sales Receipt	8,500.00	0.00	T9	Y	8,500.00	-	N
73	PP	28/02/2013	DE001	1200	0	BACS	Purchase Payment	5,174.00	0.00	T9	Y	5,174.00	-	N
74	PP	28/02/2013	EL001	1200	0	BACS	Purchase Payment	8,500.00	0.00	T9	Y	8,500.00	-	N
75	PP	28/02/2013	MA001	1200	0	BACS	Purchase Payment	4,454.40	0.00	T9	Y	4,454.40	-	N
76	SR	20/02/2013	KD001	1200	0	BACS	Sales Receipt	523.80	0.00	T9	Y	523.80	-	N
77	SD	20/02/2013	KD001	4009	0	BACS	Sales Discount	13.50	0.00	T9	Y	13.50	-	-
78	BR	08/02/2013	1200	4000	0	10736	Hardware sales	12,500.00	2,500.00	T1	Y	15,000.00	N	N
79	BR	08/02/2013	1200	4001	0	10737	Software sales	4,680.00	936.00	T1	Y	5,616.00	N	N
80	BR	15/02/2013	1200	4000	0	10738	Hardware sales	15,840.00	3,168.00	T1	Y	19,008.00	N	N
81	BR	15/02/2013	1200	4001	0	10739	Software sales	3,680.00	736.00	T1	Y	4,416.00	N	N
82	BR	22/02/2013	1200	4000	0	10740	Hardware sales	17,800.00	3,560.00	T1	Y	21,360.00	N	N
83	BR	22/02/2013	1200	4001	0	10741	Software sales	4,800.00	960.00	T1	Y	5,760.00	N	N
84	BP	12/02/2013	1200	5000	0	122992	Cash purchases	15,500.00	3,100.00	T1	Y	18,600.00	N	N
85	BP	14/02/2013	1200	6201	0	122993	Advertising	10,200.00	2,040.00	T1	Y	12,240.00	N	N
86	BP	15/02/2013	1200	0040	0	122994	Furniture	5,000.00	1,000.00	T1	Y	6,000.00	N	N
87	BP	22/02/2013	1200	7200	0	122995	Electricity	158.00	31.60	T1	Y	189.60	N	N
88	BP	26/02/2013	1200	7550	0	122996	Telephone	310.00	62.00	T1	Y	372.00	N	N
89	BP	26/02/2013	1200	7502	0	122997	Stationery	340.00	68.00	T1	Y	408.00	N	N
90	BR	28/02/2013	1200	3000	0	10742	Share capital	5,000.00	0.00	T9	Y	5,000.00	-	N
91	JC	01/02/2013	1200	1200	0	122991	From bank to petty cash	100.00	0.00	T9	Y	100.00	-	N
92	JD	01/02/2013	1230	1230	0	122991	From bank to petty cash	100.00	0.00	T9	Y	100.00	-	-
93	CP	07/02/2013	1230	7502	0	PC101	Copy paper	36.00	7.20	T1	Y	43.20	N	-
94	CP	14/02/2013	1230	7501	0	PC102	Postage stamps	25.00	0.00	T2	Y	25.00	N	-
95	CP	20/02/2013	1230	7502	0	PC103	Envelopes	16.00	3.20	T1	Y	19.20	N	-
96	CP	28/02/2013	1230	7501	0	PC104	Postage stamps	5.00	0.00	T2	Y	5.00	N	-
97	CP	28/02/2013	1230	5003	0	PC105	Packing tape	4.00	0.80	T1	Y	4.80	N	-
98	CR	26/02/2013	1235	4000	0	10743	Hardware sales	5,000.00	1,000.00	T1	Y	6,000.00	N	-
99	CR	26/02/2013	1235	4001	0	10743	Software sales	480.00	96.00	T1	Y	576.00	N	-
100	CR	27/02/2013	1235	4000	0	10744	Hardware sales	1,200.00	240.00	T1	Y	1,440.00	N	-
101	CR	27/02/2013	1235	4001	0	10744	Software sales	890.00	178.00	T1	Y	1,068.00	N	-
102	CR	28/02/2013	1235	4000	0	10745	Hardware sales	600.00	120.00	T1	Y	720.00	N	-
103	CR	28/02/2013	1235	4001	0	10745	Software sales	120.00	24.00	T1	Y	144.00	N	-
104	BR	15/02/2013	1200	4904	0	STO	Rent 10A High St	456.00	91.20	T1	Y	547.20	N	N
105	BP	16/02/2013	1200	7100	0	DD	Broadwater Properties rent paid	4,500.00	900.00	T1	Y	5,400.00	N	N
106	BP	19/02/2013	1200	7103	0	STO	Wyvern DC	350.00	0.00	T2	Y	350.00	N	N
107	BP	28/02/2013	1200	7701	0	DD	Xerax 566 maintenance	19.80	3.96	T1	Y	23.76	N	N
108	BP	28/02/2013	1200	2300	0	DD	Loan repayment	850.00	0.00	T9	Y	850.00	-	N
109	BP	28/02/2013	1200	7903	0	DD	Loan interest	150.00	0.00	T2	Y	150.00	N	N

The order of transactions may alter slightly depending on whether you have worked through Chapters 6 and 7 or whether you have worked through Chapter 8 instead.

Task 5 (b)

Pronto Supplies Limited
Period Trial Balance

Page: 1

To Period: Month 2, February 2013

N/C	Name	Debit	Credit
0020	Plant and Machinery	35,000.00	
0030	Office Equipment	15,760.00	
0040	Furniture and Fixtures	30,000.00	
1100	Debtors Control Account	5,610.00	
1200	Bank Current Account	54,835.24	
1230	Petty Cash	2.80	
1235	Cash Register	9,948.00	
2100	Creditors Control Account		12,044.20
2200	Sales Tax Control Account		31,922.50
2201	Purchase Tax Control Account	35,717.36	
2300	Loans		34,150.00
3000	Ordinary Shares		80,000.00
4000	Computer hardware sales		139,242.00
4001	Computer software sales		30,100.00
4002	Computer consultancy		2,628.00
4009	Discounts Allowed	13.50	
4904	Rent Income		456.00
5000	Materials Purchased	93,362.00	
5003	Packaging	4.00	
6201	Advertising	22,600.00	
7000	Gross Wages	16,230.00	
7100	Rent	9,000.00	
7103	General Rates	800.00	
7200	Electricity	308.00	
7501	Postage and Carriage	30.00	
7502	Office Stationery	567.00	
7550	Telephone and Fax	585.00	
7701	Office Machine Maintenance	19.80	
7903	Loan Interest Paid	150.00	
	Totals:	330,542.70	330,542.70

Chapter 13

Task 5

Pronto Supplies Limited

Period Trial Balance

To Period: Month 2, February 2013

N/C	Name	Debit	Credit
0020	Plant and Machinery	35,000.00	
0030	Office Equipment	15,760.00	
0040	Furniture and Fixtures	30,000.00	
1100	Debtors Control Account	5,610.00	
1200	Bank Current Account	54,785.24	
1230	Petty Cash	2.80	
1235	Cash Register	9,948.00	
2100	Creditors Control Account		12,044.20
2200	Sales Tax Control Account		31,922.50
2201	Purchase Tax Control Account	35,717.36	
2210	P.A.Y.E.		2,200.00
2211	National Insurance		2,570.00
2220	Net Wages		13,330.00
2300	Loans		34,150.00
3000	Ordinary Shares		80,000.00
4000	Computer hardware sales		139,242.00
4001	Computer software sales		30,100.00
4002	Computer consultancy		2,628.00
4009	Discounts Allowed	13.50	
4904	Rent Income		456.00
5000	Materials Purchased	93,362.00	
5003	Packaging	4.00	
6201	Advertising	22,600.00	
7000	Gross Wages	33,010.00	
7006	Employers N.I. (Non-Directors)	1,320.00	
7100	Rent	9,000.00	
7103	General Rates	800.00	
7200	Electricity	150.00	
7201	Gas	158.00	
7501	Postage and Carriage	30.00	
7502	Office Stationery	567.00	
7550	Telephone and Fax	585.00	
7701	Office Machine Maintenance	19.80	
7901	Bank Charges	50.00	
7903	Loan Interest Paid	150.00	
	Totals:	348,642.70	348,642.70

Interlingo Translation Services Extended Exercise: Activity 2

Task 3

Interlingo Translation Services

Day Books: Customer Invoices (Detailed)

Date From:	01/07/2013									Customer From:		
Date To:	31/07/2013									Customer To:	ZZZZZZZZ	
Transaction From:	1									N/C From:		
Transaction To:	99,999,999									N/C To:	99999999	
Dept From:	0											
Dept To:	999											

Tran No.	Type	Date	A/C Ref	N/C	Inv Ref	Dept.	Details	Net Amount	Tax Amount	T/C	Gross Amount	V	B
1	SI	06/07/2013	RS001	9998	10010	0	Opening Balance	850.00	0.00	T9	850.00	-	-
2	SI	12/07/2013	PL001	9998	10011	0	Opening Balance	795.00	0.00	T9	795.00	-	-
3	SI	19/07/2013	HD001	9998	10013	0	Opening Balance	345.00	0.00	T9	345.00	-	-
4	SI	20/07/2013	SC001	9998	10014	0	Opening Balance	800.00	0.00	T9	800.00	-	-
							Totals:	2,790.00	0.00		2,790.00		

Task 6

Interlingo Translation Services

Day Books: Supplier Invoices (Detailed)

Date From:	01/07/2013									Supplier From:		
Date To:	31/07/2013									Supplier To:	ZZZZZZZZ	
Transaction From:	1									N/C From:		
Transaction To:	99,999,999									N/C To:	99999999	
Dept From:	0											
Dept To:	999											

Tran No.	Type	Date	A/C Ref	N/C	Inv Ref	Dept	Details	Net Amount	Tax Amount	T/C	Gross Amount	V	B
5	PI	05/07/2013	TD001	9998	2347	0	Opening Balance	780.00	0.00	T9	780.00	-	-
6	PI	06/07/2013	BB001	9998	9422	0	Opening Balance	420.00	0.00	T9	420.00	-	-
							Totals	1,200.00	0.00		1,200.00		

Task 7

Interlingo Translation Services

Period Trial Balance

To Period: Month 1, July 2013

N/C	Name	Debit	Credit
1100	Debtors Control Account	2,790.00	
2100	Creditors Control Account		1,200.00
9998	Suspense Account		1,590.00
	Totals:	2,790.00	2,790.00

Interlingo Translation Services Extended Exercise: Activity 3

Task 2

Interlingo Translation Services

Period Trial Balance

To Period: Month 1, July 2013

N/C	Name	Debit	Credit
0020	Plant and Machinery	5,000.00	
0030	Office Equipment	2,500.00	
0040	Furniture and Fixtures	3,000.00	
1100	Debtors Control Account	2,790.00	
1200	Bank Current Account	8,295.00	
2100	Creditors Control Account		1,200.00
2200	Sales Tax Control Account		814.00
2201	Purchase Tax Control Account	623.00	
2210	P.A.Y.E.		700.00
2211	National Insurance		900.00
2300	Loans		5,000.00
3000	Ordinary Shares		15,000.00
4000	Sales Type A		3,660.00
4100	Sales Type D		456.00
4101	Sales Type E		950.00
5000	Materials Purchased	300.00	
5001	Materials Imported	750.00	
6201	Advertising	550.00	
7000	Gross Wages	3,600.00	
7100	Rent	250.00	
7103	General Rates	129.00	
7200	Electricity	61.00	
7501	Postage and Carriage	86.00	
7502	Office Stationery	471.00	
7550	Telephone and Fax	275.00	
	Totals:	**28,680.00**	**28,680.00**

Interlingo Translation Services Extended Exercise: Activity 4

Task 3

Interlingo Translation Services
Day Books: Customer Invoices (Detailed)

Date From:		01/08/2013							Customer From:				
Date To:		31/08/2013							Customer To:		ZZZZZZZ		
Transaction From:		1							N/C From:				
Transaction To:		99,999,999							N/C To:		99999999		
Dept From:		0											
Dept To:		999											

Tran No.	Type	Date	A/C Ref	N/C	Inv Ref	Dept.	Details	Net Amount	Tax Amount	T/C	Gross Amount	V	B
53	SI	10/08/2013	HD001	4000	10015	0	Translation of sales contracts	520.00	104.00	T1	624.00	N	-
54	SI	16/08/2013	PL001	4000	10016	0	Translation of sales literature	120.00	24.00	T1	144.00	N	-
55	SI	20/08/2013	RS001	4000	10017	0	Translation of shipping docs	100.00	20.00	T1	120.00	N	-
56	SI	20/08/2013	SC001	4000	10018	0	Translation of sales contracts	160.00	32.00	T1	192.00	N	-
57	SI	22/08/2013	RT001	4101	10019	0	16 Beginners' French CDs	320.00	62.40	T1	382.40	N	-
58	SI	31/08/2013	RT001	4100	10020	0	10 German First Course books	180.00	0.00	T0	180.00	N	-
59	SI	31/08/2013	RT001	4100	10020	0	10 French Second Course books	220.00	0.00	T0	220.00	N	-
60	SI	31/08/2013	RT001	4101	10020	0	20 Advanced Italian CDs	480.00	93.60	T1	573.60	N	-
							Totals:	2,100.00	336.00		2,436.00		

Interlingo Translation Services
Day Books: Customer Credits (Detailed)

Date From:		01/08/2013							Customer From:				
Date To:		31/08/2013							Customer To:		ZZZZZZZ		
Transaction From:		1							N/C From:				
Transaction To:		99,999,999							N/C To:		99999999		
Dept From:		0											
Dept To:		999											

Tran No.	Type	Date	A/C Ref	N/C	Inv Ref	Dept.	Details	Net Amount	Tax Amount	T/C	Gross Amount	V	B
61	SC	31/08/2013	HD001	4000	501	0	Refund invoice 10015	52.00	10.40	T1	62.40	N	-
							Totals:	52.00	10.40		62.40		

Interlingo Translation Services Extended Exercise: Activity 5

Task 3

<table>
<tr><td colspan="2" align="center">**Interlingo Translation Services**
Day Books: Supplier Invoices (Detailed)</td></tr>
</table>

Date From:	15/08/2013	Supplier From:
Date To:	20/08/2013	Supplier To: ZZZZZZZ
Transaction From:	1	N/C From:
Transaction To:	99,999,999	N/C To: 99999999
Dept From:	0	
Dept To:	999	

Tran No.	Type	Date	A/C Ref	N/C	Inv Ref	Dept	Details	Net Amount	Tax Amount	T/C	Gross Amount	V	B
62	PI	15/08/2013	TD001	5001	2561	0	Beginners French CDs	1,000.00	200.00	T1	1,200.00	N	-
63	PI	15/08/2013	TD001	5001	2561	0	Advanced Italian CDs	600.00	120.00	T1	720.00	N	-
64	PI	20/08/2013	BB001	5000	11231	0	German First Coure	537.00	0.00	T0	537.00	N	-
65	PI	20/08/2013	BB001	5000	11231	0	French Second Course	492.75	0.00	T0	492.75	N	-
66	PI	15/08/2013	RS002	5100	72/554	0	Same day delivery to London	100.00	20.00	T1	120.00	N	-
							Totals	2,729.75	340.00		3,069.75		

Task 4

<table>
<tr><td colspan="2" align="center">**Interlingo Translation Services**
Day Books: Supplier Credits (Detailed)</td></tr>
</table>

Date From:	28/08/2013	Supplier From:
Date To:	28/08/2013	Supplier To: ZZZZZZZ
Transaction From:	1	N/C From:
Transaction To:	99,999,999	N/C To: 99999999
Dept From:	0	
Dept To:	999	

Tran No.	Type	Date	A/C Ref	N/C	Inv Ref	Dept	Details	Net Amount	Tax Amount	T/C	Gross Amount	V	B
67	PC	28/08/2013	TD001	5001	1919	0	Faulty CDs returned	100.00	20.00	T1	120.00	N	-
							Totals	100.00	20.00		120.00		

Interlingo Translation Services Extended Exercise: Activity 6

Task 1

Interlingo Translation Services

Product Details

				Category From:	1
Product From:					
Product To:	ZZZZZZZZZZZZZZ			**Category To:**	999

Product Code:	FR2	**Product Description:**	French Second Course		
Category:	2	In Stock:	11.00	Units of Sale:	each
Category Desc:	Books	On Order:	0.00	Supplier part refn:	
Department Code:	0	Allocated:	0.00	Supplier A/C:	BB001
Tax Code:	T0	Location:		Purchase Price:	10.95
Nominal Code:	4100	Selling Price:	22.00	Reorder Level:	0.00
Date Last Pur:		Last Purchase Qty:	0.00	Date Last Sale:	

Product Code:	FRB	**Product Description:**	Beginners French CD		
Category:	1	In Stock:	33.00	Units of Sale:	each
Category Desc:	CDs	On Order:	0.00	Supplier part refn:	
Department Code:	0	Allocated:	0.00	Supplier A/C:	TD001
Tax Code:	T1	Location:		Purchase Price:	10.00
Nominal Code:	4101	Selling Price:	20.00	Reorder Level:	0.00
Date Last Pur:		Last Purchase Qty:	0.00	Date Last Sale:	

Product Code:	GE1	**Product Description:**	German First Course		
Category:	2	In Stock:	19.00	Units of Sale:	each
Category Desc:	Books	On Order:	0.00	Supplier part refn:	
Department Code:	0	Allocated:	0.00	Supplier A/C:	BB001
Tax Code:	T0	Location:		Purchase Price:	8.95
Nominal Code:	4100	Selling Price:	18.00	Reorder Level:	0.00
Date Last Pur:		Last Purchase Qty:	0.00	Date Last Sale:	

Product Code:	ITA	**Product Description:**	Advanced Italian CD		
Category:	1	In Stock:	29.00	Units of Sale:	each
Category Desc:	CDs	On Order:	0.00	Supplier part refn:	
Department Code:	0	Allocated:	0.00	Supplier A/C:	TD001
Tax Code:	T1	Location:		Purchase Price:	12.00
Nominal Code:	4101	Selling Price:	24.00	Reorder Level:	0.00
Date Last Pur:		Last Purchase Qty:	0.00	Date Last Sale:	

Task 2

Interlingo Translation Services
Purchase Order List

Order Number From 1	**Order Date From** 01/01/1980	**Supplier From**
Order Number To 9,999,999	**Order Date To** 31/12/2019	**Supplier To** ZZZZZZZZ

Stock Code From
Stock Code To ZZZZZZZZZZZZZZZZZZZZZ

Order Number 13   **Order Date** 07/08/2013   **Account Ref** TD001   **Name** TDI Wholesalers

Stock Code	Description	Unit Of Sale	Quantity Order	Discount	Net Amount	Tax Amount	Gross Amount
FRB	Beginners French CD	each	100.00	0.00	1,000.00	200.00	1,200.00
ITA	Advanced Italian CD	each	50.00	0.00	600.00	120.00	720.00
			150.00	0.00	1,600.00	320.00	1,920.00

Order Number 14   **Order Date** 07/08/2013   **Account Ref** BB001   **Name** Bardners Books

Stock Code	Description	Unit Of Sale	Quantity Order	Discount	Net Amount	Tax Amount	Gross Amount
FR2	French Second Course	each	45.00	0.00	492.75	0.00	492.75
GE1	German First Course	each	60.00	0.00	537.00	0.00	537.00
			105.00	0.00	1,029.75	0.00	1,029.75
			255.00	0.00	2,629.75	320.00	2,949.75

Task 4

Interlingo Translation Services
Day Books: Supplier Invoices (Detailed)

Date From:	01/08/2013	**Supplier From:**
Date To:	31/08/2013	**Supplier To:** ZZZZZZZZ
Transaction From:	1	**N/C From:**
Transaction To:	99,999,999	**N/C To:** 99999999
Dept From:	0	
Dept To:	999	

Tran No.	Type	Date	A/C Ref	N/C	Inv Ref	Dept	Details	Net Amount	Tax Amount	T/C	Gross Amount	V	B
53	PI	15/08/2013	TD001	5001	2561	0	Beginners French CD	1,000.00	200.00	T1	1,200.00	N	-
54	PI	15/08/2013	TD001	5001	2561	0	Advanced Italian CD	600.00	120.00	T1	720.00	N	-
55	PI	20/08/2013	BB001	5000	11231	0	French Second Course	492.75	0.00	T0	492.75	N	-
56	PI	20/08/2013	BB001	5000	11231	0	German First Course	537.00	0.00	T0	537.00	N	-
							Totals	2,629.75	320.00		2,949.75		

Task 8

Interlingo Translation Services
Update Ledgers

Inv	Type	Tran	Date	A/C	N/C	Stock Code	Details	Quantity	Net	Tax	Gross
501	SC	58	31/08/2013	HD001	4000		Refund of 10% discount on invoice no. 10015 dated 10 08 13		-52.00	-10.40	-62.40
							Total for Invoice 501		-52.00	-10.40	-62.40
10015	SI	59	10/08/2013	HD001	4000		Translation of sales contracts		520.00	104.00	624.00
							Total for Invoice 10015		520.00	104.00	624.00
10016	SI	60	16/08/2013	PL001	4000		Translation of sales literature		120.00	24.00	144.00
							Total for Invoice 10016		120.00	24.00	144.00
10017	SI	61	20/08/2013	RS001	4000		Translation of shipping documents		100.00	20.00	120.00
							Total for Invoice 10017		100.00	20.00	120.00
10018	SI	62	20/08/2013	SC001	4000		Translation of sales contracts		160.00	32.00	192.00
							Total for Invoice 10018		160.00	32.00	192.00
10019	SI	63	22/08/2013	RT001	4101	FRB	Beginners French CD	16.00	320.00	62.40	382.40
							Total for Invoice 10019		320.00	62.40	382.40
10020	SI	64	31/08/2013	RT001	4101	ITA	Advanced Italian CD	20.00	480.00	93.60	573.60
	SI	65	31/08/2013	RT001	4100	GE1	German First Course	10.00	180.00	0.00	180.00
	SI	66	31/08/2013	RT001	4100	FR2	French Second Course	10.00	220.00	0.00	220.00
							Total for Invoice 10020		880.00	93.60	973.60
							Grand Total for All:		2,048.00	325.60	2,373.60

Interlingo Translation Services Extended Exercise: Activity 7

Task 2

Interlingo Translation Services
Day Books: Customer Receipts (Summary)

Date From: 01/08/2013
DateTo: 31/08/2013

Transaction From: 1
Transaction To: 99,999,999

Customer From :
Customer To: ZZ

Bank   1200   **Currency**   Pound Sterling

No	Type	Date	Account	Ref	Details	Net £	Tax £	Gross £ B
68	SR	09/08/2013	HD001	100110	Sales Receipt	345.00	0.00	345.00 N
69	SR	16/08/2013	PL001	100112	Sales Receipt	795.00	0.00	795.00 N
70	SR	23/08/2013	RS001	100114	Sales Receipt	850.00	0.00	850.00 N
71	SR	26/08/2013	RT001	100116	Sales Receipt	374.40	0.00	374.40 N
73	SR	31/08/2013	SC001	100118	Sales Receipt	800.00	0.00	800.00 N
					Totals £	3,164.40	0.00	3,164.40

Task 4

Interlingo Translation Services

Day Books: Bank Receipts (Detailed)

Transaction From:	1
Transaction To:	99,999,999

Dept From:	0
Dept To:	999

Bank: 1200   **Currency:** Pound Sterling

No	Type	N/C	Date	Ref	Details	Dept	Net £	Tax £	T/C	Gross £	V	B
74	BR	4000	09/08/2013	100111	Cash sales	0	96.00	19.20	T1	115.20	N	N
75	BR	4101	09/08/2013	100111	Cash sales	0	240.00	48.00	T1	288.00	N	N
76	BR	4100	09/08/2013	100111	Cash sales	0	160.00	0.00	T0	160.00	N	N
77	BR	4000	16/08/2013	100113	Cash sales	0	116.00	23.20	T1	139.20	N	N
78	BR	4101	16/08/2013	100113	Cash sales	0	180.00	36.00	T1	216.00	N	N
79	BR	4100	16/08/2013	100113	Cash sales	0	107.00	0.00	T0	107.00	N	N
80	BR	4000	23/08/2013	100115	Cash sales	0	104.00	20.80	T1	124.80	N	N
81	BR	4101	23/08/2013	100115	Cash sales	0	220.00	44.00	T1	264.00	N	N
82	BR	4100	23/08/2013	100115	Cash sales	0	84.00	0.00	T0	84.00	N	N
83	BR	4000	30/08/2013	100117	Cash sales	0	82.00	16.40	T1	98.40	N	N
84	BR	4101	30/08/2013	100117	Cash sales	0	190.00	38.00	T1	228.00	N	N
85	BR	4100	30/08/2013	100117	Cash sales	0	113.00	0.00	T0	113.00	N	N
						Totals £	1,692.00	245.60		1,937.60		

Task 6

Interlingo Translation Services

Day Books: Credit Card Receipts (Detailed)

Transaction From:	1	**N/C From:**	
Transaction To:	99,999,999	**N/C To:**	99999999

Dept From:	0
Dept To:	999

Bank: 1250   **Currency:** Pound Sterling

No	Type	N/C	Date	Ref	Details	Dept	Net £	Tax £	T/C	Gross £	V	B
88	VR	4101	30/08/2013	Cards	Card sales CDs	0	100.00	20.00	T1	120.00	N	N
89	VR	4100	30/08/2013	Cards	Card sales books	0	72.00	0.00	T0	72.00	N	N
						Totals £	172.00	20.00		192.00		

Interlingo Translation Services Extended Exercise: Activity 8

Task 2

Interlingo Translation Services

Day Books: Supplier Payments (Summary)

Date From:	02/08/2013	Bank From: 1200
DateTo:	02/08/2013	Bank To: 1200
Transaction From:	1	Supplier From:
Transaction To:	99,999,999	Supplier To: ZZZZZZZ

Bank 1200   **Currency** Pound Sterling

No	Type	Date	Supplier	Ref	Details	Net £	Tax £	Gross £	B	Bank Rec
90	PP	02/08/2013	TD001	120006	Purchase Payment	780.00	0.00	780.00	N	
91	PP	02/08/2013	BB001	120007	Purchase Payment	420.00	0.00	420.00	N	
					Totals £	1,200.00	0.00	1,200.00		

Task 4

Interlingo Translation Services

Day Books: Bank Payments (Detailed)

Transaction From:	1	N/C From:
Transaction To:	99,999,999	N/C To: 99999999
Dept From:	0	
Dept To:	999	

Bank: 1200   **Currency:** Pound Sterling

No	Type	N/C	Date	Ref	Details	Dept	Net £	Tax £	T/C	Gross £	V	B
92	BP	0040	07/08/2013	120009	Office furniture	0	140.00	28.00	T1	168.00	N	N
93	BP	6201	08/08/2013	120010	Advertising	0	600.00	120.00	T1	720.00	N	N
94	BP	7100	15/08/2013	120011	Rent	0	250.00	50.00	T1	300.00	N	N
95	BP	7502	17/08/2013	120012	Stationery	0	126.00	25.20	T1	151.20	N	N
96	BP	7103	20/08/2013	120013	Rates	0	129.00	0.00	T2	129.00	N	N
97	BP	2210	22/08/2013	BACS	HMRC	0	700.00	0.00	T9	700.00	-	N
98	BP	2211	22/08/2013	BACS	HMRC	0	900.00	0.00	T9	900.00	-	N
99	BP	7550	22/08/2013	120014	Telephone	0	186.00	37.20	T1	223.20	N	N
100	BP	7200	24/08/2013	120015	Electricity	0	84.00	16.80	T1	100.80	N	N
101	BP	7501	30/08/2013	120016	Postages	0	45.60	0.00	T2	45.60	N	N
					Totals £		3,160.60	277.20		3,437.80		

Task 5

Interlingo Translation Services
Day Books: Credit Card Payments (Detailed)

Transaction From:	1								N/C From:			
Transaction To:	99,999,999								N/C To:	99999999		
Dept From:	0											
Dept To:	999											

Bank: 1240 Currency: Pound Sterling

No	Type	N/C	Date	Ref	Details	Dept	Net £	Tax £ T/C	Gross £	V	B
102	VP	6201	19/08/2013	C/Card	Mereford	0	70.00	14.00 T1	84.00	N	N
						Totals £	70.00	14.00	84.00		

Interlingo Translation Services Extended Exercise: Activity 9

Task 3

Interlingo Translation Services
Day Books: Cash Payments (Detailed)

Date From:	07/08/2013											
DateTo:	22/08/2013											
Transaction From:	1								N/C From:			
Transaction To:	99,999,999								N/C To:	99999999		
Dept From:	0											
Dept To:	999											

Bank: 1230 Currency: Pound Sterling

No	Type	N/C	Date	Ref	Details	Dept	Net £	Tax £ T/C	Gross £	V	B
105	CP	7502	07/08/2013	0001	Copy paper	0	16.00	3.20 T1	19.20	N	N
106	CP	7501	07/08/2013	0002	Postage stamps	0	24.00	0.00 T2	24.00	N	N
107	CP	7502	15/08/2013	0003	Box files	0	20.00	4.00 T1	24.00	N	N
108	CP	7501	22/08/2013	0004	Postage stamps	0	12.00	0.00 T2	12.00	N	N
						Totals £	72.00	7.20	79.20		

Interlingo Translation Services Extended Exercise: Activity 11

Task 3

Interlingo Translation Services

Day Books: Nominal Ledger

Date From:	26/08/2013							**N/C From:**			
Date To:	26/08/2013							**N/C To:**	99999999		
Transaction From:	1							**Dept From:**	0		
Transaction To:	99,999,999							**Dept To:**	999		

No	Type	N/C	Date	Ref	Ex.Ref	Details	Dept	T/C	Debit	Credit	V	B
111	JD	6203	26/08/2013	13/11		Correction of posting error	0	T1	200.00		N	-
112	JC	6201	26/08/2013	13/11		Correction of posting error	0	T1		200.00	N	-
113	JD	7000	26/08/2013	13/12		Gross pay	0	T9	4,210.00		-	-
114	JC	2210	26/08/2013	13/12		Tax	0	T9		718.00	-	-
115	JC	2211	26/08/2013	13/12		Employee NI	0	T9		433.00	-	-
116	JC	2211	26/08/2013	13/12		Employer NI	0	T9		500.00	-	-
117	JD	7006	26/08/2013	13/12		Employer NI	0	T9	500.00		-	-
118	JC	2220	26/08/2013	13/12		Net pay 31 Aug	0	T9		3,059.00	-	-
								Totals:	4,910.00	4,910.00		

Interlingo Translation Services Extended Exercise: Activity 12

Task 1

Interlingo Translation Services
Bank Reconciliation

Page: 1

Bank Ref:	1200		**Date To:**	31/08/2013
Bank Name:	Bank Current Account		**Statement**	310813
Currency:	Pound Sterling			

Balance as per cash book at 31/08/2013: 8,565.70

Add: Unpresented Payments

Tran No	Date	Ref	Details	£
99	22/08/2013	120014	Telephone	223.20
100	24/08/2013	120015	Electricity	100.80
101	30/08/2013	120016	Postages	45.60
				369.60

Less: Outstanding Receipts

Tran No	Date	Ref	Details	£
				0.00

Reconciled balance : 8,935.30

Balance as per statement : 8,935.30

Difference : 0.00

Task 2

Interlingo Translation Services

Aged Debtors Analysis (Summary)

Report Date:	31/08/2013	
Include future transactions:	No	
Exclude later payments:	No	

Customer From:
Customer To: ZZZZZZZZ

** NOTE: All report values are shown in Base Currency, unless otherwise indicated **

A/C	Name		Credit Limit	Turnover	Balance	Future	Current	Period 1	Period 2	Period 3	Older
HD001	Hill & Dale & Co, Solicitors	£	0.00	813.00	561.60	0.00	561.60	0.00	0.00	0.00	0.00
PL001	Playgames PLC	£	0.00	915.00	144.00	0.00	144.00	0.00	0.00	0.00	0.00
RT001	Rotherway Limited	£	0.00	1,200.00	973.60	0.00	973.60	0.00	0.00	0.00	0.00
SC001	Schafeld Ltd	£	0.00	960.00	192.00	0.00	192.00	0.00	0.00	0.00	0.00
	Totals:			3,888.00	1,871.20	0.00	1,871.20	0.00	0.00	0.00	0.00

Task 2 (continued)

Interlingo Translation Services

Audit Trail (Summary)

Customer From:
Customer To: ///////

Supplier From:
Supplier To: ///////

Dept From: 0
Dept To: 999

N/C From:
N/C To: 99999999

Exclude Deleted Tran: No

No	Type	Date	A/C	N/C	Dept	Ref	Details	Net	Tax	T/C	Pd	Paid	V	B
1	SI	06/07/2013	RS001	9998	0	10010	Opening Balance	850.00	0.00	T9	Y	850.00	-	-
2	SI	12/07/2013	PL001	9998	0	10011	Opening Balance	795.00	0.00	T9	Y	795.00	-	-
3	SI	19/07/2013	HD001	9998	0	10013	Opening Balance	345.00	0.00	T9	Y	345.00	-	-
4	SI	20/07/2013	SC001	9998	0	10014	Opening Balance	800.00	0.00	T9	Y	800.00	-	-
5	PI	05/07/2013	TD001	9998	0	2347	Opening Balance	780.00	0.00	T9	Y	780.00	-	-
6	PI	06/07/2013	BB001	9998	0	9422	Opening Balance	420.00	0.00	T9	Y	420.00	-	-
7	JD	31/07/2013	0020	0020	0	O/Bal	Opening Balance	5,000.00	0.00	T9	Y	5,000.00	-	-
8	JC	31/07/2013	9998	9998	0	O/Bal	Opening Balance	5,000.00	0.00	T9	Y	5,000.00	-	-
9	JD	31/07/2013	0030	0030	0	O/Bal	Opening Balance	2,500.00	0.00	T9	Y	2,500.00	-	-
10	JC	31/07/2013	9998	9998	0	O/Bal	Opening Balance	2,500.00	0.00	T9	Y	2,500.00	-	-
11	JD	31/07/2013	0040	0040	0	O/Bal	Opening Balance	3,000.00	0.00	T9	Y	3,000.00	-	-
12	JC	31/07/2013	9998	9998	0	O/Bal	Opening Balance	3,000.00	0.00	T9	Y	3,000.00	-	-
13	JD	31/07/2013	1200	1200	0	O/Bal	Opening Balance	8,295.00	0.00	T9	Y	8,295.00	-	-
14	JC	31/07/2013	9998	9998	0	O/Bal	Opening Balance	8,295.00	0.00	T9	Y	8,295.00	-	-
15	JC	31/07/2013	2200	2200	0	O/Bal	Opening Balance	814.00	0.00	T9	Y	814.00	-	-
16	JD	31/07/2013	9998	9998	0	O/Bal	Opening Balance	814.00	0.00	T9	Y	814.00	-	-
17	JD	31/07/2013	2201	2201	0	O/Bal	Opening Balance	623.00	0.00	T9	Y	623.00	-	-
18	JC	31/07/2013	9998	9998	0	O/Bal	Opening Balance	623.00	0.00	T9	Y	623.00	-	-
19	JC	31/07/2013	2210	2210	0	O/Bal	Opening Balance	700.00	0.00	T9	Y	700.00	-	-
20	JD	31/07/2013	9998	9998	0	O/Bal	Opening Balance	700.00	0.00	T9	Y	700.00	-	-
21	JC	31/07/2013	2211	2211	0	O/Bal	Opening Balance	900.00	0.00	T9	Y	900.00	-	-
22	JD	31/07/2013	9998	9998	0	O/Bal	Opening Balance	900.00	0.00	T9	Y	900.00	-	-
23	JC	31/07/2013	2300	2300	0	O/Bal	Opening Balance	5,000.00	0.00	T9	Y	5,000.00	-	-
24	JD	31/07/2013	9998	9998	0	O/Bal	Opening Balance	5,000.00	0.00	T9	Y	5,000.00	-	-
25	JC	31/07/2013	3000	3000	0	O/Bal	Opening Balance	15,000.00	0.00	T9	Y	15,000.00	-	-
26	JD	31/07/2013	9998	9998	0	O/Bal	Opening Balance	15,000.00	0.00	T9	Y	15,000.00	-	-
27	JC	31/07/2013	4000	4000	0	O/Bal	Opening Balance	3,660.00	0.00	T9	Y	3,660.00	-	-
28	JD	31/07/2013	9998	9998	0	O/Bal	Opening Balance	3,660.00	0.00	T9	Y	3,660.00	-	-
29	JC	31/07/2013	4100	4100	0	O/Bal	Opening Balance	456.00	0.00	T9	Y	456.00	-	-
30	JD	31/07/2013	9998	9998	0	O/Bal	Opening Balance	456.00	0.00	T9	Y	456.00	-	-
31	JC	31/07/2013	4101	4101	0	O/Bal	Opening Balance	950.00	0.00	T9	Y	950.00	-	-
32	JD	31/07/2013	9998	9998	0	O/Bal	Opening Balance	950.00	0.00	T9	Y	950.00	-	-
33	JD	31/07/2013	5000	5000	0	O/Bal	Opening Balance	300.00	0.00	T9	Y	300.00	-	-
34	JC	31/07/2013	9998	9998	0	O/Bal	Opening Balance	300.00	0.00	T9	Y	300.00	-	-
35	JD	31/07/2013	5001	5001	0	O/Bal	Opening Balance	750.00	0.00	T9	Y	750.00	-	-
36	JC	31/07/2013	9998	9998	0	O/Bal	Opening Balance	750.00	0.00	T9	Y	750.00	-	-
37	JD	31/07/2013	6201	6201	0	O/Bal	Opening Balance	550.00	0.00	T9	Y	550.00	-	-
38	JC	31/07/2013	9998	9998	0	O/Bal	Opening Balance	550.00	0.00	T9	Y	550.00	-	-
39	JD	31/07/2013	7000	7000	0	O/Bal	Opening Balance	3,600.00	0.00	T9	Y	3,600.00	-	-
40	JC	31/07/2013	9998	9998	0	O/Bal	Opening Balance	3,600.00	0.00	T9	Y	3,600.00	-	-
41	JD	31/07/2013	7100	7100	0	O/Bal	Opening Balance	250.00	0.00	T9	Y	250.00	-	-
42	JC	31/07/2013	9998	9998	0	O/Bal	Opening Balance	250.00	0.00	T9	Y	250.00	-	-
43	JD	31/07/2013	7103	7103	0	O/Bal	Opening Balance	129.00	0.00	T9	Y	129.00	-	-
44	JC	31/07/2013	9998	9998	0	O/Bal	Opening Balance	129.00	0.00	T9	Y	129.00	-	-
45	JD	31/07/2013	7200	7200	0	O/Bal	Opening Balance	61.00	0.00	T9	Y	61.00	-	-
46	JC	31/07/2013	9998	9998	0	O/Bal	Opening Balance	61.00	0.00	T9	Y	61.00	-	-
47	JD	31/07/2013	7501	7501	0	O/Bal	Opening Balance	86.00	0.00	T9	Y	86.00	-	-
48	JC	31/07/2013	9998	9998	0	O/Bal	Opening Balance	86.00	0.00	T9	Y	86.00	-	-
49	JD	31/07/2013	7502	7502	0	O/Bal	Opening Balance	471.00	0.00	T9	Y	471.00	-	-
50	JC	31/07/2013	9998	9998	0	O/Bal	Opening Balance	471.00	0.00	T9	Y	471.00	-	-
51	JD	31/07/2013	7550	7550	0	O/Bal	Opening Balance	275.00	0.00	T9	Y	275.00	-	-
52	JC	31/07/2013	9998	9998	0	O/Bal	Opening Balance	275.00	0.00	T9	Y	275.00	-	-
53	SI	10/08/2013	HD001	4000	0	10015	Translation of sales contracts	520.00	104.00	T1	N	0.00	N	-
54	SI	16/08/2013	PL001	4000	0	10016	Translation of sales literature	120.00	24.00	T1	N	0.00	N	-
55	SI	20/08/2013	RS001	4000	0	10017	Translation of shipping docs	100.00	20.00	T1	Y	120.00	N	-
56	SI	20/08/2013	SC001	4000	0	10018	Translation of sales contracts	160.00	32.00	T1	N	0.00	N	-
57	SI	22/08/2013	RT001	4101	0	10019	16 Beginners' French CDs	320.00	62.40	T1	Y	382.40	N	-
58	SI	31/08/2013	RT001	4100	0	10020	10 German First Course books	180.00	0.00	T0	N	0.00	N	-
59	SI	31/08/2013	RT001	4100	0	10020	10 French Second Course books	220.00	0.00	T0	N	0.00	N	-
60	SI	31/08/2013	RT001	4101	0	10020	20 Advanced Italian CDs	480.00	93.60	T1	N	0.00	N	-
61	SC	31/08/2013	HD001	4000	0	501	Refund invoice 10015	52.00	10.40	T1	N	0.00	N	-
62	PI	15/08/2013	TD001	5001	0	2561	Beginners French CDs	1,000.00	200.00	T1	N	0.00	N	-
63	PI	15/08/2013	TD001	5001	0	2561	Advanced Italian CDs	600.00	120.00	T1	N	0.00	N	-
64	PI	20/08/2013	BB001	5000	0	11231	German First Course	537.00	0.00	T0	N	0.00	N	-
65	PI	20/08/2013	BB001	5000	0	11231	French Second Course	492.75	0.00	T0	N	0.00	N	-
66	PI	15/08/2013	RS002	5100	0	72/554	Same day delivery to London	100.00	20.00	T1	Y	120.00	N	-
67	PC	28/08/2013	TD001	5001	0	1919	Faulty CDs returned	100.00	20.00	T1	N	0.00	N	-
68	SR	09/08/2013	HD001	1200	0	100110	Sales Receipt	345.00	0.00	T9	Y	345.00	-	R
69	SR	16/08/2013	PL001	1200	0	100112	Sales Receipt	795.00	0.00	T9	Y	795.00	-	R

Task 2 (continued)

No	Type	Date	A/C	N/C	Dept	Ref	Details	Net	Tax	T/C	Pd	Paid	V	B
70	SR	23/08/2013	RS001	1200	0	100114	Sales Receipt	850.00	0.00	T9	Y	850.00	-	R
71	SR	26/08/2013	RT001	1200	0	100116	Sales Receipt	374.40	0.00	T9	Y	374.40	-	R
72	SD	26/08/2013	RT001	4009	0	100116	Sales Discount	8.00	0.00	T9	Y	8.00	-	-
73	SR	31/08/2013	SC001	1200	0	100118	Sales Receipt	800.00	0.00	T9	Y	800.00	-	R
74	BR	09/08/2013	1200	4000	0	100111	Cash sales	96.00	19.20	T1	Y	115.20	N	R
75	BR	09/08/2013	1200	4101	0	100111	Cash sales	240.00	48.00	T1	Y	288.00	N	R
76	BR	09/08/2013	1200	4100	0	100111	Cash sales	160.00	0.00	T0	Y	160.00	N	R
77	BR	16/08/2013	1200	4000	0	100113	Cash sales	116.00	23.20	T1	Y	139.20	N	R
78	BR	16/08/2013	1200	4101	0	100113	Cash sales	180.00	36.00	T1	Y	216.00	N	R
79	BR	16/08/2013	1200	4100	0	100113	Cash sales	107.00	0.00	T0	Y	107.00	N	R
80	BR	23/08/2013	1200	4000	0	100115	Cash sales	104.00	20.80	T1	Y	124.80	N	R
81	BR	23/08/2013	1200	4101	0	100115	Cash sales	220.00	44.00	T1	Y	264.00	N	R
82	BR	23/08/2013	1200	4100	0	100115	Cash sales	84.00	0.00	T0	Y	84.00	N	R
83	BR	30/08/2013	1200	4000	0	100117	Cash sales	82.00	16.40	T1	Y	98.40	N	R
84	BR	30/08/2013	1200	4101	0	100117	Cash sales	190.00	38.00	T1	Y	228.00	N	R
85	BR	30/08/2013	1200	4100	0	100117	Cash sales	113.00	0.00	T0	Y	113.00	N	R
86	SR	31/08/2013	RS001	1200	0	CONTRA	Contra Receipt	120.00	0.00	T9	Y	120.00	-	R
87	PP	31/08/2013	RS002	1200	0	CONTRA	Contra Payment	120.00	0.00	T9	Y	120.00	-	R
88	VR	30/08/2013	1250	4101	0	Cards	Card sales CDs	100.00	20.00	T1	Y	120.00	N	N
89	VR	30/08/2013	1250	4100	0	Cards	Card sales books	72.00	0.00	T0	Y	72.00	N	N
90	PP	02/08/2013	TD001	1200	0	120006	Purchase Payment	780.00	0.00	T9	Y	780.00	-	R
91	PP	02/08/2013	BB001	1200	0	120007	Purchase Payment	420.00	0.00	T9	Y	420.00	-	R
92	BP	07/08/2013	1200	0040	0	120009	Office furniture	140.00	28.00	T1	Y	168.00	N	R
93	BP	08/08/2013	1200	6201	0	120010	Advertising	600.00	120.00	T1	Y	720.00	N	R
94	BP	15/08/2013	1200	7100	0	120011	Rent	250.00	50.00	T1	Y	300.00	N	R
95	BP	17/08/2013	1200	7502	0	120012	Stationery	126.00	25.20	T1	Y	151.20	N	R
96	BP	20/08/2013	1200	7103	0	120013	Rates	129.00	0.00	T2	Y	129.00	N	R
97	BP	22/08/2013	1200	2210	0	BACS	HMRC	700.00	0.00	T9	Y	700.00	-	R
98	BP	22/08/2013	1200	2211	0	BACS	HMRC	900.00	0.00	T9	Y	900.00	-	R
99	BP	22/08/2013	1200	7550	0	120014	Telephone	186.00	37.20	T1	Y	223.20	N	N
100	BP	24/08/2013	1200	7200	0	120015	Electricity	84.00	16.80	T1	Y	100.80	N	N
101	BP	30/08/2013	1200	7501	0	120016	Postages	45.60	0.00	T2	Y	45.60	N	N
102	VP	19/08/2013	1240	6201	0	C/Card	Mereford Publications	70.00	14.00	T1	Y	84.00	N	N
103	JC	06/08/2013	1200	1200	0	120008	From bank to petty cash	80.00	0.00	T9	Y	80.00	-	R
104	JD	06/08/2013	1230	1230	0	120008	From bank to petty cash	80.00	0.00	T9	Y	80.00	-	-
105	CP	07/08/2013	1230	7502	0	0001	Copy paper	16.00	3.20	T1	Y	19.20	N	N
106	CP	07/08/2013	1230	7501	0	0002	Postage stamps	24.00	0.00	T2	Y	24.00	N	N
107	CP	15/08/2013	1230	7502	0	0003	Box files	20.00	4.00	T1	Y	24.00	N	N
108	CP	22/08/2013	1230	7501	0	0004	Postage stamps	12.00	0.00	T2	Y	12.00	N	N
109	BP	10/08/2013	1200	7104	0	DD	Suresafe Insurance (premises	98.50	0.00	T2	Y	98.50	N	R
110	BP	25/08/2013	1200	7901	0	STO	Albion Bank (standing charge)	15.00	0.00	T2	Y	15.00	-	-
111	JD	26/08/2013	6203	6203	0	13/11	Correction of posting error	200.00	0.00	T1	Y	200.00	N	-
112	JC	26/08/2013	6201	6201	0	13/11	Correction of posting error	200.00	0.00	T1	Y	200.00	N	-
113	JD	26/08/2013	7000	7000	0	13/12	Gross pay	4,210.00	0.00	T9	Y	4,210.00	-	-
114	JC	26/08/2013	2210	2210	0	13/12	Tax	718.00	0.00	T9	Y	718.00	-	-
115	JC	26/08/2013	2211	2211	0	13/12	Employee NI	433.00	0.00	T9	Y	433.00	-	-
116	JC	26/08/2013	2211	2211	0	13/12	Employer NI	500.00	0.00	T9	Y	500.00	-	-
117	JD	26/08/2013	7006	7006	0	13/12	Employer NI	500.00	0.00	T9	Y	500.00	-	-
118	JC	26/08/2013	2220	2220	0	13/12	Net pay 31 Aug	3,059.00	0.00	T9	Y	3,059.00	-	-

Task 3

Interlingo Translation Services
Customer Activity (Detailed)

Date From:	01/01/1980	
Date To:	31/08/2013	

Customer From:	RT001
Customer To:	RT001

Transaction From: 1
Transaction To: 99,999,999

N/C From:
N/C To: 99999999

Inc b/fwd transaction: No
Exc later payment: No

Dept From: 0
Dept To: 999

** NOTE: All report values are shown in Base Currency, unless otherwise indicated **

A/C: RT001   Name: Rotherway Limited   Contact: Tel:

No	Type	Date	Ref	N/C	Details	Dept	T/C	Value	O/S	Debit	Credit	V	B
57	SI	22/08/2013	10019	4101	16 Beginners' French CDs	0	T1	382.40			382.40	N	-
58	SI	31/08/2013	10020	4100	10 German First Course books	0	T0	180.00 *	180.00	180.00		N	-
59	SI	31/08/2013	10020	4100	10 French Second Course	0	T0	220.00 *	220.00	220.00		N	-
60	SI	31/08/2013	10020	4101	20 Advanced Italian CDs	0	T1	573.60 *	573.60	573.60		N	-
71	SR	26/08/2013	100116	1200	Sales Receipt	0	T9	374.40			374.40	-	R
72	SD	26/08/2013	100116	4009	Sales Discount	0	T9	8.00			8.00	-	-
					Totals:			973.60	973.60	1,356.00	382.40		

Amount Outstanding   973.60
Amount Paid this period   374.40
Credit Limit £   0.00
Turnover YTD   1,200.00

Task 4

Interlingo Translation Services
Supplier Activity (Detailed)

Date From:	01/01/1980
Date To:	31/08/2013

Supplier From:	TD001
Supplier To:	TD001

Transaction From: 1
Transaction To: 99,999,999

N/C From:
N/C To: 99999999

Inc b/fwd transaction: No
Exc later payment: No

Dept From: 0
Dept To: 999

** NOTE: All report values are shown in Base Currency, unless otherwise indicated **

A/C: TD001   Name: TDI Wholesalers   Contact: Tel:

No	Type	Date	Ref	N/C	Details	Dept	T/C	Value	O/S	Debit	Credit	V	B
5	PI	05/07/2013	2347	9998	Opening Balance	0	T9	780.00	0.00		780.00	-	-
62	PI	15/08/2013	2561	5001	Beginners French CDs	0	T1	1,200.00 *	1,200.00		1,200.00	N	-
63	PI	15/08/2013	2561	5001	Advanced Italian CDs	0	T1	720.00 *	720.00		720.00	N	-
67	PC	28/08/2013	1919	5001	Faulty CDs returned	0	T1	120.00 *	-120.00	120.00		N	-
90	PP	02/08/2013	120006	1200	Purchase Payment	0	T9	780.00	0.00	780.00		-	R
					Totals:			1,800.00	1,800.00	900.00	2,700.00		

Amount Outstanding   1,800.00
Amount paid this period   780.00
Credit Limit £   0.00
Turnover YTD   2,280.00

Task 5

Hill & Dale & Co, Solicitors
17 Berkeley Chambers
Penrose Street
Mereford
MR2 6GF

Playgames PLC
Consul House
Viney Street
Mereford
MR2 6PL

RS Export Agency
46 Chancery Street
Mereford
MR1 9FD

Rotherway Limited
78 Sparkhouse Street
Millway
MY5 8HG

Schafeld Ltd
86 Tanners Lane
Millway
MY7 5VB

INDEX

308

for your notes

for your notes

for your notes

for your notes

for your notes

for your notes

for your notes